MANAGEMENT
Challenge and Response

MANAGEMENT

Challenge and Response

Case Histories
from
FORTUNE

Edited by

Martin B.Carter • Charles A.Ray • Walter Weintraub
SCHOOL OF COMMERCE, NEW YORK UNIVERSITY

Holt, Rinehart and Winston, Inc.

New York • Chicago • San Francisco
Toronto • London

3056

Contents

ANALYZING
BUSINESS CASES

CHAPTER 1

Introduction

Objectives

The application of the basic concepts, principles, and techniques of management often proves to be confusing when attempts are made to bridge the gap between theory and practice. Paradoxically, this is true even of those who have had actual on-the-job experience at the lower levels in business organizations. It is not until the junior executive has experienced membership in the management team that he realizes both the significance of theory and its limitations in decision making.

One way to acquire broad-gauge experience would be to visit a variety of companies and to observe whether theory was being implemented in actual company situations. This, of course, is not feasible for many reasons, the least of which is time. But just as the biologist may dissect a frog to verify his theoretical knowledge of its nervous system, so may the potential administrator use company histories for his verification of the value of management theories. The study of a company's history, its method of operation, and the people identified with its rate of growth provides realism and practicality for the field of management. In addition, such an approach mirrors the many facts and complexities of modern business and furnishes a comparative view of the "art" of administration.

This book presents case histories of specific companies, which describe the problems they faced and how they solved them. All of these company situations have appeared in *Fortune* in recent years. The problems are those which resulted from social and economic forces in the business environment as they were reported. In a number of instances the articles discuss pivotal management decisions made in situations of company crisis. These represent management at the crossroads.

The material is based on interviews with key personnel of the companies as well as on research documentation by the author of the article. In a sense, each case is a bird's-eye view of the company at one point of time, providing material for both micro- and comparative analysis.

The case histories in this book differ from those normally used in the so-called "case method" of instruction. The latter usually contain a specific major problem along with related data and the reader is required to analyze the case, identify the problem, and present his decision or recommendation. The company situations in this book are different in that they describe the manner in which the problems were solved by management, leaving for analysis and identification the extent to which management theory was applied.

The length of the cases varies as a result of editing the original articles and eliminating material consisting of charts and photos not particularly germane to the objective of this book. However, the resultant cases are not rewrites, and each contains all of the detail necessary to analyze the operation of the company.

Analyzing the Cases

When this volume is used as part of educational or management development programs, the material may become the focus of a number of analytical approaches. The method selected should be the one that best meets the needs of the individual instructor, taking into consideration the experience and academic background of training group participants. It may be useful to comment briefly on two possible approaches that have worked out well in the past. Without being too preoccupied with sophistication of terminology, we may designate these two approaches as (1) "intensive" analysis and (2) "comparative" analysis.

In using intensive analysis each company case history is handled as a self-contained unit. The objective of this approach is to require a comparison of a single company's practice with the universals or principles of the field of management. The student is required to read the case and then to organize his findings around an analytical outline furnished by the instructor. Such an outline may be developed from the major topical breakdown of a preferred text in management. Under the guidance of the instructor's outline, all participants approach their analysis in a uniform manner, and a comparison of their findings is facilitated. A very brief example of such an outline is appended to the end of this chapter.

In using comparative analysis, two or more company case histories are handled as a unit assignment. The objective of this approach is concerned with the recognition and description of fundamental similarities, or unique differences, among different organizations. The analysis of similarities may thus point the way to the value of the universals of management; the recognition of unique differences tends to delimit the area to which generalizations may apply and emphasizes a "diagnostic guide" attitude toward management principles.[1]

Although the total number of cases presented in this volume has been limited by the usual considerations, the authors have attempted a selection which lends itself to the two foregoing analytical approaches. In several instances a given company has been represented at two points of time in its development; some industries are represented by a number of companies. Several articles refer the student to earlier issues of *Fortune* for additional material concerning the company under discussion. Additionally, a selective index of companies by back issues of *Fortune* is included at the end of Part II.

Whether a case should be assigned to an individual or a committee for analysis will depend largely on the size of the group and on the length and complexity of the assignment. Where the group is small, it seems advisable to assign cases to the individuals for analysis. In this way the individual will gain much satisfaction and skill in applying himself to a company situation, and in working by himself he is able to move along with the analysis at his own pace. Working by himself the individual is also in a position to make observations without being influenced by the opinions of others. The end result can be a high degree of self-confidence and satisfaction of an analysis well done.

However, where the group is large, it becomes too time-consuming and burdensome either to listen to or to read individual analyses. In situations of this nature it has been found advantageous to have committee presentations. The strength of the committee approach lies in the fact that each member is exposed to the judgments of the others and is able to evaluate his judgment with theirs. The committee members also tend to "teach" as well as "learn" from each other. Furthermore, longer and more complex assignments may be handled better by a group than by an individual. In addition, if each committee is required to report on the analysis of its case, all the other members of the group will profit from its findings. Finally, the committee method makes each participant realistically aware of the need and problems of working together for a common purpose.

---

[1] See Ernest Dale, *The Great Organizers*, 1960; McGraw-Hill Book Company, Inc., Chapter 1.

INTENSIVE ANALYSIS CASE OUTLINE

I. *Identification of the Company*
A. Name. B. Type of business. C. Present size (number of people, plants, etc.). D. Names of officers (simple organization chart if possible). E. Private or public ownership; proprietary or management control.

II. *Brief Summary of Early Company History*
A. When founded. B. By whom. C. Where. D. Circumstances leading to "birth."

III. *Philosophy of the Company*
Direct statements and/or implications of such revealed in case analysis.

IV. *Objectives of the Company*
Prefer actual quotes from research, and value judgment of them.

V. *Policies of the Company*
Actual statements and/or implications of such revealed in case analysis.
Note: If possible, policies should be identified by level, type, or function, that is, Sales, Finance, Labor Relations, etc.

VI. *Type of Organization Structure of Company*
(1) Centralized or decentralized
(2) Pattern of departmentation
(3) Committee structure
(4) Line and staff applications

VII. *Authority, Responsibility, and Accountability*
Examples and/or indicators of company operations.

VIII. *Planning*
Citations or examples—long-range and short-range.

IX. *Decision Making*
Evidence and/or citations of key decisions and how made.

X. *Directing (Leadership)*
Evidence and/or citations of approach—autocratic, bureaucratic, democratic, charismatic.

XI. *Control*
Evidence and/or citations of control.
Note: Group under Finance, Marketing, and so on, if possible.

XII. *Company Relations*
A. Public. B. Employee. C. Stockholder. D. Union. E. Government. F. Supplier. G. Distributor. H. International. I. Community.

XIII. *Human Relations*

      A. Executive leadership.   B. Conflicts.

XIV. *Ethics and Morality*

      Societal obligations and corporate behavioral values.

 XV. *Summary*

      Critique of the practices of the company as related to management theories.

      Whether the findings should be submitted in oral, outline, or essay form is a matter of individual choice of the instructor.

CHAPTER 2

Analysis of a Case

*The Durable Threads of J. P. Stevens**_____
by RICHARD J. WHALEN

That gloomiest of U.S. manufactures, the textile industry, recently interrupted its laments and dirges to join in the jaunty, brassy celebration of a happy textile birthday: the one hundred and fiftieth anniversary of J. P. Stevens & Co., Inc. In the whole history of U.S. business there has never been anything quite like Stevens. Its uniqueness goes beyond being the world's oldest diversified textile company. Over the century and a half, the management of the firm has passed from father to son in a direct line (even the du Ponts had to rely on an occasional son-in-law) from the founder, Captain Nathaniel Stevens, who began it all by weaving woolen broadcloth in a converted gristmill in North Andover, Massachusetts. Among some one hundred families who started woolen mills in the U.S. in the years 1800 to 1815, the Stevenses are the sole survivors. And generation after generation of Stevenses has shown the industry how to survive and prosper by sinuously working around obstacles, by unsentimentally jettisoning outmoded traditions—in short, by adapting to the world's constant changes.

The Stevens example was never more needed than in today's situation, which admittedly is a challenge to even Stevens staying power. Expansion to meet the demands of World War II and the Korean war left the industry with overcapacity, inventory gluts, and in a dog-eat-dog market; so far as textiles are concerned, the real hell comes after the war. Since the mid-Fifties, a rising number of overseas competitors have invaded domestic markets, intensifying the traditionally brutal price competition. In addition, textiles have become so entangled in the web of wool and cotton politics that only more logically absurd involvement seems to promise relief. Under the impact of all this, the liquidation has

* *April 1963*

8

been murderous. Since the Korean war, cotton-system spindles have declined 17 percent and woolen and worsted looms a staggering 52 percent. The rewards for running high risks are below average. The seventeen largest U.S. textile companies included in the 1962 *Fortune* Directory of the 500 showed a median return on invested capital of 6.1 percent (vs. 8.3 percent for the 500 as a group). All in all, the liveliest talk concerning textiles seems to be speculation as to an old industry's life expectancy.

But somber statistics and doom-crying about cheap imports, while reflecting real problems, cast a disproportionate shadow across a basic industry, a pall obscuring vitality and even radical change. In its sesquicentennial year, J. P. Stevens is living up to its own tradition by making a yard of goods and ingeniously striving to make a better profit.

"The Business Is in Stronger Hands"

Optimism about the outcome would be misplaced if Stevens were scratching along by turning out staple goods. Last year the company's 1,200,000 spindles and nearly 30,000 looms poured out more than 800 million linear yards of fabric, which almost defy classification by end use. A billowing ocean of cloth, this output included luxurious woolens (at $6 a yard), lightweight cotton muslins (at 17¼ cents a yard), sheer dress fabrics of 65 percent Dacron and 35 per cent cotton, fiberglass to be laminated and machined into missile nose cones and other components, snowy damask tablecloths and flower-bedecked printed sheets, and a synthetic fabric for tents that will be pitched on the roof of the world this year, if the American climbers conquer Mount Everest. Also, Stevens sold 150 million yards of fabric for outside mills.

Handling nearly a billion yards of goods implies unusual size and scope in an industry commonly described as "fragmented" among some 5,500 small companies. Stevens is big. In eight states from Maine to Georgia, the company employs some 35,000 workers in fifty-five plants. (The word "mill" is passing out of fashion among modern textile men.) With record sales of $586 million in fiscal 1962, the company boosted volume 18 percent over 1961. Stevens is the second-largest textile company in the U.S. (and the world), surpassed only by Burlington Industries, which last year became the first billion-dollar textile company. With a diversified base dating from before and immediately after World War II, Stevens has been on the leading edge of a glacial trend toward ever larger textile entities: there were fourteen

$100-million textile companies in 1962, compared to ten a decade earlier. Large companies like Stevens, by transforming themselves, are gradually transforming the industry. "The shake-out has been good for textiles," says Treasurer A. J. Smith. "The business is now in stronger hands."

Weak, undercapitalized companies, stepping up production and beating down prices to gain a little business, have long kept textiles a weak industry. Even though it still calculates prices to the fourth decimal place, the large diversified company operates quite differently. For example, the loom and the shuttle, the main tools of the old business, are now joined to a new tool—the computer. In Stevens' giant synthetics division (1962 sales: $240 million) the industry's most advanced system of data processing applies customers' orders to goods in inventory, and is moving toward full control of production. A parallel program is exploring the possibilities of forecasting market trends.

Smaller textile companies argue, plausibly, that they cannot afford research. Stevens has decided it cannot afford to be without it. In Garfield, New Jersey, the company maintains a 66,000-square-foot central research laboratory and pilot plant, one of the pioneering basic research facilities in the industry. Foreseeing changes in traditional markets and seeking new ones, Stevens is engaged in joint ventures with a paper company in the field of nonwoven materials, and with a chemical company in the development of plastics and new fibers such as polypropylene. It also has made a deliberate but growing commitment to the markets of Western Europe.

The Uses of Diversity

Stevens has propelled itself light-years away from the one-mill, one-fiber textile business because it meant to stay in the game. The old business of supplying staple goods to huge markets was production-obsessed; the new business lives by merchandising. "We're continually fitting equipment to fabric," says Harry Carter, a vice president of the synthetics division. "It's not the business it was ten years ago, when we ran crepes for five years in one mill. Now it's a style and merchandising business." Eighty-four Stevens selling departments in the New York City headquarters tailor the mills' output to the specialized wants of hundreds of distinct markets. An enormous 73 percent of Stevens' production goes into the volatile apparel trade, which rips apart the familiar pattern every season.

To make a profit and enjoy reasonable stability, Stevens must be diversified across the board. Chairman and President Robert T. Stevens, Captain Nat's great-grandson, explains: "The broad and comprehensive base of our product lines crosses the market in its style and popularity swings, and enables us to be at almost all times in the position of having something going for us."

A newcomer might lose his head (not to say his business) in the swings. In 1961 and 1962, Stevens' cotton and synthetics divisions each provided about two-fifths of the company's total volume, and the woolen and worsted division the remaining one-fifth. But consider the relative profitability of fibers in these years: in 1961 the cotton division was the leading money-maker, contributing 44 percent of company profits, followed by synthetics (29 percent) and woolens (27 percent). In 1962, however, synthetics, especially spun rayons and blends of natural and man-made fibers, made a strong comeback, and the synthetics division contributed 47 percent of company profits. Meanwhile, the cotton and woolen divisions tailed off, contributing 32 percent and 21 percent of profits respectively. The ups and downs from year to year, even quarter to quarter, are extreme. Since 1950, for example, the synthetics division has made as much as 75 cents of each dollar of company profit in a year—and as little as 18 cents. Despite the swing, 1962 was a good year for Stevens: the company's volume of $586 million produced a net income of $16 million.

Quiet, mild-mannered Chairman Stevens, the former Secretary of the Army under Eisenhower who did battle with the late Senator McCarthy before a television audience of millions, is frankly sentimental about the company founded by his great-grandfather. He is unsentimental about how his company spins a profit. "We go to the marketplace and attempt to find out what the public wants. If the public wants straw, we'll weave straw. We're not wedded to any particular product or fiber."

That philosophy has an oddly radical ring in an industry still composed largely of "cotton men," "wool men," and the like. Indeed, so deep is the attachment to a fiber (and so difficult the adjustment to new ones) that a Stevens executive, lecturing not long ago at Manhattan's Fashion Institute of Technology, was hissed by "silk men" in the audience after what they took to be a slur against their true love. But Nathaniel Stevens was nothing if not adaptable, and he would approve the trait in his heirs and their company.

The Bride Could Wait

Nathaniel Stevens, known familiarly as "Captain Nat" in recognition of his rank in the Massachusetts militia, was typical of the early Yankee entrepreneurs. One of fourteen children of a farmer who fought the British at Concord and Lexington, Nathaniel shipped out at twenty-one on a merchant vessel, returned to clerk in a general store, and showed a talent for trading. War with Great Britain in 1812 decided young Nathaniel on his career. With the westward push of population, U.S. markets for cloth were expanding, and imports would be cut off for the duration. Borrowing money from his father, Nathaniel, with two friends as partners, took over the gristmill and converted it to woolens. Family lore provides an illustration of his diligence. On his wedding day, in 1815, while his bride-to-be waited at the church, Captain Nat was discovered in his mill, absorbed in dyeing a piece of cloth.

Postwar resumption of imports drove many infant mills out of business and posed an early test of Captain Nat's flexibility. He converted from broadcloth to flannels, a daring diversification: up to then no one had successfully produced flannel in the U.S. Captain Nat succeeded, and reinvested the profits. However, a Boston importer, Abbot Lawrence, advised Captain Nat to "shut down your mill and save what you have, for we can bring goods in here and sell them for less than it costs you to manufacture them." Unconvinced, Captain Nat chose instead to whip the invader.

He parted company with one partner and bought out the other to become sole proprietor, served a term in the Massachusetts legislature, and sired nine children. He kept on improving the mill. The Panic of 1837 hit New England hard and every mill closed down for a spell, except the one at North Andover, which kept running and was even expanded as Captain Nat took advantage of the scare to steal a march on the competition. He drove himself and his help through a six-day seventy-six-hour week, for which he paid above-average wages: $4.50 a week, plus board of $2.

One of his sons, Moses Tyler, became a partner in 1850; his help was needed. For the Stevenses soon acquired a mill in Haverhill, Massachusetts, and became the first family owning more than one flannel mill. Sons were a blessing in the growing business. Captain Nat sent a second son, George, to Haverhill, summoning a third, Horace, from his studies at Harvard to assist Moses at North Andover. When the Civil War broke out, the mills worked overtime, under flickering whale-oil lamps, to supply the Union Army with blankets.

Captain Nat died a month before Lee's surrender, and Moses was his natural successor among the three sons who had become partners. Like their resourceful father, they were willing to experiment. They bought a bale of cotton and proceeded to whip up a blended fabric, an indigo-dyed mixture of 60 percent wool and 40 percent cotton. The blend sold well, and the Stevenses were in a position to ride out the collapse of the postwar boom in 1873. They acquired two mills. The deaths of Horace and George left Moses alone but, once again, there was a son on hand. On the day the name of the firm was changed—from Nathaniel Stevens & Sons to M. T. Stevens—another Nathaniel Stevens, son of Moses, quit school and went to work for his father.

A Salesman in the Family

However, one young Stevens, John P., the son of Horace, did *not* enter the family business, at least not in the usual way. Instead, he went (at a salary of $150 a year) into the commission house that handled the goods from the Stevens mills. He learned to sell and to sniff out a poor credit risk. A blood tie with a commission house being thus established, expansion from manufacturing into merchandising soon seemed an obvious move, so the family created its own selling house. On August 1, 1899, J. P. Stevens & Co., with capital of $25,000 and twenty-one employees, opened its doors on Thomas Street in lower Manhattan's textile district. True to the time-honored script, the day before it opened John P. had occasion to wire cousin Nathaniel in North Andover, announcing the arrival of a "new office boy," later christened Robert Ten Broeck.

While the selling house was gaining its feet, the mill company prospered. Like his father, Moses admitted his three sons to partnership early, and served in the state legislature and Congress, where he was pointed out as the largest individual woolen manufacturer in the country. But the Stevenses were also reaching out for cotton. John P. crisscrossed the rapidly developing South, lining up cotton mills for the selling house and investing in likely ones. When Moses died, in 1907, after sixty-four years in the business, the family already had laid the foundation of diversification.

By World War I, J. P. Stevens & Co. from its New York office was selling the output of nine cotton mills and was doing the bulk of its business in that fiber. The usual bust after the war boom found the Stevenses shopping as usual; they acquired five mills. Experiments with the new-fangled synthetic, rayon, were begun in the Twenties. John P.'s son Robert served an apprenticeship in the mills, and got a start in his father's firm selling the handkerchief trade. He assumed command in the selling house when J.P. died two days before the crash in 1929. Over the next decade Bob and his older brother, John P. Jr., hustled the house to a volume of better than $100 million.

As a result of acquisitions and investments, the Stevens textile interests sprawled in all directions. The explosive expansion of World War II, and a death in the family, produced a crisis. Moses' son Nathaniel, "Mr. Nat," who had run the mill company since 1907, died in 1946 at the age of eighty-eight. His estate needed to sell stock to settle with the tax collector. The selling house, which now dwarfed the family's mill operations, needed access to the capital markets to continue growing. Everything pointed to the wisdom and necessity of going public.

In September, 1946, after months of negotiations, a merger was arranged, uniting the Stevens selling house and mill company with eight other companies. J. P. Stevens & Co., Inc., with Bob Stevens as chairman and J. P. Stevens Jr. as president, was listed on the New York Stock Exchange, the ninth-oldest company on the big board. Within two years the family sold 375,000 shares. Going public brought only a passing twinge. "I think the change was a good thing," reflects Chairman Stevens. "The discipline of public ownership is a stimulus to management to do a better job. We wouldn't retrace our steps."

The Trek to Dixie

Bob Stevens' contribution to the evolving family fortunes has been his successful handling of size and diversity. The 1946 merger created an administrative monstrosity, composed of fourteen divisions (operating twenty-nine mills) that would go on operating as fourteen companies if allowed to. Just back from wartime service as a colonel in the Office of the Quartermaster General, where he had been deputy director of purchases, Bob Stevens had learned something about efficient systems management and large-scale organization. Within a few years the divisions were reduced to a manageable three, organized by fiber.

In the immediate postwar years all the organization seemed

to need was order takers. Profits in 1947 were a fat 12.7 percent on sales of $224 million. While textile stocks boomed and industry figures voiced bullish forecasts, Bob and John Stevens cautioned the stockholders out of the depths of family experience that "textile earnings are on a higher level than is likely to be maintained over any long period." From 1948 to 1949, Stevens' profits slumped 18 percent. Just as the hangover from the war boom began to be felt, however, the U.S. was involved in Korea. From 1949 to 1950, Stevens' profits rebounded. The boom was on again.

It was short-lived. When the bust of 1953-54 arrived, Stevens' margin on sales sank below 2 percent. At that, the company was luckier than the scores that sank out of sight. It also was—as ever— a little bit more farsighted and adaptable.

For one thing, the company began earlier than most to shift operations southward. In the Army, Bob Stevens had met an affable fellow colonel with a Georgia drawl, John P. Baum, who had been manager of a cotton mill before the war. In 1945, Baum joined J. P. Stevens and, although he had never been in a woolen mill, he was commissioned to begin moving woolen and worsted manufacturing to Dixie. The reasons were obvious, at least to those who saw through the euphoria of what the Stevens executives call "the fake years." Old buildings and high costs were a killing combination, and then there were the unions. In a typical case, the Stevens mill at Rockville, Connecticut, was struck in 1951, after the Textile Workers Union of America local refused a change in work assignments. A company ultimatum was ignored, the workers stayed out, and the mill was closed. Only seven Stevens woolen mills remain in the North, and their future is uncertain. "The New England mills are struggling," says Whitney Stevens, vice president for woolen and worsted sales, and Bob's son. "They survive on special skills and experience." Another executive puts the situation bluntly: "Bob Stevens would close even the North Andover mill if it didn't make a profit; he's not running any museums." Since 1947, Stevens has closed four northern mills (and acquired two); in the same span it has established eight new mills in the South. It also has said goodby to the unions. Stevens now pays an average hourly wage of $1.55 in the South (vs $1.72 in New England).

While J. P. Stevens was about rebuilding, it built a different kind of business, integrating such operations as finishing, which had formerly been done by outsiders. A cotton-finishing plant at Wallace, South Carolina, built in 1950, has been automated and expanded to five times its original size. In synthetics, Stevens used to sell its entire output of tricot as gray goods; now it finishes most of its tricot, and has seen sales grow from $10 million to $30 million. Vertical integration is profitable, but mainly it shortens the channel of trade between manufacturing a yard of goods and the final sale at the retail counter. This long channel, in which goods pass through the hands of the converter, the jobber, the cutter, the wholesaler, and other specialists, has been the grave of many a primary producer. For the message signaling the turn of the retail market from one product to another travels slowly along this complex network, usually not reaching the manufacturer until he is buried in unwanted inventory. Stevens wants to control its goods through as many processes as are profitable, with the aim of getting closer to the consumer.

The most ambitious move in this direction came in 1952 with the stock purchase of Utica & Mohawk Cotton Mills, a leading producer of sheets and pillowcases. Stevens, while no stranger to acquisitions, had memorable headaches shaking this one down. Utica-Mohawk was moving south from upstate New York when Stevens took over, and it was months before personnel and equipment were sorted out. Stevens soon discovered it had overrated the management of the company, and had acquired fewer experts than it had hoped for. While a new management was being created and integrated with the parent, Stevens painfully learned how to make a quality bed sheet. "We had seconds running out of our ears," recalls a veteran of the ordeal. Years were required to establish Utica-Mohawk as a solid money-maker. A mill built at Clemson, South Carolina, in 1952, and since expanded, now opens bales of raw cotton (650 a week) at one end and ships packaged sheets and pillowcases at the other. Stevens, which does an estimated $40 million in sheets and pillowcases annually, is neck and neck with Springs Cotton Mills for second place in the business (first: Cannon Mills).

While reaching out to the consumer, Stevens in the early postwar years also moved deeper into synthetic fibers—and into new problems. For example, glass fiber, which had been introduced in the late Thirties, offered desirable properties—resistance to flame, high dimensional stability—but weaving it seemed wellnigh impossible because of cutting and breaking. "At first," says Andrew J. Sokol, recently retired vice president for synthetics merchandising, "we threw the glass salesman out the door until he could prove it was practical. Then we hired him to head our department."

Entering the field in 1947, Stevens passed up the seeming

shortcut of acquiring one of the few glass weaving companies and learned the business the hard way. Special machinery had to be designed to provide the new precision required in weaving. Improving the appearance and texture of the inert glass fiber, to exploit its promise in household markets, plunged Stevens into the chemistry of dyestuffs and the technology of ceramics. Breaking into glass was time consuming and costly. The Stevens plant at Slater, South Carolina, which has become the largest combined glass-fiber weaving and finishing installation in the world, represents a new investment of $10 million. Stevens and Burlington are the leaders in the glass-fiber business, in which Stevens has a volume of about $35 million annually, divided between household and industrial markets.

The Shooting War in Washington

In the midst of the scrambling at Utica-Mohawk, the experimenting with glass, and the weakening of the Korean boom, Chairman Stevens resigned from the company, in January, 1953, to join the incoming Eisenhower Administration as Secretary of the Army. He was a stranger to politics and politicians. His name had been suggested to Ike by Defense Secretary Charles E. Wilson, who knew of Stevens and his good World War II record in the Office of the Quartermaster General. "I went to Washington for one reason," says Bob Stevens. "A shooting war was going on and kids were getting killed." John P. Stevens Jr. moved into the chairmanship left vacant by his brother, and continued in the post until his retirement last year.

Bob Stevens performed competently as Army Secretary, and traveled 74,000 miles in the course of four trips to the front in Korea. About the bitter, bruising episode that culminated in the so-called Army-McCarthy hearings, he prefers to say nothing, except to remark wryly that his tour of duty taught him something about "human relations." A friend who counseled the harassed Army Secretary comments: "Bob Stevens is a gentlemanly, reserved fellow, and I can see someone going into a conference with him thinking, 'I'm going to take this guy's hide off.' But you don't do this to Bob Stevens. He matured in Washington, and was abler and more skillful when he went back to his company."

On his return in September, 1955, Stevens stepped into the presidency and, with his embattled brother John, faced up to a bad situation. The textile business had plummeted the year before: J. P. Stevens' profits were off $6 million, although the dividend was cut, earnings had failed to cover it. Nevertheless, Stevens took a familiar tack in hard times and acquired D. B. Fuller & Co., of Easthampton, Massachusetts, Cheney Brothers of Manchester, Connecticut, which was faltering after a hundred and seventeen years, and the ninety-five-year-old Worumbo Manufacturing Co., of Lisbon Falls, Maine. Stevens also purchased the textile properties of the Simmons Co., the mattress manufacturer, which gave the company another consumer line in Simtex napkins and tablecloths.

A Sizable Impression

Growth by acquisition would be an illusion, however, if the textile business were to keep sliding downhill. In the Army, Bob Stevens had been exposed to military and industrial research on a vast scale. "It made a profound impression," he recalls. Here were companies spending money that might not yield a return for several years, if at all—quite a change from the textile industry's practice of never losing sight of a dollar. Recognizing the need to tackle basic textile problems, J. P. Stevens in 1957 set out to create a research program that would provide answers while staying within limited means.

At the most generous estimate, the textile industry annually spends *one-tenth of 1 percent of sales*, or $14 million, on research, compared with 2 percent of sales spent by U.S. industry as a whole. Though J. P. Stevens does not disclose R. and D. expenditures, knowledgeable outsiders guess it spends about $3 million annually—or one-half of 1 percent of sales. Since 1957, a staff of eight researchers and technicians has grown to 130, of whom forty-five hold degrees. Organic chemistry, promising products hitherto unattainable, receives major attention. One notable success has been the development of a superior wash-and-wear finish, created by building new cotton cellulose molecules with reactive sulfone, a process now licensed to chemical producers. Stevens also has gained a good share of automotive markets through research yielding improved one-piece tufted and molded carpets (a $10-million-plus business for the company). Stevens hopes to apply the experience to the manufacture of tufted floor carpeting, which has grown from nothing to 75 percent of U.S. carpet sales in the past dozen years.

With textiles losing out to paper in some markets, J. P. Stevens teamed up with Kimberly-Clark Corp. in September, 1959, to form the jointly owned Kimberly-Stevens Corp., which is making fabric through processes that eliminate spinning and weaving. In addition to tapping markets falling between textiles and paper, nonwoven materials promise the economies of continuous-process manufacturing. Some nonwoven fiber products have been marketed—e.g., disposable aprons, pillowcases, and surgical drapes and gowns (used on the hospital ship, SS. *Hope*). Kimberly-Stevens, starting from scratch, has made only modest progress. In 1962 the company had estimated sales of $2 million.

Experiments in nonwoven materials are being conducted at the Stevens research laboratory. A needle punch "loom," for example, intertwines jute fibers to make the backing for automotive carpets. Blankets also are being made on the loom. In a $200,000 pilot plant at the Stevens lab, fibers are being combined and bonded to a scrim backing electrostatically.

Another joint venture growing out of Stevens' research is in plastics. In August, 1961, Stevens and Enjay Chemical Co., a division of Humble Oil & Refining Co., bought the National Plastic Products Co., of Odenton, Maryland. Approximately half of National's $20-million volume is in Nevamar, a high-pressure laminate used for tabletops and counters. A major aim of the joint venture is to develop the manufacture and use of fibers made from polypropylene, a byproduct of petroleum refining. National will begin commercial production of multifilament and staple polypropylene this summer. While Stevens does not plan to go into the synthetic-fiber business in a big way, it feels textiles have been too dependent on the fiber producers. "If we have proficiency in the fiber area, it gives us flexibility," says Dr. Paul B. Stam, Stevens' vice president for research.

How to "Find" $11 Million

There's an obvious symbolism about the profits arising from Stevens' research laboratory; it is housed in buildings once occupied by a company that died because it couldn't adapt—the old Forstmann Woolen Co., of New Jersey. Forstmann, founded in 1904, had established its reputation by turning out high-quality woolens, and when postwar markets changed under the impact of imports and overcapacity, Forstmann continued to run 500 looms on high-priced (i.e., around $5 a yard) goods. "The only way they could have survived," says a woolen man at Stevens, "would have been to keep fifty looms on Forstmann goods and put the rest on $1.50-a-yard stuff that they called something else."

Forstmann couldn't bring itself to do that, and Stevens acquired the stricken company in September, 1957.

Forstmann was acquired for 280,000 shares of Stevens' stock, which was selling at $23 a share at the time, and its assets were transferred to Stevens' records at book value. Stevens tried to operate Forstmann but soon concluded its old mills could not be run competitively and would have to be liquidated. In anticipation of losses involved in running out and selling the Forstmann mills, a reserve fund was created. The proceeds of the liquidation, plus the reserve, produced a cash flow of $11 million for Stevens. In effect, Stevens realized $41 a share for its 280,000 shares of stock. "It took two years of hard work and a lot of explanation to the board," says Kenneth W. Fraser, Stevens' financial vice president, "but this deal enhanced our equity by $11 million."

Financial resourcefulness, like diversity, is essential in the modern textile business. So is close control, and Bob Stevens recognized early that an expanding and increasingly complex company could not be controlled effectively by traditional methods. He gave the green light to data processing. Since 1957 the computer program in the synthetics division has cost J. P. Stevens some $500,000, a scandalous amount in the eyes of some old-timers, but it is saving the company more than $300,000 a year.

The man behind the computer is compact, precise J. Roy Lawing, Stevens' assistant treasurer, who found that his difficult campaign to sell the computer concept was a breeze compared to the job of making it work. Orders from twenty-four merchandising departments in New York had to be coordinated with the capabilities of twenty-nine manufacturing units. The variables were staggering: a given fabric may be available in 250 classes of quality. The average weekly production of five million yards could encompass an almost infinite variety of items. Moreover, the flow of orders had to be matched with the flow of fibers through the manufacturing processes. What began as two fibers could become sixteen woven items, each with a different delivery date. The new system would have to avoid both inventory pileups and late deliveries resulting in canceled orders.

Beginning with the consolidation of manufacturing and merchandising records at the Greensboro divisional headquarters, the computer program moved by stages from an I.B.M. 607 to the present I.B.M. 1410 (monthly rental: $30,000). Once an order is received, it now goes by teletype from New York directly into the computer, which matches the order against inventory data stored in its memory unit, selects the desired yardage from appropriate

warehouses on a first-in, first-out basis, and teletypes to the plant
(or plants) the invoice and bill of lading. As a byproduct, the
computer supplies figures on costs, inventory, and theoretical
profit and loss more quickly (by at least two weeks) and far less
expensively than under the old methods. When data processing
invaded plant supply rooms, the results were spectacular. In the
first six plants, data processing uncovered $300,000 worth of ex-
cess inventory, which was sold and the cash applied to working
capital.

In the next phase, extending perhaps into 1966, the computer
is expected to procure raw materials, control inventories, and
assign orders to looms. Just beginning is work toward the predic-
tion of trends, based on data disclosing historical patterns in
market variables. "This should give us clues soon enough to enable
us to see the weak spots and shift to the strong," says Lawing.
Can the textile business be reduced to pushing buttons? "The
computer is another tool to compete with," Lawing believes, "but
it isn't going to replace any creative thinking."

Fashion Is a Form of Divorce

Whatever Captain Nat might think of computers, he would
doubtless applaud, and marvel at, his great-grandson's attention
to style and fashion. With almost three-fourths of its yardage
going into apparel markets, J. P. Stevens is goaded by the generally accepted estimate that half of the apparel fabrics in use
in 1970 will be constructions now unknown. The firm employs
140 stylists. Some of their ideas are exuberant—e.g., the decision
a few years ago to splash bright colors through the lingerie line.
("Fashion is the desire to change," says a stylist. "For a woman,
it's a mild form of divorcing her husband.") Other style ideas
are coldly practical, such as the application of a relatively underpriced fiber to an emerging trend. "We caught the market unaware on the development of mohair fabrics in the fashion cycle
of luxury and style," says a Stevens man. "We bought mohair
near the beginning of a rise from $1.50 to $2 a pound, and had a
good thing going for a year and a half."

The household markets, which took 16 percent of Stevens'
output last year (vs. 3 percent ten years earlier), are regarded as
a major growth area. Stevens' over-all strategy has been to upgrade its product line from staple to styled goods, and to continue upgrading the latter. Early this year the company introduced
a line of styled terry towels, produced in mills converted from

low-margin industrial goods that have run into stiff import competition. Another consideration was that towels fit into the distribution pattern established for Utica-Mohawk sheets and pillowcases. At Utica-Mohawk, printed goods have grown from nothing to 25 percent of sales in five years, evidence that styling pays. Although it also produces unbranded sheets (for J. C. Penney and other retailers), Stevens pursues the higher-margin, branded market (e.g., Utica-Mohawk, Beauticale) that accounts for some 50 percent of U.S. sheet and pillowcase volume.

"Seven years ago," says Irving Cohen, vice president for marketing services, "it was decided that Stevens had to be brought closer to the retailer." Stevens does only 10 percent of its volume directly with retailers, but by leapfrogging its own middleman customers to get at *their* customers, Stevens tries to promote brand identification and to spot shifts in markets early enough to check inventory buildups.

In today's textile markets, size, once it is under skilled management control, tends to attract sizable customers. In 1952, Stevens had about fifty million-dollar-plus accounts. Last year it had twice as many, and the ninety-nine largest among its 17,000 customers accounted for 40 percent of Stevens' total volume. Large retailers, apparel manufacturers, and other customers, witnessing wholesale liquidation of primary textile producers, have given new weight to the continuity of supply offered by a large company, and relatively less to the lower price sometimes offered by a small company that may go under. The trend toward lean inventories in U.S. industry also favors the larger, more efficient supplier. Stevens' transportation fleet of 450 units, with headquarters at Greensboro, can make delivery to warehouses on the West Coast within seventy-two hours. In Kenosha, Wisconsin, American Motors operates on a three-day supply of auto carpets, depending on Stevens to deliver every fourth day. The interaction of large customers and large producers is an important force affecting the structure of the textile industry. Bigness breeds bigness.

Growth also inspires a search for fertile new ground, even as far afield as Europe. Stevens took its time getting started overseas, and did not make its first move until December, 1960. A joint venture in the Netherlands, Stevensten Cate N.V., was arranged with Royal Textile Mills Nijverdal-ten Cate N.V., to make and sell cotton work-clothing, rainwear, and sportswear fabrics. In 1961, Stevens purchased a minority interest in France's S. A. Pierre Genin & Cie., the largest weaver of glass fabric in Europe (1962 sales: about $5 million). Last August, Stevens formed a British subsidiary to distribute decorative glass fabrics. George Roderick, an Assistant Secretary of the Army under Bob Stevens, who joined the company as a vice president for overseas operations in 1961, explains that Stevens picked glass fabric as the best bet abroad because it is entirely new. Stevens has bigger plans for the future. "Our foreign operations will be smaller, but we want to duplicate our diversity in the U.S." However, nothing made overseas, he emphatically declares, will be shipped back to the American market.

Woebegone Wool and Balled-up Cotton

The reason for this odd-sounding declaration is, of course, that "import" is a dirty word in the textile business. J. P. Stevens, as an expanding overseas enterprise and as a leading spokesman for an industry asking government protection against overseas production, finds itself in a somewhat ambivalent position. But Bob Stevens insists that the plea of American textile manufacturers is not a violation of principle so much as a case of principle made impracticable.

Woolen and worsted imports undeterred by tariffs (which average 40 percent of value) amounted to an estimated one-fifth of U.S. woolen consumption in 1962. Chief exporters to the U.S. are the United Kingdom, Japan, and Italy, with Italy's trade expanding explosively. Although style and market changes are factors, rising imports are generally regarded as the overriding cause of the 50 percent liquidation of the U.S. woolen business since the end of World War II. (Woolen manufacturers tend to play down the effects of high raw-material costs, the result of long-time government protection of domestic woolgrowers). J. P. Stevens did 20 percent of its business in woolens and worsteds last year, and, along with the rest of the industry, it wants protection. "What remains of the woolen and worsted industry," says Bob Stevens, "is utterly incapable of handling military and essential civilian needs in case of an emergency." A petition to the Office of Emergency Planning, seeking import restraints on the ground of U.S. security, has been pigeonholed for almost two years.

In cotton, the industry's case for government help is strongest because it is government that has made free trade in cotton textiles impossible. "How can we compete," asks Bob Stevens, "when the federal government ties one hand behind our back?"

The Two-price Tangle

One must go back to 1956 to see how the knot was tied. That year the government, which has supported domestic cotton prices since 1933, took fright at the buildup of government-owned cotton in federal warehouses. Congress authorized payment of a subsidy to exporters, to bring the subsidized raw cotton into line with world prices and so dispose of it. Thus began the so-called two-price system: domestic manufacturers pay the government-imposed price for cotton; foreign textile manufacturers may buy U.S. cotton at the lower world price. (Annual U.S. imports of raw cotton are restricted by law to less than one day's domestic consumption.) In 1956, when the two-price system started, the U.S. was a substantial net exporter of cotton textiles.

In 1962, U.S. imports of cotton textiles exceeded exports by more than 40 percent. Thanks to an increase in the support price by the Kennedy Administration in 1961, the export subsidy for cotton has risen to 8½ cents a pound, or $42.50 a bale. Multiply that figure by the 450,000 bales of cotton Stevens uses annually (it works out to about $19 million) to get an inkling of the inequity textile manufacturers are stridently opposing. Their case boils down to an unassailable complaint: fabrics made overseas from U.S. cotton bought at the world market price of 24 cents a pound, and shipped back to the U.S., can undersell goods made in the U.S. from cotton bought at the government-fixed minimum price of 32½ cents a pound. Not even soaring textile productivity, which has risen 57 percent in the past dozen years, can overcome the competitive disadvantage imposed on the U.S. textile industry by the political pricing of its chief raw material.

Logic argues for an end of two-price cotton and a return to the free market. In practice, though, politics has overruled logic. Nearly 75 percent of U.S. cotton farmers hold government allotments of fifteen acres or less, but each farmer has a vote and is vocally represented in Washington. Highly efficient cotton growers in Texas, Arizona, and California can operate profitably without the government subsidy; indeed, many growers blame it for the loss of cotton's markets to the synthetic fibers. "The difficult thing to get across to the farmer in, say, South Carolina, is that cotton has to compete with other fibers," says Gordon McCabe, Stevens' vice president for cotton and wool purchasing. "Rayon staple is selling at 25 cents a pound; medium-quality cotton sells for 36 cents a pound. With the waste factor in cotton, this means it is selling about 15 cents higher than competitive fibers." Although the number of farmers is declining in poor cotton-growing areas such as the Carolinas, unused acreage allotments by law must remain in these areas, and cannot be transferred to the Southwest, where growers are hungry for acreage.

Since textile men think it is useless to tackle the cotton price-support program head on, the subsidy to exporters is deemed indispensable, even though it has at best slowed the decline of U.S. cotton sales abroad. Therefore, in response to textile-industry pleas for relief from two-price cotton, the drift of congressional thinking is toward a new government subsidy, which would be paid to one of the middlemen who handle the cotton between the grower and the textile manufacturer. At the mill gate, the government, in effect, would knock down the price it had propped up on the farm. To put it another way, the scheme calls for a subsidy to offset a subsidy that offsets a price support.

Textile men aren't happy about this "solution," but they have embraced it. "If we can't get the loaf," reasons James Finley, Stevens' vice president for cotton merchandising, "we'll take a slice." Less is said about another slice that is already in hand. In late 1962 a five-year agreement went into effect between the U.S. and twenty-one other textile-exporting countries, enabling the U.S. to restrain each country's imports by category of cotton fabric if domestic markets were disrupted. In effect, the U.S. can resort to quotas. Hickman Price Jr., recently resigned Assistant Secretary of Commerce, who negotiated and administered the pact, estimates that between 75 and 90 percent of the categories of cotton textile and apparel imports are now under restraint.[1] Even so, imports in 1962 were a record 1.1 billion yards, or about 7 percent of domestic consumption. Without the quota system, Price estimates that imports might have been well over three billion yards. "Looking at it broadly," he says, "if the U.S. can restrain cotton imports for five years and meanwhile get around the two-price system, the U.S. cotton-textile industry can breathe."

Artificial respiration has been purchased at a stiff price that few in the industry appreciate. "The stress so many of us put on imports has had a depressing effect on textiles and hasn't helped us with the financial community," admits Ken Fraser, Stevens' financial vice president. "But it was a calculated risk; we finally got Washington to do something."

The Rewards of Self-help

It is something of a paradox that Bob Stevens has spearheaded the industry's drive for help from Washington when the

---

[1] For the first time in history, the U.S. last year imposed a peacetime embargo and impounded imported goods ruled in excess of quotas.

history of his company so clearly reflects the rewards of self-help. If J. P. Stevens had dug in its heels and kept its pocketbook shut in the face of sweeping change, it would be in no better shape than those who clamor desperately for protection. Perhaps the most striking contrast between the textile industry as a whole and J. P. Stevens in particular is provided in the company's woolen and worsted division. Vice President John Baum expertly reviews the steep decline of domestic woolens, then notes that "Stevens' experience has been absolutely counter to the trend." It has. From 1952 to 1962, while U.S. woolen and worsted capacity was shrinking by one-half, Stevens' output more than doubled. "In this business," says Baum, "you either stay modern or you're dead."

Still, the more things change at Stevens, the more they remain the same, in at least one respect. When John P. Stevens Jr. retired a year ago, he turned the chairmanship over to brother Bob. But the role he had loved best was being chief woolen and worsted merchant for the company. Both John and Bob were particularly careful about filling that vacancy. Now selling a tough line in a tough business is thirty-six-year-old Whitney Stevens, one of Bob's four sons. And in the generation right behind are more sons, whose job it may be to stretch the durable Stevens threads from North Andover around the world.

REPRESENTATIVE ANALYSIS—INTENSIVE APPROACH

The Durable Threads of J. P. Stevens*
by Richard J. Whalen

I. Identification of the Company
   A. J. P. Stevens Company.
   B. Textiles.
   C. 35,000 employees in 55 plants from Maine to Georgia. 1962 output—800 million linear yards of fabric; 1,200,000 spindles, 30,000 looms. Record sales of $586 million in fiscal 1962 (18 percent over 1961). Second largest textile company of the U.S. (and the world).
   D. Chairman and President: Robert T. Stevens. Financial Vice-President: Kenneth W. Fraser. Executive Vice-President: William J. Carter.
   E. Public ownership.

* April 1963

II. *Brief Summary of Early Company History*
  A. Founded in 1812.
  B. By Captain Nathaniel Stevens.
  C. At North Andover, Massachusetts.
  D. Circumstances: with the westward push of population, U.S. markets for cloth were expanding and imports would be cut off for the duration of the War of 1812. Nathaniel Stevens and two friends took over a gristmill and immediately converted to produce woolens.

III. *Philosophy of the Company*
  Mr. Stevens has said, "We go to the market place and attempt to find out what the public wants. If the public wants straw, we'll weave straw. We're not wedded to any particular product or fiber." In brief, the company's philosophy is basically merchandising oriented.

IV. *Objectives of the Company*
  A. *Profitability*—"Bob Stevens would close even the North Andover mill if it didn't make a profit; he's not running any museums."
  B. *Growth* through product diversification and acquisitions.
  C. *Survival* in a highly competitive market.

V. *Policies of the Company*
  A. *Product diversification*, "across the board."
  B. *Vertical integration*, starting with raw material purchasing, moving to production, finishing, and the selling trades.
  C. *Horizontal integration*, for example, Kimberly Stevens Corporation—for markets falling between paper and textiles (nonwoven materials); joint venture with Humble in petroleum fibers field (polypropylene).
  D. *Growth*, through mergers, and acquisitions made during depressed periods.
  E. *Public ownership*—Chairman Stevens, "The discipline of public ownership is a stimulus to management to do a good job. . . ."
  F. *Basic research*—at Garfield, New Jersey, 66,000 square foot central research laboratory and pilot plant. Research budget estimated at $3 million annually, or one half of 1 percent of sales. Staff of 130, major emphasis on organic chemistry.
  G. *Aggressive merchandising*—84 Stevens selling departments in New York City headquarters tailor the mills'

output to the specialized wants of hundreds of distinct markets. Promotion of brand identification.

H. *Overseas sales*—commitment to markets of Western Europe starting in 1960, including the Netherlands, France, and Great Britain.

I. *Geographic displacement*—post-World War II movement to new southern mill location; since 1947, 8 new mills in the South.

VI. *Type of Organization Structure of Company*
   A. Domestic corporate parent.
   B. Joint ventures, both domestic and foreign.
   C. Product departmentation—under Bob Stevens, the 1946 merger structure composed of 14 divisions was reorganized to three divisions by fiber.

VII. *Authority, Responsibility, and Accountability*
   Not expressly covered.

VIII. *Planning*
   Long-range planning in the field of product development (synthetics); same for overseas operations, data processing, and production techniques.
   Financial planning in regard to mergers, acquisitions, liquidations, etc.

IX. *Decision Making*
   Emphasis on the quality of management in any acquisitions. Some executive staffing from external new fields sources, tradition of family top management developed from within company.
   Heavy emphasis on top executive creative thinking, and decision making based on industry experience.

X. *Directing*
   Board controlled, top level corporate direction.

XI. *Control*
   A. Integrated data processing in order and inventory system, advances being made in production control.
   B. Almost three-fourths of company yardage goes to apparel markets. Company employs 140 stylists—attempts to catch fashion trends early in the cycle thus regulating production and inventory from New York.
   C. Large-block stockholder control in hands of company executives.

XII. *Company Relations*
   A. *Public*—not expressly covered.
   B. *Employee*—not expressly covered.

C. *Stockholders*—not expressly covered.

D. *Union*—hard-line approach with antiunion company sentiment.

E. *Government*—protective in nature—against overseas production and for import restraints.

Enabling pact between United States and 21 textile-exporting countries which established an import quota system by category of cotton fabric if domestic markets were disrupted.

This agreement has led to a peacetime embargo, which resulted in impounding imported goods ruled in excess of quotas.

F. *International*—joint ventures and harbinger of the adoption of multinational concept. See Government.

G. *Community*—not expressly covered.

XIII. *Human Relations*

Not expressly covered.

XIV. *Ethics and Morality*

Not expressly covered.

XV. *Summary*

Here is the second largest textile company of its kind in the world, and it continues to survive and grow as the industry as a whole contracts.

Key factors in its success include the ability to perpetuate effective top-level management, programs of basic and applied research, modernization of company organization structure and internal systems of management control, and an aggressive merchandising policy.

The challenge of obsolescent plants and equipment (and high labor costs) has been met by a program of plant relocation in the South.

The philosophy of the company is well perceived—profitability and survival through research and merchandising.

Through skillful mergers, brilliant financing, foresightedness, overseas growth, diversification, respect for his subordinates' wisdom and judgment, Chairman Stevens would certainly make his great-grandfather proud of him.

_____*part II*

CASES

What Happened at Burlington
When the King Dropped Dead*_____

BY SEYMOUR FREEDGOOD

A conspicuous feature of most executive offices in Burlington Industries' modest headquarters building in Greensboro, North Carolina, is a framed color photograph of a slender, youthful-looking man with a lean, freckled face, smiling blue eyes, and a wide, generous mouth. This was James Spencer Love, Burlington's diffident but fantastically hard-working founder, who dropped dead on a tennis court two and a half years ago. But when, as they often do, Love's corporate heirs glance at his portrait, they do so with mixed emotions. Many of them believe that Love, who escalated the company he started from scratch as a small cotton mill in 1923 into what is now by far the nation's biggest and most diversified textile manufacturer, ranks with Thomas Watson and George Eastman as an industrial and financial genius. But under Charles F. Myers Jr., Spencer Love's successor as chief executive, Burlington's managers find life, as one of them put it recently, "a hell of a lot more relaxed."

But not only more relaxed. For to the total amazement of outsiders as well as some insiders, Burlington today also appears to be more successful than ever. By 1962, the year Love died, he had acquired textile companies at such a rate during his thirty-nine years as Burlington's boss that his empire consisted of upwards of 120 plants located in eighteen states, plus operations in Puerto Rico and eight foreign countries. From these there cascaded a seemingly endless flow of fabrics suitable for almost every conceivable use in the apparel, home-furnishings, and industrial fields. Organized in thirty-six divisions or "profit centers," each with its own president, manufacturing staff, and sales organization, and all largely autonomous within the corporate frame, Burlington for the first time broke the industry's sound barrier by producing consolidated sales of $1 billion, almost twice those of J. P. Stevens, its closest publicly owned competitor.

* June 1964

33

Yet in President Myers' first full fiscal year after Love's death, the company's sales came to $1,084,919,000 and this year they may well reach $1.2 billion. Profits have kept up with the sales growth. Burlington had a net of $40,620,000 in fiscal 1963, which represented a 10.5 percent return on stockholders' equity. This compares with 5.3 percent achieved by Stevens and about 6 percent averaged by the industry. A return of 9.8 percent on stockholders' equity was the highest during the last five years of Love's life. In part as a result, Wall Street has come to view Burlington with such enthusiasm that its common stock has doubled in value from about $24 a share when Myers took over.

Thus Burlington has accomplished that most difficult feat in a corporation's life, successfully managing the transition from what many considered unorthodox, unpredictable one-man rule to a modern team operation. This transition is all the more remarkable because Spencer Love did not seem to be the type of man capable of gathering and keeping a strong, talented management group about him. Quite the contrary. A brilliant, complex, and often contradictory entrepreneur who has been variously described by his associates as a "thinking machine," "impulsive, sharp tongued, and full of whims," a "perfectionist" with an "incredible flair for detail," a "lucky sharpshooter willing to take outside chances," and "the most demanding and most considerate boss in the business," Love was the very epitome of the nonorganization man and his difficulties with his lieutenants were legendary.

Outspoken, frank, mercurial, and capable, as one Burlington director puts it, "of falling in and out of love with an executive faster than anybody I've ever seen," he constantly shifted about those who did not meet his high standards. Unused to sharing the throne and wishing to have the final say on all major decisions, he was unable to work for very long with a second-in-command: the few whom he elevated to this difficult position were soon demoted or left the company. And his troubles with his managers were by no means confined to the senior men. Throughout the 1950's, when he was gobbling up companies, some of them giants, at the rate of about two a year, his need for competent managers became so acute that he made it a practice to hire young men, some just out of college, train them briefly by having them serve as assistants either to himself or to some other senior officer, and then, if he liked their style, hand them a key job at corporate headquarters or in one of the divisions. From then on, as one of the more successful of these recalls it, "You were on your own. With Love, the company always came first. He judged only by

results. If you got them, O. K. If you didn't, you were through."
As a result there were inevitable casualties. Although the number
of these has undoubtedly been exaggerated, there were enough
so that in the mid-Fifties, when Burlington was in the midst of its
acquisition boom, a joke in the industry had it that Love was contemplating setting up a separation center for fired vice presidents.

Management by Memo

Love had a final trait that made him a difficult chief executive
to serve. Essentially a shy man, he preferred to manage Burlington's affairs by the written word rather than by face-to-face en-
counters and did so by way of what came to be called "pen notes."
These were short memoranda that he either dictated to his four
secretaries or scribbled on small pads of yellow paper which he
carried in his pockets; the secretaries reproduced the memos for
the files and then distributed them to all concerned parties. Working seven days a week and up to eighteen hours a day as he
shuttled between his Greensboro and New York offices and his
homes in Greensboro and Palm Beach—a schedule he interspersed ·
with ritual bouts of tennis, touch football, and bridge—Love might
be expected to write fifty or more such notes daily in addition to ·
regular correspondence and formally typed memos. Since he encouraged his executives to use the memo system to make their
own suggestions, he usually received thrice that many in return.
In this way, he managed to keep track of Burlington's minutest
details.

Love's pen notes had other functions. He encouraged the
hugger-mugger of intracompany politics and found it instructive,
as another survivor of the process puts it, "to hear a young guy
take a crack at an old guy," which he liked to get in writing. "He
thought that kind of competitiveness kept everybody on their
toes." Naturally, some older men would feel obliged to reply in
kind, thus further adding to Love's knowledge of the situation.
In his efforts to keep tabs on everything that went on in the
company, he thought nothing of asking subordinates what they
thought of their bosses. Recalls the president of one division,
"He'd call up one of my junior salesmen and ask how he thought
I was doing. It was murder." "The boss," adds another Burlington
man, "got results but lots of them were by needling and reminding
people of their shortcomings."

Considering Love's peculiar genius, it is not surprising that many outsiders expected Burlington to blow apart after his demise, particularly since he had never formally appointed a successor. At the very least, they expected a period of political infighting before a new chief executive was chosen, a period that would be followed by the inevitable wounds and bad feelings.

Yet there was one important point the outsiders had missed. This was the fact that, despite Love's showers of paper and his heckling and needling, he did inspire loyalty toward himself and the company. Strong men did stay with him—each fully trained in his ways and all fully able to say no to him on occasion—any one of whom was capable of taking over as chief executive officer. Some, like J. C. Cowan Jr. and Stephen L. Upson, now vice chairmen of the board, William A. Klopman, head of Klopman Mills, a major Burlington subsidiary, and Edward R. Zane, general counsel and chairman of the executive finance committee, had been Love's associates almost from the start and were thoroughly versed in the company's operations. Others, like Executive Vice President Walter E. Greer Jr. and Herbert M. Kaiser, head of Burlington's hosiery operations, Henry E. Rauch, then the corporation's controller, and Charles F. Myers Jr., its treasurer and in effect financial vice president, although post-World War II acquisitions, were also thoroughly knowledgeable about what makes Burlington tick. In fact, Love had built such a topflight group of men around him that it explains at least in part why he died without choosing a successor. "Spencer was afraid," explains one of the group, "that if he did choose an heir apparent and then lived on for some time, he might change his mind afterward."

When, in January, 1962, Love died of a heart attack at sixty-five while playing tennis at Palm Beach, that choice became a stark necessity and was, as matters turned out, accomplished smoothly. Burlington's board members met in Greensboro and selected a nominating committee from among themselves to choose a new head. Although the committee in its month's deliberations considered the possibility of going outside the company, in the end they unanimously tapped Myers, now fifty-two and the youngest of the senior group, with a background in international operations as well as corporate finance, to be president and chief executive officer. To back him up, they selected Henry Rauch, sixty-one, to serve as a working board chairman. One member of the nominating committee recalls, "We knew that no single man could replace Spencer. He was one of a kind. There was a desire for a team operation."

The New Team

This is precisely what Burlington has got under its new regime and the company has probably gained by the transition. For while one man may build a great organization, it is seldom that he can pass on his own peculiar style to any single person. Myers and Rauch haven't tried to imitate. Both professional finance men, they quickly agreed that, as Rauch puts it, "Charlie and I would split Love's job."

In doing so they appear to have reversed the usual roles of chairman and president. Rauch, an exceedingly hard-working chairman, who, in the opinion of his colleagues, knows more about the company's internal operations than anyone else in it, spends much of his time touring Burlington's vast network of plants in an effort to increase productivity and profits. President Myers, while very much Burlington's chief executive, concentrates on broad policy decisions and on administering the company's over-all affairs.

Myers differs temperamentally in almost all respects from his predecessor. A native-born Southerner who graduated from Davidson College and the Harvard Business School and worked as a banker in New York and the South before joining Love as a financial adviser in 1947, he is an urbane, gregarious, outgoing man and a top-notch administrator who likes and works well with people in a relaxed yet firm manner. Myers prefers to deal with his subordinates directly rather than in writing, as a result of which the stream of pen notes has disappeared. And instead of emulating Love's practice of intervening personally in matters of small detail, he leaves that to others.

There are other important differences of both style and substance between Myers and his predecessor. Like Love, Myers keeps a tight rein on the activities of Burlington's large array of divisions by way of a management committee chaired by himself and consisting of Rauch and seven other top officers, each responsible for a group of divisions whose presidents report to them and whose operations they discuss at frequent meetings held at the company's Greensboro or New York offices. But in his dealings with the committee Myers, according to one of its members, "is more patient than Love, more willing to prolong discussion. Spencer was quick and brought things to a head quickly. Also, we've got more teamwork now. We arrive at decisions jointly. Charlie is firm but he doesn't start out knowing all the answers."

Soon after attaining the presidency, Myers in fact changed both the composition and function of the committee. As constituted by Love, it was a rotating body on which he placed younger executives to give them a sense of the broad sweep of company operations. Myers reduced the role of the younger men in top management by replacing them on the committee with a number of their elders, like William G. Lord, president of Galey & Lord, one of Burlington's most profitable divisions, and Frank H. Leslie, who has primary responsibility for Burlington's cotton and synthetic greige-goods sales, because "at the time of transition I wanted to be able to call on our senior merchants." Today Myers is proud of the wealth of youthful executive talent in the company, upon which he is depending to replace the older men as they retire: about half of Burlington's seventy top manufacturing and sales executives are still in their thirties or early forties and there are a dozen more in other top posts. On the other hand, he does not use the system of preparing young executives for important posts by having them serve as his assistants and, in further contrast to Love, he tends to turn for advice to his seniors rather than the juniors. "In Spencer's time," observes one of the founder's old associates, "Burlington was on a youth kick that sometimes got out of hand." In addition, Myers has transformed the committee from what, under Love, was at least partially an educational and coordinating body into one primarily concerned with operations.

There are other major differences. In the twelve years between the turn of the 1950's and Love's death he put out $284 million in cash and stock to acquire seven large and a score of smaller companies. Since Myers and Rauch took over, the firm has acquired a substantial interest in Stoffel AG, a Swiss manufacturer of high-quality combed cotton and synthetic blended fabrics with sales of about $14 million annually. The venture will expand Burlington's overseas operations and give it a larger foothold in the European market. Domestically, however, Burlington has not made one acquisition of any importance. The reasons for this are not hard to find. Having diversified by acquisition very heavily in the Fifties, company executives feel that they have picked the available fields fairly clean and that few good offers remain at reasonable prices. Needless to say, Burlington is being approached by people wishing to sell companies and it, of course, considers such offers: the textile industry continues to include a great many family-owned businesses, the inheritors of which often wish to sell out, and in looking for potential purchasers they naturally approach the biggest companies first. But in contemplating such offers Burlington must, of course, be exceedingly circumspect: as its counsel, Douglas M. Orr, points out, although the company accounts for only about 7 percent of the industry's $15 billion to $16 billion in sales, "the anti-trust boys are keeping an eye on us all the time even though they know textiles is terrifically competitive." While Burlington may conceivably acquire some new companies in the few fields in which it does not yet have a foothold, or not a major one, the pace of such acquisitions will certainly be much slower than in the past.

Growth from Inside

Consequently, Burlington's considerable growth since Myers took over has and will continue to come primarily from internal expansion and plant improvement, on which the company is spending huge sums. Indeed, as Myers observes, it is now spending more on improvements than Love did on acquisitions. Between 1959 and the time he made his last acquisition—the day before he died—Love spent $177 million on expansion and modernization, about a third of which went into new acquisitions. Between February, 1962, and the end of the company's 1964 fiscal year, Burlington will have spent $153 million, virtually all for additions and improvements to existing plants. "Through internal expansion," says Myers, "we can concentrate on profit improvement in areas where we already have a strong position and proven management, rather than tackling the unknowns that come with acquisitions."

As Myers and Rauch have gone about consolidating Love's empire and expanding it from within, they have turned their hands to a number of new areas. Among other things, they cleaned up Burlington's balance sheet, which until a year and a half ago had four issues of preferred stock piled on top of the common. To correct this they borrowed $25 million in subordinated debentures and called the preferred, a move that will save Burlington some $4 million over the life of the preferreds. Explains Myers: "It made sense to convert to debt. The money market was fairly free and we were able to borrow on a subordinated basis instead of on a senior debt basis. This ability reflected the improving status of the company." Again with an eye on the financial community, Burlington's dividend policy now favors more stable payments than in the past.

Under its new regime Burlington has also concentrated more on research and development. Although the divisions have had their own R. and D. operations for years and a central research lab has existed at Greensboro headquarters since 1959, these various activities were not fully coordinated until recently and the bulk of the investment and effort was concentrated on near-term research problems like proper dyeing applications. Soon after Myers took over, however, he appointed a vice president, George E. Norman Jr., to coordinate R. and D. centrally. Norman, among other things, has expanded the central lab's research library to include a technical information service that will store, retrieve, and communicate all pertinent information to the some 300 technicians working in the twenty-five divisional labs. At the same time the central lab has begun long-range research on such problems as the adhesive characteristics of polymers and elastomers. To keep up with all of this, the central staff has been beefed up from fifty-five to seventy-five technicians in the past two years. In its current fiscal year, the company will spend $12 million on broad R. and D. (including some product development and quality-control work). While industry statistics are sketchy, Burlington's research-and-development investment, amounting to 1 percent of its sales, is probably ten times the average of the industry.

Yet when it comes to actual operations, Burlington today continues to function substantially the way it did under its founder. Like Love, who developed the principle in the first place, Myers puts great stress on divisional autonomy in manufacturing and sales. As he points out, this fragmentation is important in the fast-moving, style-conscious textile industry because "It gives us a chance to move faster with the styles. We're trying to do what G.M. does—give independence to the divisions to hit a special segment of the market." In those segments where Burlington's product lines overlap, like, for example, casual-wear fabrics, which are manufactured by several divisions, Myers also encourages competition. And again like Love, Myers has tried to make Burlington more market-oriented than most textile companies. In contrast to the typical small company, where the plant boss is apt to call the turn on what the company may have for sale, at Burlington the merchandising men in the divisions' thirty-six principal sales offices in New York and elsewhere tell the plants what and how much to produce and are held primarily responsible for profits.

Up the Rope

In going about this, they are dealing with elements of an enormously diversified business that Spencer Love put together in a remarkably short period of time. "It was like watching the Indian rope trick," says one of Love's old associates. "One minute Spencer was standing there with nothing in his pocket but that one hocked cotton mill in North Carolina. The next, he was climbing upward so fast he was practically out of sight."

To understand Burlington as it exists today it is well to recall how Love wove the strands of his rope together. The process involved no fixed plan but rather a series of astute moves that bit by bit shaped a spreading empire. Starting with a mere $3,000 of savings after World War I, Love persuaded a New York commission house and a North Carolina bank to put up some $80,000 for the purchase of an antiquated mill in Gastonia, North Carolina. Came a drop in cotton prices and Love realized this investment could operate successfully only in boom times. Turning around fast, Love sold off the mill's real estate for $200,000, and persuaded civic boosters in Burlington, North Carolina, to underwrite a more efficient plant into which he moved his best looms.

A Plunge into "Poor Man's Silk"

That was the beginning of Burlington Mills and also the beginning of an involvement in the market for synthetic greige (unfinished) goods, then a primitive rayon fabric woven from yarn made by Celanese Corp., Du Pont, and American Viscose, and used primarily for apparel. Today synthetic greige goods are an estimated $500-million business and in it Burlington now ranks among the leaders. Love astutely saw that rayon had big possibilities and proceeded to widen his beachhead into a major undertaking largely through debt. In essence, his practice was to build up one of his companies into a sound enough position so that he could borrow from banks and yarn makers, and this money in turn was used to build up new and struggling ventures. By 1937, Love had some thirty companies on the string with consolidated sales of $27 million and profits of $767,000. In that year he merged them together, got Burlington's stock listed on the Big Board, and raised more than $3 million through a new stock issue.

All this took financial genius, but there was more to Love's success than that. From the beginning, he recognized that he was neither a manufacturing man nor a salesman and that he needed lieutenants. Accordingly, in the first decade or so of his entrepreneurial life, he acquired the charter members of the team that helped him lift the company to the heights—some of them are helping President Myers operate it today. In 1931 he hired John C. Cowan, now a board vice chairman, who became his manufacturing executive. Because Love himself was a Cambridge-born Harvard graduate of southern extraction, he was somewhat at a loss in his dealings with the predominantly Jewish New York converters. So he next hired William Klopman, today the head of one of Burlington's biggest divisions, Klopman Mills, as vice president in charge of New York rayon-greige-goods sales. Then thirty and a crackerjack salesman with a passion for selling rayon or "poor man's silk," Klopman persuaded the New York converters to make generous use of the then novel fabric for lower-priced dress goods and other apparel, and was thus in part responsible for the rise in Burlington's sales right through the depression.

Far from interrupting Burlington's rise, World War II opened new opportunities. Love entered the international field for the first time by acquiring rayon-weaving plants in, among other places, Columbia and Australia. Indeed, the company did so well during the war and immediate postwar periods that it made $91 million in profits from 1942 through 1948, of which Love retained over $61 million to acquire and operate new properties. By that time, he had floated some $29 million worth of preferred stock and borrowed $26 million in long-term insurance-company loans for the same purposes. By war's end, Burlington had also undergone two major transformations: it began to manufacture finished as well as unfinished goods, and at the same time it expanded horizontally into ribbons, tricot-knit goods, and other textile fields in the synthetic area where it had had little or no foothold.

Still wedded to synthetics in the immediate postwar period, Love continued Burlington's expansion in that area by acquiring the women's hosiery manufacturing firm of May McEwen Kaiser for Burlington stock, then worth about $11 million. Love had nudged into this field in the late Thirties when he organized six small companies to manufacture full-fashioned hose, and in 1944 he bought Harriman Hosiery Mills of Harriman, Tennessee, a producer of seamless stockings, for $1,500,000. But May McEwen Kaiser, with its Cameo line, provided Love with a top-line branded stocking, which Burlington lacked. It also provided him with Herbert M. Kaiser, a founding partner of M.M.K. and a top merchandiser who joined Love to head up his hosiery operations and continues to be active under President Myers. Today, through Burlington's hosiery division, the company has the biggest single share (about 10 to 15 percent) of the $460-million hosiery market.

By then Love was discovering that synthetics were not the whole show. Just after the war he socked $12 million into Cramerton Mills, a top North Carolina producer of high-style cotton dress goods and, soon afterward, bought Galey & Lord, Cramerton's New York sales outlet, intending to convert Cramerton to spun rayon. But these acquisitions proved so profitable that Love changed his mind and kept to cottons. In the Fifties he made another series of major moves that just about tripled the company's sales in a decade. The first came in 1952 when Love, concerned about the waning demand for rayon products, paid $22 million in cash and stock for Peerless Woolen Mills of Rossville, Georgia, owner of the nation's largest woolen-manufacturing plant. As it turned out, the Peerless acquisition was one of his few failures: though it was eminently successful at first, a combination of rising woolen imports after 1956 and a consumer trend away from bulky woolens toward lighter worsted-synthetic and cotton-synthetic blends put the division in such a bind that Love was eventually forced to liquidate all but a Cleveland woolen operation.

Two years after acquiring Peerless, however, he got into the worsted business by buying, for $48 million, the big Pacific Mills of Boston, a major producer of wool worsteds and cotton printcloth, whose cotton operation Love soon sold off at a nice profit. Today Burlington's Pacific division, along with another worsted operation, Raeford, which Love acquired in 1956, make it the biggest factor in the U.S. worsted business (which probably comes to some $400 million annually at manufacturers' prices, including some $125 million in imports).

Encouraged by the success of the Galey & Lord lines of fancy cottons produced by the Cramerton Mills, Love broadened Burlington's base in cotton. In 1955 he acquired, for $5,500,000, Mooresville Mills of Mooresville, North Carolina, a supplier of a somewhat simpler line of cotton fabrics, and in the same year paid $63 million for Ely & Walker, a St. Louis drygoods firm that owned some big printcloth mills. In addition, just before his death in 1962, he acquired, for about $25 million, Erwin Mills of Durham, North Carolina, now the largest producer of stretch denim for casual clothes and sportswear, and a substantial factor in other finished goods, including sheets and pillowcases.

Love also jumped into two new fields. He bought Hess, Goldsmith & Co., through which Burlington today is the largest producer of decorative glass fabrics (draperies, bedspreads, shower curtains) in a market of some $40 million to $45 million. He likewise acquired control of Sidney Blumenthal & Co., a major producer of fake fur, pile linings, and toy and upholstery fabrics. In the same period he made an even more important acquisition. In 1947 his former sales vice president, William Klopman, had left

Burlington to found his own company, Klopman Mills, a rival producer of synthetic greige goods. In 1956, Love and Klopman got together again when Love bought stock control of Klopman ("A Man You Can Lean On") Mills, which now gives Burlington by far the biggest share (upwards of $100 million) of an estimated $250-million market in polyester-cotton fabrics. Klopman is still the boss of this operation.

Rounding out his acquisitions, Love made Burlington one of the three largest outfits (along with Mohasco and Bigelow-Sanford) in the current $950-million woolen and blended-fiber carpet market when he bought, for $44 million worth of stock, the more-than-a-century-old Philadelphia carpet-manufacturing firm of James Lees & Sons Co. And that was not the end of it. By a wide variety of smaller acquisitions during the 1950's, Love also got Burlington into fields as diverse as men's socks and vinyl fabrics. Indeed, of the many product lines that make up the textile industry, he may be said to have bequeathed his corporate heirs a major beachhead or at least a foothold in virtually all except blankets and towels.

Benefits of Bigness

To hold all of this together is now the business of President Myers and his associates, and it is obvious that they have their hands full. While Burlington breaks down neither its sales nor its profits, it is evident that it has a dominant position in many segments of the $15-billion to $16-billion textile industry. Not only is it the leader in worsteds, but it is also at the top or near the top of the heap in the production of both cotton and synthetic greige goods, of polyester-cotton fabrics, of stretch fabrics, and of fancy cotton fabrics by way of Galey & Lord and Mooresville Mills. And by its prominence in hosiery, carpets, and decorative glass fabrics, it has a strong position in consumer items as well.

In this diversification there is, of course, great inherent strength. In an industry as volatile as textiles the trouble with the small company is that it must concentrate on one segment of the market, and, because of shifts in fashion, its products may go sour. In contrast, the big company operating in many market areas can compensate for the profit downturns of some operations by the upturns of others. Moreover, with the high cash flow of $78 million at the end of 1963, Burlington is in a better position than its smaller competitors to cash in on the more profitable areas.

Yet life in even the textile industry's biggest company is certainly not all roses. Last year, for example, Burlington earned only 3.74 percent on its sales of $1,084,919,000. While this was slightly higher than the median of the top twenty publicly owned companies in the industry, the margin is, of course, on the slim side as manufacturing operations go. The reason is that while textiles have been integrating, the industry still contains a great many independent operators with lots of capacity and it is also plagued by the problem of foreign imports. Thus the business is fiercely competitive and the net effect is to hold prices down.

But Burlington's 10.5 percent return on investment after taxes is higher than it has been in years and Myers is determined to make it better. According to him, the average pretax return on investment[1] for Burlington's thirty-six divisions came to about 16 percent in fiscal 1963 as against 12 percent in the five previous years. Moreover, despite the ups and downs of the textile business, Myers anticipates that by next year 80 percent of Burlington's divisions will yield a minimum pretax return of 12.5 percent on investment. Until now, divisional pretax returns have varied from close to breaking even in the case of two small divisions all the way up to 40 percent for some of the divisions producing high-style fabrics.

An Accent on Profits

One reason behind Burlington's much better than average investment returns undoubtedly lies in its huge expenditures on new plant and equipment, now running at the rate of more than $60 million a year. In addition, Myers and Chairman Rauch have moved in two other ways to improve Burlington's productivity and profitability. For one thing, they have gone out of their way to improve the company's employee relations. Like most big textile operators with the majority of their plants in the Southeast, Burlington has very few union members in its work force. Traditionally, however, it has paid its 52,000 hourly wage earners at a higher scale than the average for the industry in seven southern states where the bulk of Burlington's plants are located; this comes to average earnings of $1.76 an hour compared to the $1.70 industry average in those states. To add to this, the company in the past year has provided a profit-sharing plan for the hourly workers. While both Burlington and some of its bigger competitors

---

[1] The company defines divisional investment as total inventory plus net fixed assets and customer accounts receivable less trade accounts payable.

have had comparable plans for their salaried employees for years, the new program is unique among the industry's large operators. At the same time, under a company-wide profit-enhancement program, plant workers are encouraged to make suggestions about cost cutting and productivity increases. Company executives are convinced that the two programs are paying off in positive results.

The net effect of all of this has already provided Burlington's 32,000 stockholders with some good news. For the company's first six months (ending March 28) of fiscal 1964 it had consolidated net sales of $587,839,000 compared to $537,491,000 for the same period last year, up 9 percent. Of this, net earnings came to $22,731,000, equal to $1.89 a share on 12,008,000 outstanding common shares, of which the company plans to distribute 37.3 percent. For the same period last year, net earnings were $21,099,000, equal to $1.70 a share. There is probably more good news to come: for the whole of fiscal 1964, the company expects its net profits to rise by about 15 percent over last year to some $46 million. Confident, expert, and extremely flexible in its adjustments to the volatile textile market, Burlington under its new team of managers appears to be in extremely good shape.

G.M.'s Remodeled Management* _____

BY ROBERT SHEEHAN

Almost a year before Harlow Curtice's retirement was due, a special committee of the board of directors of General Motors was quietly formed. Its franchise: to reassess the whole question of G.M.'s top management structure; and to recommend, to the board at large, a successor to Curtice as chief executive officer of the company.

There was a great deal at stake in the impending decision—both for G.M. and for the U.S. economy. The past twelve months have not been cheerful ones in the automobile industry; even today, with a general business recovery well under way, there is a question whether Detroit will be a drag or stimulant. With its

* *November 1958*

completely redesigned line of 1959 cars just hitting the market, much of the burden of proof lies with G.M. Some 588,000 employees sign its $3-billion payroll, 718,000 stockholders draw approximately $568 million in annual dividends, and 26,000 prime supplier firms throughout the U.S. depend on G.M. for $5 billion in orders yearly. The fortunes of millions of people, and the flow of billions of dollars, are highly sensitive to any variation in touch on the tiller of giant G.M.

Yet the responsibility for choosing the new leadership had to lie with a select few. It was obviously not a matter that could be frankly debated before the full board of G.M. The leading candidates for the big job to be filled were all members of the board.

The chairman of the special committee was G.M.'s eighty-three-year-old chairman emeritus, Alfred P. Sloan Jr., who laid out the corporation's first effective organization chart thirty-eight years ago, and whose remarkably durable energies have never since ceased to be absorbed in the corporation's affairs. The other members of the committee were Board Chairman Albert Bradley, Walter S. Carpenter Jr. (who is chairman of the board of du Pont), General Lucius D. Clay (a "public" member of G.M.'s board), and Harlow Curtice himself.

What the committee finally did was to rearrange rather radically, all things considered, the power lines of the world's largest industrial organization. For Curtice was replaced, in effect, not by one officer, but two—Frederic G. Donner, fifty-six, former executive vice president for finance, who became chairman of the board; and John F. Gordon, fifty-eight, former vice president in charge of the body-and-assembly group, who was named president. Strictly speaking, of course, Donner succeeded the retiring chairman, Albert Bradley. But the distinctive point is that Chairman Donner was designated chief executive officer of the company, and is therefore principal heir to the power that once was Curtice's. It is the first time in over a dozen years that this power has resided in the office of the chairman in New York (who traditionally has a close relationship with the shareholders) rather than in the presidency in Detroit (traditionally the voice and arm of management).

To the U.S. business community these changes have been an engrossing subject of speculation. There is naturally an overwhelming curiosity as to what really went on in G.M.—after all, the jobs up for grabs were among the highest-paid in American industry. But there is also a genuinely studious interest, among corporate executives everywhere, in the complex management problem posed by the changes, and the thinking that went into its solution.

Beneath the surface of General Motors, furthermore, one can begin to discern the makings of a momentous change in the whole character of the corporation, perhaps involved only marginally in the choice of Donner and Gordon, but bound to come in their time. In this article, *Fortune* explores some of the implications of this approaching change at General Motors, as well as the more immediate considerations involved in the choice of the Donner-Gordon team for the top command.

Breaking Up the Burden

For Mr. Sloan's special committee, the picking of Curtice's successor was in a sense secondary to a re-evaluation of G.M.'s whole top-management concept. Except for fiscal affairs, which came under the financial policy committee, Curtice had pretty much the whole show on his hands. As the discussions went on, it became the firm belief of the committee that the full load of responsibility for government relations, labor relations, public relations, and the running of the multiple manufacturing establishments of G.M. was just too great a burden for one man.

From this conclusion it was logical to move on to consideration of a setup in which G.M. would have as chairman a full-time employee of the company who would be responsible for broad policy and the external equilibrium of the company. And with him would serve a president responsible for operations and the internal equilibrium of the company. This is the pattern of organization observed by such corporations as U.S. Steel, General Electric, Standard Oil (New Jersey), and many others. Indeed, it is not too different from the old G.M. pattern when Sloan was chairman and chief executive officer, with first William S. Knudsen, and later Charles E. Wilson, as president. It was broken off in 1946, when Mr. Sloan, then seventy-one, finally retired as chief executive officer in favor of the president, Mr. Wilson, but was induced to remain as chairman of the board.

While Mr. Sloan's entirely unpublicized committee, meeting principally in New York, went about its work, there was plenty of gossip inside G.M. and out. Many of the gossipers had only one solid fact to go on: Harlow Curtice's sixty-fifth birthday would fall on August 15, 1958. One rumor was that G.M. might change the rules to enable Mr. Curtice to stay on in his post for an ad-

ditional six months, or a year; or that he might move on to chairman of the board. But this did not enter into the committee's
thinking. In the first place, all hands agreed it would be unwise to
make an exception to the mandatory retirement rule in favor of
the president. And in the new conception of the chairman as employee, subject to retirement at sixty-five just like anybody else,
neither Curtice nor Bradley, who is sixty-seven, was eligible for
that post. They both remain on the board, however, and both are
members of the newly named Finance Committee, which is now
the senior G.M. committee.

Clearly, the burden on the top command of G.M., and the
desirability of splitting the job among two men, was the primary
and immediate reason for the organizational change. But there
are other forces that are also working a change in G.M.'s structure
and control.

The Potent 26 Percent

Because G.M. is not only so huge, but such a model of
modern corporate efficiency, even sophisticated observers tend to
forget what anybody can learn from a glance at the proxy statement: that G.M. is really a proprietary company with a concentration of ownership that is far more characteristic of small business
than of large business in the U.S. today. In this respect it is
virtually an anachronism among giant corporations.

There is, first of all, the 23 per cent interest of du Pont,
represented by four family members on the board—Walter S.
Carpenter Jr., Lammot du Pont Copeland, and Emile F. and
Henry B. du Pont. Of course, it has always been said that the du
Ponts do not vote as a bloc, and that they studiously refrain from
flexing their muscles in the G.M. board room. But forget the
du Ponts for a moment, and consider the five members of the
board—some of them with close du Pont ties—who together own
approximately 3 percent of General Motors' 279 million outstanding shares. They are Alfred P. Sloan Jr., with 1,297,261 shares;
Charles F. Kettering, 3,281,970; Charles S. Mott, 2,458,000; John
L. Pratt, 642,426; and Donaldson Brown, 415,432 shares. To be
sure, 3 percent of ownership hardly represents naked control of
the company. But few would quarrel with the assertion that this
combination of directors, if they chose to act as a combination
(and assuming the neutrality of the du Ponts), certainly constitutes the dominant voice in General Motors. The shareholdings
of all the other twenty-five directors combined add up to only

slightly more than one-third of 1 percent of the total shares out-standing. (The biggest institutional investor, Massachusetts Investment Trust, with 675,000 shares, holds less than one-quarter of 1 percent of the total.)

But now observe the ages of these men. Sloan is eighty-three; Kettering, eighty-two; Mott, eighty-three; Pratt, seventy-nine; and Brown, seventy-three. None has any progeny who are associated with General Motors or who aspire to any direct relationship with the company. Also, bear in mind that under the recent Supreme Court decision du Pont will probably divest itself of all—or a large part—of its G.M. holdings, and however the divestiture is worked out, it is almost a certainty that the du Pont members will be required to retire from the G.M. board.

It Can't Happen Again

So the moving finger writes. And it is doubtful, indeed, that any similar concentration of ownership will ever rise again in G.M. It is inconceivable that any company or coalition will ever have the opportunity to "save" G.M., as du Pont did some forty years ago, in return for a quarter interest in the company. Nor is it likely that circumstances (and taxes) will ever again permit individual accumulations on the Sloan-Mott-Kettering scale. All three established their ground-floor positions with the sale, several decades ago, of their small companies to Billy Durant. (Sloan sold Hyatt Roller Bearing Co., of Harrison, New Jersey, and Kettering sold his Dayton Engineering Laboratories—Delco—to United Motors, later merged into General Motors. Mott sold the Weston-Mott Axle Co. of Flint, Michigan, direct to General Motors.) They took a large part of their payments in stock, and "never had the sense to sell it." In addition, Sloan and Kettering (and similarly Pratt and Brown) participated in the famed Managers Securities Co. bonanza, the original stock-purchase plan that set up the early officers of G.M. so handsomely.

Latter-day G.M. managers, for all their spanking salaries and stock bonuses, can't begin to approach such levels of financial influence in the company. Harlow Curtice, after forty-four years of service with G.M. (he missed out on the Managers Securities deal), owns 44,113 shares today. Frederic G. Donner has 26,080 shares; John F. Gordon, 5,640. When former President Charles E. Wilson was named Secretary of Defense, and had to unload his G.M. stock in deference to the "conflict of interest" principle, he owned 39,470 shares, which he sold for $2,680,000 (he has since bought 500 shares to qualify him for his recent return to the G.M. board).

Tempering the Revolution

As General Motors passes from proprietary to professional management, and turns from a board representing huge blocks of stock ownership to one representing the stockholders at large, the much-advertised Managerial Revolution is finally arriving at the world's largest industrial corporation. How much did the anticipation of this ultimate change influence the changes in the top command that were put into effect two months ago?

In speculating, one runs the risk of reading into the minds of the decision-makers certain complications and abstractions of thought that may have played no conscious part in the decision-making process. After all, these were practical businessmen tackling a practical and concrete problem. In the words of Mr. Sloan, "We simply sat down, and in the light of the size and nature of the task, and of the capabilities of the people available, recommended what we thought was best for both the short-term and long-term interests of the Corporation."

Nevertheless, it may be assumed that if the coming managerial revolution was foreseen, the instinct—among the senior members of the board, at least—would be to slow it down. Prudent businessmen usually take that approach ("Let it be evolutionary, not revolutionary"). And one way to adjust the balance and prepare for management's ascendancy would be to make the chairman, who has a close relationship with the shareholders, the chief executive officer. In the past twelve years the chairman of the board of G.M. has had only an advisory role. But since he represented those huge blocks of stock, he exerted a very real influence. That would not be the case, however, with the boards of the future. Hence it can be said that the change which has just been made ties management and shareholders together while there is still time to do it.

Owners vs. Managers

That is not to suggest that in the past there has been any noticeable divergence in the interests of management and shareholders in G.M. In corporations where such conflict occurs, it is usually over long-range policies, favored by management, that work to the temporary disadvantage of the shareholders. Thus management may prefer to issue new stock rather than borrow; to plow back earnings rather than pay the high dividends that some directors might feel the smaller shareholders deserved; to pay what may seem to be disproportionately large salaries and bonuses in order to keep the organization intact and strong in depth. But in G.M. these issues do not appear to be controversial. Most of the large shareholders on the board were a part of management at one time. They still have the management approach to problems, and they have a fantastic attachment and loyalty to the organization as a whole.

Most important, the company has been very successful, and G.M. shareholders, large and small, can scarcely quarrel with what management has accomplished in their interests. Under Harlow Curtice's regime, for example, though G.M. spent tremendous sums for expansion and development, it regularly paid out between half and two-thirds of earnings in dividends to stockholders. It was under Curtice, also, that G.M. elected to sell new stock to the tune of $325 million, a move that some old stockholders might have felt constituted a "dilution" of their share in the company's ownership. The fact is that when Curtice became president, in 1953, one share of G.M. stock sold for $68. When he retired last September, the old shareholder had three shares for the price of one, and the market price was $43 a share. So the $68 share of 1953 had grown to an equity of $129 in 1958. Curtice's management at G.M. produced record-breaking sales and profits. It was a resilient management, too, and after a mediocre year in 1957, it came back more strongly, in the first half of 1958, than its major competitors.

Yet Curtice's was also an extremely independent management from an organizational point of view. Though he was meticulous in observing company protocol, and scrupulously avowed his deference to the powers of the governing committees and to the board, he was such a crisp and confident executive, and moved so fast and forcefully, that he usually got his way. Again, there is no suggestion that Curtice and the board diverged seriously on fundamentals of policy. But conceivably some of the senior members may have blinked a bit at the way policy was whipped through, and felt that their role was tending more toward affirmation that formulation. Suppose you had a powerful manager of this type who missed, instead of hit, the target? At any rate, with "Red" Curtice, the G.M. board got a foretaste of what life will be like when the Managerial Revolution is fully accomplished. And perhaps a subconscious voice whispered, "If we must have strong management, let it be vested, closer to home, in the chairman of the board."

How the Choice Was Narrowed

When it came to picking the people for the new setup, the special committee benefited from a Darwinian kind of force that is always at work in General Motors, a process that might be called the natural selection of the competent. Like all companies, G.M. has its factions and informal coalitions. But in its executive promotions, G.M. is actually rather cool to cliques and favorite sons, and there is absolutely no nepotism at all. "The good of the organization" is the ultimate test, and every general officer of the company is presumed to have passed it.

This might have led to a confusing overabundance of candidates except for the critical matter of age. The committee felt that any chairman or president needed a minimum tenure of five years if his administration were to have the necessary continuity and freedom from speculation over "who's next?" For all practical purposes this eliminated any candidate over sixty. (Harlow Curtice might never have been president of G.M. had not Charles E. Wilson joined Eisenhower's Cabinet in 1953. At Wilson's normal retirement date—1955—Curtice would have been sixty-two.) Among the able and vigorous executives thus disqualified as successors to Curtice were Sherrod E. Skinner, sixty-two, group executive for accessories, and Cyrus R. Osborn, sixty-one, vice president in charge of the engine group. (Another highly qualified officer, Executive Vice President Ivan Wiles, sixty, had retired at the first of the year for reasons of health.)

When the age test was applied, it left less than a dozen G.M. officers even remotely qualified for the top posts. Among these men, "natural selection" had already brought five to places on the board of directors. Whether the committee looked seriously beyond these five, or precisely how hard they found it to choose among the five, is a matter the committee members are understandably closemouthed about. But two of the five—Donner and his first lieutenant, George Russell—were "financial" or "New York" men, and once the decision had been made that the new chairman should be a full-time employee with responsibility for finance and broad policy, the choice of Donner was virtually inevitable.

Picking the President

The choice of the new president, from the three "operating" or "Detroit" men, may have been more difficult. One was Roger M. Kyes, fifty-two, group executive in charge of household appliances and the GMC Truck Division. But Kyes, who was once president of the Ferguson tractor outfit, has had only ten years of service with G.M., and was also away from the company for fifteen rugged months as Wilson's deputy in the Pentagon. It may be, too, that Kyes was, as the phrase goes in G.M., "too controversial" for the presidency. Another of the "Detroit" men was Louis C. Goad, fifty-seven, executive vice president in charge of the car divisions, a job that many thought tabbed Goad as heir apparent. But, as one of the selection committee members puts it, "There are no heirs apparent in G.M." It has always been G.M.'s boast that it could cast up, at any given time, several fully qualified men for the presidency. Goad was certainly one of them, like Gordon who got the job. To many outsiders it looked like a fielder's choice. Goad, incidentally, along with Gordon, has been elected a member of the top-policy Finance Committee.

How Will Donner Do?

In the two months he has been chairman, many a reporter has probed Fred Donner for his views on vital points of G.M. policy. His debut would have indeed been sensational had he announced that he was panting to build a small car, or that he thought annual model changes were antisocial, or that he was worried about G.M.'s being too successful. Donner preferred a quiet debut. On major issues his statement of the G.M. case often sounds like a synthesis of Sloan, Wilson, and Curtice, except that it is possibly a mite more precisely phrased. And in the transition stage, this is probably all to the good. But Donner is booked to be chief executive officer for nine years. In due time he'll have to decide on problems for which there are no precedents, and meet change with change in a creative way. Except in the financial area, however, there is not much in the record on Donner as a policy *maker*. One can report only on his general assets. They are very impressive assets.

Fred Donner was born to modestly prosperous parents in Three Oaks, Michigan. He went to the University of Michigan where, as an economics major, he pulled straight A's (except for one B in a history course) for all four years, and was graduated in 1923—a Phi Beta Kappa, of course. For the next three years he worked for a public accounting firm in Chicago. But in 1926, G.M.'s Albert Bradley, also a Michigan graduate, wrote to his old classmate William A. Paton, who had become professor of economics at Michigan, and asked him to recommend a bright young accountant with "an analytical type of mind." Dr. Paton sent Fred Donner to him, and in G.M.'s financial hierarchy, in New York City, Donner's rise was swift. In 1941, at thirty-eight, he was made vice president in charge of the financial staff—one of the youngest V.P.'s ever in G.M. history. Six months later he was elected to the board of directors. In 1956 he was elected an executive vice president of G.M. and chairman of the Financial Policy Committee.

Though "financial man" is hardly a term of opprobrium, to tab Donner as that, and strictly that, is to underestimate his range. The G.M. financial staff has always been much on the order of a general staff, and broadly concerned with operations. One of Donner's first big tasks, back in the Thirties, was to make an extensive study of G.M.'s distribution system, and he has been regularly engaged in the analysis of dealer policies, sales, and marketing reports—and even consumer research—ever since. On the labor side he has been responsible for formulating pension plans, benefit programs, wage scales. He has never built an automobile, but he is the company-wide expert on cost controls and product pricing. He was the group executive in charge of General Motors Acceptance Corp. and the G.M. insurance subsidiaries. He handled the renegotiation of G.M.'s huge defense contracts. And through many a Washington hearing he's served as one of G.M.'s most resourceful witnesses.

The Answer Man

Donner's knowledge of G.M. is encyclopedic—"a more extensive knowledge of all operations," says one director, "than that of any other single person in the corporation." He carries about with him, in his inside pocket, a small black notebook into which he has compressed a series of charts that seem to hold the answer to any question of fact you can ask him about the automobile industry. Taunt him with a careless assertion about the automobile's declining prestige, and he whips out the notebook, traces, with stern finger, the correlation of consumer spending for automobiles to U.S. disposable income (in constant dollars) from 1948 to 1958. You were wrong, of course.

But Donner is not a mere collector of facts. They are his tools, and he is highly regarded, in G.M. board and committee meetings, for the caliber of his analyses and judgments. In alternate years, for the past ten years, he has taken his vacations abroad, spending much of his time touring G.M. establishments there. When he returns, he writes a paper analyzing economic conditions in the United Kingdom, Belgium, and Germany, and discussing the outlook for General Motors operations abroad, which is distributed to the corporation's officers and board members. He is a reader, principally in economics and history, and it is a strange and wonderful experience to hear a G.M. executive, in discussing the problem of G.M.'s bigness, casually cite a parallel from Thucydides' *Peloponnesian Wars*.

Like the men who have preceded him in the top command, Donner yields not an inch in his defense of General Motors' size, and its share of the auto market. He is determined that G.M. shall do more business rather than less. He thinks the best way to defend the corporation from political attack is to keep it progressive and keep it clean, "to be able to be proud of our dealer relations, labor relations, community relations, and of our product." He bristles at the faintest suggestion that he, Donner, may ever be expected to plan for or preside over a G.M. retreat, and he compares such thinking to the reported Pentagon study of surrender plans that made Mr. Eisenhower so furious a while back.

Nevertheless, one feels that if G.M. ever should be forced to compromise on the issue of size or monopoly, it would have a useful strategist and spokesman in the person of Donner. He is a generally well-informed man who knows what's going on in the U.S., and in the world. An orthodox economist himself, he is conversant with left-of-center economic theory—he has read *The Affluent Society* as well as *The Wealth of Nations*—and in any economic or ideological controversy he can be depended upon to parry as well as thrust. It is not to be doubted that the G.M. directors felt that a leader of Donner's intellectual and analytic capacities was particularly called for at this stage in G.M.'s history; and that if he was to have the time to handle the task as it should be handled, he should be relieved of direct responsibility for operations, an equally large order in itself.

Engineer-President

For its president and operations chief, G.M. chose in Jack Gordon a solid man who has handled a diversity of important jobs in thirty-five years with the company, and has never had a failure. He is the engineer who developed for Cadillac, in 1948, the first genuinely new V-8-type engine. Virtually all high-compression engines in use today are based on that design.

Recently a press photographer, aiming his camera down on Gordon's nearly bald pate and square-cut features, exclaimed, "Why this guy looks just like Ike!" As it happens, Gordon is an Annapolis man. Ohio-born, he entered the academy through a competitive examination during the World War I period, but like some 150 other midshipmen in the class of 1922—when the world's navies were piously undergoing reduction—he was permitted to resign on the day of his graduation. (One classmate who didn't: Admiral Hyman Rickover.)

Gordon took his master's in engineering at the University of Michigan, then went to work at Cadillac's experimental laboratory division. It was in 1939 that Gordon was assigned to head a product-study group in forward engine design. It was a blue-sky project, and the group designed a high-compression engine, calling for 100-plus octane, that was at least a dozen years ahead of its time: such fuel wasn't available then.

When World War II approached, Gordon took his entire forward engine group over to Allison, in Indianapolis, to build airplane engines on a volume basis. In 1943 he returned to Cadillac as chief engineer and three years later was made general manager of Cadillac, where he was "lucky enough," he says, "to put the Cadillac in a position where the car always deserved to be—superlatively competitive."

In 1950, Charlie Wilson picked Gordon to be vice president in charge of G.M.'s engineering staff. Gordon wasn't sure he wanted to leave the exciting Cadillac operation for a staff job. Wilson said to him prophetically, "We never make promises about the future to any man in G.M., but—I strongly advise you to take it." He did, and six months later was promoted to group executive in charge of body and assembly plants. In this job he practically lived with all the car divisions of the company, and was in the closest contact with the styling, engineering, and production of every automobile in the G.M. family.

This family of cars, 1959 edition, has just been brought to market, and for the first time in history all five of them are completely new in the same year. Of this legacy from Harlow Curtice, Gordon says, "I think they are at the zenith of eye appeal and quality. I feel fortunate to move into this job at a time when we have never been in better shape from the standpoint of product and organization."

An Agonizing Appraisal

These cars are, in general, longer, lower, and wider than ever. As Gordon bent to the task of selling them, it was perhaps an inopportune time to request his opinion and prophecy on the small car. But Mr. Gordon is an accommodating man, and it can solemnly be reported that (1) G.M. "has been watching the small car with interest"; (2) G.M. is not sure whether small car sales in the U.S. are at the top of a leveling curve, or whether the curve is still rising; (3) if G.M. becomes convinced there is a sizable small-car market it will be ready to be in that market because (4) G.M. has always been the first to participate in any *volume* U.S. market, and the present administration has no intention of departing from that policy.

Mr. Gordon is not rocking the boat either. His actual phrase is, "I do not intend to quarrel with the success of G.M." But it would hardly be in order for either Donner or Gordon to fill the air with explosive comment at this juncture. Both men are working unconscionable hours in an effort to establish an entente with each other, and jointly with the division heads and dealers. Except for the necessary replacements, they contemplate no substantial changes in executive personnel (James E. Goodman was named to Gordon's old job; George Russell succeeded Donner as executive vice president for finance). And so G.M. rolls on, without disruption, under dual controls.

It certainly seems like a prudent way to run a company of such size and complexity. The men at the controls are highly competent. They appear to be—as they must be—fully compatible. What remains to be seen is whether the system can supply the intuitiveness, imagination, and intensity of the single leadership of the past.

It's a New Kind of Ford Motor Co.*_____

BY ROBERT SHEEHAN

Henry Ford II has the candor and grace to say, when questioned on the point, that he "badly misses" the services of Ernest R. Breech, who chose to retire as chairman of Ford Motor Co. in the summer of 1960, and of Robert McNamara, summarily snatched from the presidency of Ford a year ago for a post in the Kennedy Cabinet. But for his subsequent one-man stewardship of the company (later supplemented by the promotion of sixty-three-year-old John Dykstra to president), Henry II, as chairman and chief executive officer, clearly has no need to apologize. Rarely, as in the year just past, has Ford come forth with such a continuous drumfire of hard and highly significant news—some of it reporting Ford's aggressive maneuvers in the grim battle of Detroit; some of it pregnant with augury of an exciting Ford future in new lines of endeavor, and in far parts of the world.

First, a rundown of the battle reports. For the U.S. automobile industry, 1961, up until the wildly resurgent fourth quarter, was a grueling and treacherous year in which the principal gauge of individual performance was the ability to cut losses. Of all carmakers, during the hard infighting of the first nine months, Ford had the smallest slippage in sales (off 3.8 percent vs. 16.4 percent for General Motors), and in profits (off 8.5 percent to G.M.'s 24.6 percent). When industry sales went through the roof in the final quarter Ford was somewhat short of cars owing to the U.A.W.'s October strike. At the finish of the year Ford appeared to be just short of its 1960 figures in sales and profits. With its great, latent power, G.M., too, made up most of its lost ground in sales and profits.

More positively, Ford in 1961 pushed its penetration of the domestic car market up more than two full points to 31 percent, the highest since 1959. The company could also exult in the ability of the Ford Falcon once again to outsell all other compact cars by a wide margin (though the standard Ford is still selling well below the standard Chevrolet). And thanks to the sustained

* February 1962

success of another hot compact, the Comet, plus a 50 percent increase in the sales of the reconceived Lincoln Continental, Ford's long-laggard Lincoln-Mercury Division made a substantial contribution to the company's over-all profit picture. Finally, despite the untimely strike, Ford boldly gave birth, late in 1961, to the Ford Fairlane and the Mercury Meteor, the company's contribution to the new concept of "in-between" compact cars. Ford seems bent on "fragmentizing" the auto industry to a fare-thee-well.

For the business community at large, however, it was the second or new-directions category of news that most whetted the imagination. First there was Henry Ford's resolute consummation, despite a chorus of criticism on both sides of the Atlantic, of the $368-million deal to achieve 100 percent ownership of Ford Motor Co., Ltd., of England. It clearly signaled Ford's intentions to press for a larger share of the growing car market abroad; more particularly, the increased flexibility the purchase gives Ford will enable the company to exploit the full potentialities of the enlarged European Common Market now shaping up. Next came the purchase, for $28 million, of the spark-plug and battery business of Electric Autolite Co., a move that thrusts Ford squarely into the raging competition for the huge U.S. "after-market" in automobile parts and accessories (and has also, incidentally, embroiled Ford in an antitrust suit). The third move was Ford's purchase, for $100 million, of Philco Corp., which, despite all its recent faltering is a big name and a big business still in electronics and household appliances.

"What in the world does Ford want with Philco?" This question, asked by many businessmen, overlooked a basic change at Ford. The Ford Scientific Laboratory in Dearborn has been quietly building up a respectable competence in far-ranging basic research; and out at Newport Beach, California, Ford's five-year-old, expertly staffed, and lavishly equipped Aeronutronic Division has been getting a growing amount of sophisticated research and development work in rocketry and space. With Philco, Ford buys into an active operating position in new-type military hardware, and in the computer, semiconductor, and transistor business. Ford is serious about becoming a creative, primary defense contractor.

In an Odd but Accurate Word

From this potpourri of news is it possible to extract a common denominator—to discern, beyond the more obvious cause-and-effect relationship of any given act of Ford's, a universal quality or attitude that epitomizes Ford's actions as a whole? At the risk of seeming sententious, it is *Fortune*'s judgment that in the perspective of the company's history the performance now going on in Dearborn distinctly heralds the arrival of Ford Motor Co. at maturity.

This may seem an odd and even uncomplimentary remark to make at this late date about the world-famous organization with which the first Henry Ford virtually established the U.S. automotive industry in 1903, and a company that, with annual sales hovering around the $5-billion mark, has for the past eight years ranked as the third-largest industrial concern in the country. But the people of Ford themselves look upon Ford as a young company. Its span is measured from 1946, when its youthful new president coolly cleaned out the almost moribund company from cellar to roof, and with the aid of a half-dozen or so hardened automobile hands, largely recruited from the ranks of General Motors alumni, undertook the most celebrated corporate reconstruction and comeback in modern history.

That story, featuring the heroic quarterbacking of "cocky, stocky Ernie Breech," scarcely needs another reprise. It is essential to recall, however, that the problem facing Breech was to get Ford back into the game that was dominated by G.M. And that couldn't be done simply by patching up Ford. So with Henry Ford II's assent, Breech set out to recreate Ford in the closest image possible to G.M. Among the ex-G.M.'ers he hired for the purpose were Lewis Crusoe, who instituted Ford's first genuine system of cost controls; Del Harder, the manufacturing expert who coined the word "automation"; and engineer Harold Youngren, who threw the existing dies out the window and designed a 1949 Ford car aimed right at Chevrolet's market. And always the battle cry was "Beat Chevrolet."

Incredibly, Ford did beat Chevrolet twice—in 1957 and in 1959—although whenever Ford attempted to compete across the board with G.M., model for model, it met with considerably less success. But the point to be emphasized is that throughout its reconstruction years Ford gave the impression of being obsessed with G.M.—and G.M., for the most part, was calling the moves, with Ford countering. Today there is evidence of a change in Ford's strategy; it is no longer playing the sedulous ape to G.M. Ford's Falcon, its outstanding success, was original in size, price, engineering, and in market concept. And it is General Motors that is countering in that market by coming up with the look-alike

Chevy II in 1962. The new Ford Fairlane, however it may fare, is also a ground-breaker. (Robert McNamara, incidentally, who came up through the company as Crusoe's understudy, is principally responsible for planning the Falcon-Comet-Fairlane programs.) And though in its venture abroad, and in the auto-parts and the defense businesses, Ford is breaking no ground that isn't already being cultivated by General Motors, Ford's present approach is not imitative, but distinctly according to its own lights and style.

Indubitably, Ford still scouts G.M. like a hawk, and respects and covets G.M.'s power and know-how. A certain amount of toe-to-toe competition between Ford and G.M. will go on as long as they're both in business (and for the foreseeable future it will probably continue to be a contest of the light heavyweight champion vs. the heavyweight champion). But it is time to stop scoring Ford's progress exclusively in terms of that contest. Among the Ford executives themselves there is no such preoccupation. If they have any tendency to boast, it is not so much about end results in sales and profits as about Ford's managerial and technical competence, the company's financial controls, planning devices, and marketing techniques. "What we're doing," says Vice President James Wright proudly, "is decreasing the cost of ownership to the American motorist." (An infringement on George Romney's copyright, maybe?)

In short, Ford is a studious company, with more quiet confidence and less locker-room boisterousness than in former years. At critical intervals over the years *Fortune* has looked closely at the changing corporate personality of Ford (see particularly "The Rebirth of Ford," May, 1947, and "Ford's Fight for First," September, 1954). It is in this sense of a developing personality that today's examination finds the Ford Motor Co. "mature."

Getting and Spending

Of Ford's physical and financial maturity, to be sure, the business world has been long aware. Even at its lowest ebb, just after World War II, Ford was hellishly big in gross assets, was absolutely debt-free, and had access to considerable cash. Since the war its rate of reinvestment in the business has been simply enormous: more than $4 billion has been poured into capital facilities, of which nearly $3 billion has gone for building and equipping new plants and modernizing older ones. Except for $250 million borrowed in 1956—the sole debt on Ford's books—all this money has come from profits.

The profits continue to roll in, but the plant, substantially speaking, is all built. Of Ford's total plant today, 90 percent is new since World War II, and 60 percent is six years old or less (which is one of the big reasons, of course, why profits are so good). Clearly, Ford has reached a point where it is not presently necessary or desirable to pour huge sums into plant. The company's last big spending sprees for this purpose were in 1956, when the program hit a peak of $487 million, and in 1957, when $329 million was spent. In 1959, by contrast, capital expenditures for expansion, modernization, and replacement were only $75 million; in 1960 they were $128 million, and last year's estimated capital spending came to no more than $130 million.

Meanwhile, Ford's cash flow (retained profits plus depreciation), despite some increases in the dividend rate, was building up powerfully. Back in 1956 the cash flow was only $252 million, considerably less than what the company laid out in capital expenditures. But by 1959 the inevitable results of Ford's big building program began to show up in the balance sheet. In the first place, there was a very substantial depreciation figure—almost $173 million. In the second place, profits, reflecting the efficiency of the new facilities, rose sharply. Consequently, Ford's cash flow in 1959 was a whopping $471 million (more than $75 million higher than in the peak car year of 1955). In 1960, Ford's cash flow was $427 million; in 1961, probably not less than $400 million.

Looking at these figures one might explain all these new ventures of Ford simply by saying that the company is making more money out of the U.S. automobile business than it can profitably re-employ in the U.S. automobile business. This is only partly true. It certainly should not be taken to mean that Ford, not quite knowing what to do with all its money, is desperately shopping around for "outlets." As a public company for more than five years now, Ford respects its obligation to earn the best possible return for its stockholders. Unless a genuine investment opportunity presents itself, it would be more appropriate for Ford to pay its surplus earnings out directly to stockholders, and let them invest it as they see fit.

"Secretary Anderson Was a Gem"

The question of diversification has long been a back-of-the-mind item at Ford. When Henry II took over from his grandfather, Ford Motor Co. was in a raft of side businesses—integrated and nonintegrated. Henry II junked a number of them, not because he opposed diversification as a policy, but for the practical reasons that they weren't profitable, and that on the basis of first things first Ford had to concentrate all its manpower and money on regaining rank in the automobile business. And for at least ten years Ford was too busy to think of anything else. But ultimately Ford reached a point where it could (*a*) measure its management and skills in depth, and (*b*) sense coming constrictions on the growth of the U.S. automobile business—what Ford economists call "a developing S-curve." So Ford undertook a systematic study of opportunities for other avenues of expansion. Primarily, Ford wants to put its money in quasi-related fields where it can exert its brains and skills and, just as important, get some brains and skills in return.

As far as the expansion of its foreign automobile operations is concerned, there is no urgent need for Ford to export capital. The vast bulk of Ford's capital expenditures overseas—and they amount to more than $700 million over the past decade—have been paid for out of the earnings of the overseas subsidiaries. The Ford payment in dollars for the remaining interests in its U.K. company was a very special action for a very special and obvious reason, and the adverse comments it caused are a source of considerable irritation to Henry Ford II. He vigorously denies, by the way, that the U.S. Government ever requested him to cancel the deal: "Secretary of the Treasury Anderson was a gem about the whole thing. He just wanted to know what we were doing, and we kept him fully informed." It was unfortunately inopportune, Ford agrees, that the deal had to be closed just when the rumble over the U.S. gold flow was at its height. But Henry II keeps handy a chart which shows that "Ford's gold flow" over the decade 1950-60 brought $1.8 billion more into the U.S. than was sent abroad.

The potential of Ford's international operation is by all odds the headiest vision in the company's horoscope. Ford is already doing close to $2 billion in foreign sales (for a ratio of two to five domestic), from which it derives 20 percent of the company's consolidated net profit. In the next decade, it is conservatively estimated, the free-world market in automobiles (outside the U.S.) will grow at a rate of around 5 percent a year. Ford is already getting 13.6 percent of this market, and if the company no more than holds its own it should be selling over a million cars a year outside the U.S. by 1970. And Ford has plans for increasing its penetration. But let the details of that story wait upon a word about the home market, which is not exactly static either, and where Ford has sales of 1,700,000 cars a year in hand.

The Flight of the Falcon

For an example of Ford's maturity as a carmaker, nothing makes the point more precisely than the company's contrasting experience with the Edsel and the Falcon. When the Edsel was plotted in 1955, Ford was still hewing to the theory that it ought to compete line by line with General Motors. At the time, the medium-price bracket accounted for 40 percent of the U.S. car market, and within that bracket G.M. was getting 60 percent of the business. But when the Edsel reached the showrooms in the fall of 1957 the economy was depressed, medium-priced cars were in a dive, and foreign economy cars were the talk of the town. After sales of 110,000 units in two and one-half years the Edsel was withdrawn at an estimated loss to Ford of $200 million.

With the Edsel, the research had been largely built around sales statistics and buying behavior. It mainly showed the past trend of buyers to move up in price class—a trend that quickly evaporated. Most of the consumer research, moreover, was concerned with the public "image" of the car, and not with the actual constitution of the product. The product decisions had been largely made in advance of the research. With the Falcon, a total of fourteen major surveys—each involving from 1,000 to 2,000 people—was made. The groups studied included buyers of foreign economy cars, owners of U.S. economy cars such as the Rambler American, and a cross section of higher-income owners of standard and medium-range cars. The undertaking was not a lonely exercise of the Ford consumer and market researchers, but the work of an integrated product-planning team that included people from finance, engineering, manufacturing, styling, and sales. After the first surveys had established that there was a substantial general interest in a small American car, the planners then postulated a series of "paper cars" of various types as to number of cylinders, length, weight, passenger capacity, etc. Each of them was accurately "sourced" and "costed," and assigned a specific price, a specific gas mileage, and a specific total cost of ownership. Thousands of Americans were then surveyed on their choice of these paper cars. The surveys were designed in such a way that market estimates could be made for each vehicle taken singly, or for any combination of vehicles that might be offered on the market simultaneously. In several hundreds of cases

the studies were supplemented and checked by having the sub-
jects perform actual driving tests of four-cylinder vs. six-cylinder
cars. The results of these studies dictated the basic plans and
objectives of the Falcon car. Whenever Ford had to modify the
objectives, for cost or engineering reasons, it returned to the
market to test alternative solutions.

The major burden of proof for the Falcon fell on the engineers. Early in the game Product Planning handed Engineering
an outline of the "impossible" objectives as to performance, weight,
size, and cost. But Engineering was not required to worry about
interchangeability, or to take anything off the shelf, nor was it
constricted in the choice of materials. The question of the engine,
naturally, was paramount. Some years earlier Ford had done considerable experimentation with all-aluminum engines and with
rear placement, and had largely decided against them. But in
the light of the weight requirements of the Falcon, the question
of these features was reopened and the research reviewed: still
negative. The end result was that Ford developed a precision-
molded, lightweight, cast-iron engine with 120 fewer parts that
was 179 pounds lighter than the Ford car's conventional six-
cylinder engine. And it was a better engine.

Similar challenges were met and mastered in body design.
A new door assembly developed for the Falcon had thirty-one
fewer parts than are in that of a standard Ford. A zinc-coated
steel was developed to solve, inexpensively, the rust problems
inherent in unitized body structures. Fenders (bolted on) and
windshields were redesigned at lower original and replacement
cost, with a resultant saving of 15 percent in a Falcon owner's
insurance premiums.

When it came to market in the late fall of 1959, the Falcon,
at 2,366 pounds, weighed three-quarters of a ton less than the
standard Ford. This enabled Robert McNamara, the executive
in charge of the program, to price the Falcon at $72 less than
G.M.'s Corvair, and offer gas mileage at least 50 percent better
than that provided by standard cars. These were the factors,
above all, that made the Falcon's astonishing record possible—
the sale, from a standing start, of 429,000 cars in the first nine
months, and a total of one million cars sold (December 6, 1961)
in a fraction over two years. Compact cars now account for approximately 36 percent of the U.S. automobile market, and within
that classification the combined share of the Falcon and its
stretched-out sister car, the Comet, is about 35 percent.

But the Falcon was also a breakthrough for Ford into new

concepts of simplified automotive design and manufacture that drastically compressed the time and the money it would take to produce new vehicles to respond to new needs as they emerged in today's violently changing market. For example, shortly after the Falcon hit the road, these interesting facts emerged: 50 percent of the buyers were willing to pay extra for automatic transmission; 42 percent wanted white-wall tires; 63 percent went for the deluxe interior job; and 30 percent ordered the optional souped-up engine though it meant a loss of a mile per gallon of gas. As Ford Division Manager Lee Iacocca has quipped, "The American public wants economy, and they don't care what they pay for it."

Falcon to Fairlane

Thus, five months after the Falcon made its debut, McNamara circulated a "blue paper" (Ford lingo for top-brass memoranda) that began, "In evaluating the market spectrum ranging from the Falcon to the Ford, it appears that there may be an important and untapped market for a product with specifications between these two." Three months later the firm decision was made to go ahead with the "Canadian-X," code name for the new Fairlane, and in just eighteen months' lead time it was produced. Never in this world could such a record have been made without the Falcon experience as a precedent. The same techniques enabled Ford to bring in a car that, at 2,900 pounds, was a complete functional substitute for the basic Ford car, and cost $200 less. Ford hopes it will become the "universal car" of the Sixties.

To match today's segmented market, therefore, the Ford Division of Ford Motor Co. views its purpose-for-purpose product line as follows: Falcon, an economy six-passenger compact car; Fairlane, a full-sized, low-priced economy car; Galaxie, a low-priced "luxury" car; Thunderbird, a high-style personal car. Also obviously in preparation, probably for 1962, is a subcompact of the Volkswagon class whose whispered working title is the Cardinal. The car has not been formally announced and Ford, as a matter of policy, is stonily silent on the subject.

As it got the Comet when the Falcon was conceived, so the Lincoln-Mercury Division now gets the Meteor as an off-shoot of the Fairlane. The division, managed by Ben Mills, one of the original Ford "Quiz Kids," has improved profits substantially since Lincoln-Mercury broke out of its character as a manufacturer of medium-priced cars, greatly increased its interchangeability with the Ford Division, and began moving along down with the market profile.

As an example of Ford's new way of looking at things, the recasting of the Lincoln Continental concept is most significant. "We decided," says Ben Mills, "that we wanted to start our own ball game instead of continuing to compete in Cadillac's ball game." The Continental, as it stood in 1959, was gradually cut down from 227 inches in over-all length to 213 inches today, and the number of models was reduced from twelve to two—a sedan and a four-door convertible. The car was completely re-engineered in 1961, to improve its life, and a new pretesting program was introduced—every Continental off the line has to go through a twelve-mile check list of 200 items. Finally, the Continental is the only U.S. car with a warranty of two years, or 24,000 miles. The car has status, Mills believes, but the status symbol is no longer the fabulous $10,000 price tag with which it started out in life. At $5,565, the Continental is in the range of the Cadillac Coup de Ville, which it has been outselling recently. With sales of about 31,800 units in 1961 (against 20,780 in 1960), the Continental is now paying its way with something more than prestige.

Much is heard, of course, about Falcon and Comet "cannibalizing" the sales of the standard Ford and Mercury. There is no doubt that the big Ford has been taking a beating. Its share of the market came down from 24.2 percent in calendar 1959 to around 13 percent in the year just past. The big Chevrolet, over the same period dropped only about two points from its 1959 penetration of 24.1 percent. And the fact that big cars make a higher unit profit than small cars is elementary. Temporizing somewhat on this question, Ford admits that sales of its compacts went way beyond expectations, and the acceptance of its 1960 standard Ford, owing to an unpopular styling change, was considerably below forecast. But Ford, looking at the progress of the Ford Division as a whole, doesn't buy the idea that its strategy has been hurtful to profits. Says Lee Iacocca, "The highest profit per unit ever known to the industry was made by Packard the year it went out of business for lack of sales. We make money on all our products, including the Falcon, but you cannot become preoccupied with the margins on a car. Our stockholders are interested in profits per share, not profits per car."

The Quest for Quality

It is Ford's judgment, in short, that the volume car of the coming market is a car of the 110 to 115-inch wheelbase class.

weighing not more than 3,000 pounds. And so it has moved into that market with all possible speed and strength. But also basic to the thinking of the modern Ford Motor Co. is the recognition that it is always possible that public preference, almost without warning, will cross up product planning. So Ford has to be flexed to get out of as well as to get into markets quickly. And it also feels it has to offer in all its products some durable ingredient that has an appeal beyond size, styling, or even price—something that will preserve customer loyalty in periods of flux, or when the product may be off target. That ingredient, in Ford's view, is quality, and its new president is making a big pitch of it.

The fact that John Dykstra was close to retirement age when appointed president last April led many to speculate that Henry Ford II was hopefully keeping the chair warm for Robert McNamara. Whatever validity that theory may have, the greater significance lies in the choice of a shirt-sleeved craftsman dedicated to the task of building durability into automobiles. Dutch-born Dykstra began his career as an apprentice diemaker, acquired his engineering knowledge through night school and correspondence courses, and was manager of manufacturing at Hudson and at Oldsmobile before coming to Ford in 1947.

Three years ago Dykstra, then vice president for manufacturing, was given an open-end assignment by Henry Ford II. The mission: to find ways of reducing the incidence of component failure in Ford products, and cut down the cost of maintenance to the consumer. He has done, in Henry Ford's words, "a fantastic job." The procedures introduced by Dykstra have endless ramifications. But essentially, he set up a comprehensive system of validation programs covering materials, tools, parts, units, and finished products, and then gave his quality-control personnel unprecedented power to enforce them.

Bull of the Woods

Dykstra himself frequently prowls Ford's facilities, going first always to look with practiced eye at the rejection pile and the scrap shed. And the first thing he does every Monday morning is to study the weekly quality-trend analysis, fresh from the test track, that charts the incidence of defects observed in the engine, chassis, body, transmission, etc., for every model car in the Ford array. "A 'defect,'" Dykstra says, "can be the fact that several drops of oil fell on the floor." There is even a specification, in the analysis, for the pressure required to open the glove compartment.

It's been a costly program, but Ford can point to tangible

evidence of a payoff. When the program began, in 1958, Ford's customer warranty was for the standard 4,000 miles, or ninety days. In 1961 Ford raised the warranty to 12,000 miles, or twelve months (the rest of the industry promptly followed suit). Ford says that its warranty costs (when adjusted for the 1961 change) are down 40 percent per car over the past three years.

Of Markets Near and Far

As 1961 was drawing to a close, Henry Ford II could confidently say to *Fortune*, "All the forces in the marketplace seem to be working for us at the moment, and we see nothing in the short-term future that will turn our situation around. Our penetration is now slightly above average, and if we can keep our mix good and our quality right, we might well push it up a point or two in 1962." But he also earnestly says, "There is no question that the overseas market is going to grow more rapidly than the U.S. market, and we regard our expanding participation in that market as not only desirable but necessary."

Preoccupation with domestic affairs long kept Ford from doing what it knew it should be doing in foreign fields. In 1957, Henry Ford II showed his good intentions by appointing one of his ablest executives and most trusted friends, John S. Bugas, to the command of the international group. But because critical union negotiations were in progress in the U.S., labor expert Bugas had to double in brass, and couldn't give his full time to overseas affairs until 1959. Now, making up for lost time, he has 108 international projects on his desk for analysis and decision.

The major plans concern the U.K. and German companies. Ford of England is the company's biggest overseas manufacturer with sales of $752 million in 1960, profits of $52 million. The German company is only about half as big, but is growing faster from its lower base. If and when the marriage of EFTA and EEC takes place, these two companies will freely share in the same huge market, which today buys a total of four million cars a year and may go to six million by 1970. Heretofore, each of the two companies has developed its own products in almost complete separation from the other because the minority U.K. interest had to be served. Now they can enjoy considerable flexibility in planning, building, and merchandising all products. Perhaps Ford will decide to set up a single wheel plant in Belgium, say, to serve both companies. In any event, they will be unhampered in undertaking any integration or interchangeability that is mutually advantageous.

Except for the capital expenditures involved (an estimated $400 million for the years 1961-63), Ford has not revealed any of the specifics of its planned expansion in the U.K. and Germany. From the stateside point of view, however, it is significant that Ford has begun to move a few of its ablest people into European operating jobs. Already in the U.K. company the chief stylist and the controller are Americans from Dearborn. And just two months ago, in response to Chairman Sir Patrick Hennessy's request for engineering help, Ford gave him, as chief engineer, one Victor Raviolo. As chairman of the engineering advisory committee at Dearborn, Raviolo was just about Ford's No. 1 man in this field. The vast majority of Ford management men abroad, of course, will continue to be drawn from the countries where the plants are located; but Ford is not being timid about installing American ideas, methods, and systems in its foreign subsidiaries. "We just think we know a little bit more about the business than they do," Henry Ford says pleasantly.

Beyond Europe, Ford is expanding aggressively in Australia, where it recently spent $50 million to introduce the Falcon, the first real competition that General Motors' Holden car in that country has ever had. And new projects are under way in Argentina, Venezuela, and Southern Rhodesia. The day could come when Ford's international division will equate, in sales and profits, the U.S. division.

Something Else Than Autos

When it comes to Ford's nonautomotive ventures in the U.S., there are, at this stage, no timetables and no hard figures, really. One can only examine Ford's motives, and its capabilities. When the Ford Scientific Laboratory was established in 1951, it went off on a somewhat different tack from what is customary with most industrial organizations. Fully half of its programs had no direct relation to automotive technology but were concerned with basic research in metallurgy, chemistry, solid-state physics, and the like. Henry Ford II placed the laboratory on a five-year budget, thus guaranteeing the continuity of research programs regardless of how Ford earnings fared. This served to create a high morale among the scientists and to attract some very good men. Many impressive scientific papers were produced, and a number of unusual patents were developed. At the same time, communication with the operations people was encouraged, and much was done to close the gap between science and engineering. The whole technological tone of the Ford Motor Co. was raised thereby, and its capabilities and confidence were enhanced.

About the same time also, Ford was re-examining its role in national defense. That role, during World War II, and again during Korea, was as a mass producer of massive weapons—tanks, bombers, jet engines, etc.—mostly of other manufacturers' designs. Looking down the road, Ford saw the diminishing need and importance of the secondary producer. In the new age of lethal weaponry and weapon systems, the major contributions—and earnings—were being made by the companies with the technological capacity to offer new ideas and designs. Cold war or hot war, the emphasis was on weapons of a relatively high technological content and relatively low production content. Ford felt that as a matter of prestige, and of good business, it ought to be in the major league.

Ford took an important step in 1956 when Ernie Breech came across a group of some twenty young physicists and engineers, formerly employed by Lockheed, who had a small missile research-and-development operation going in southern California. Ford bought control, and in 1959 took the whole group into the company as the Aeronutronic Division. Gerald J. Lynch, a Ford vice president who had been handling Ford's conventional defense products—jeeps, tanks, etc.—was sent out as general manager. Fourteen of the original group are still with the company: one of the originals is now undersecretary of the Air Force, one a special assistant on space to Secretary of Defense McNamara, and four were lost to the competition. The division's progress, for an operation of this kind, has been rather remarkable. The personnel has grown to 3,000, a hundred of them Ph.D.'s, now handsomely housed in quarters Ford built on 200 acres of ground in Newport Beach at a cost of $33 million.

Shooting for the Moon

In its five short years Aeronutronic has qualified for some important pieces of some important projects. Perhaps the most glamorous is a lunar space capsule, a part of the Ranger program, that will land on the moon sometime this year, and will radio information back to the earth for a month or longer. Aeronutronic also developed the system's retro-rocket, which will brake the capsule's speed to 300 miles an hour for the landing. Perhaps its largest R. and D. contract is for the Shillelagh, an Army surface-to-surface guided missile. Some others: the Blue Scout reconnaissance rocket, successfully fired at Cape Canaveral last year (Aeronutronic is prime contractor for this); Artoc, a mobile electronic command post for the Signal Corps; the penetration-aids program, related to the anti-missile missile program; a classified antisubmarine-warfare development; a study contract for an air-cushion vehicle to travel five feet above the ground at eighty miles an hour.

The economics of this kind of business are rather complicated. A typical missile program might encompass thirteen years. During the first two years the company would be engaged in a competitive study program. It may then win the research-and-development contract, which could take three years more. After this follow production, improved models, operation, and maintenance, which could add up to a profitable eight years more. At this stage in its life, Aeronutronic is in the middle, or R. and D., phase on most of its contracts, and by industry estimates it is doing around $65 million a year in sales. If, as hoped, Aeronutronic has adequate manufacturing facilities built and operating by 1966, and it gets "all the pieces," it could expect to be taking in $350 million in sales for pretax profits of around $28 million. Not peanuts; but not, by Ford Motor Co. standards, intoxicating. On the other hand, there is always the possibility of a bonanza. The Pershing missile, on which Aeronutronic boldly bid, but which the experienced Martin Co. got, is shaping up to be a $1-billion project.

The acquisition of Philco was Ford's next step in its development as a primary defense contractor, but it was also part of a broader, more general expansion plan. About two years ago Ford set up a business-planning office, under the direction of Charles E. Beck, now forty, to make a study of industries, and the specific opportunities within them, that offered the greatest potential growth. They were to be industries that would augment, and not conflict with, Ford's operations. And the survey included overseas as well as domestic opportunities. One of the first recommendations made was that the Ford tractor business be placed on a world-wide basis because of the economies obtainable thereby. And that was promptly done.

Beck's group also recommended the Autolite purchase, although expansion in the auto-parts replacement market was no sudden decision on Ford's part. Its Motorcraft operation was already pecking away at this market when the chance to buy

Autolite developed. At this moment Ford's situation is beclouded by the totally unexpected antitrust suit, which would void the purchase. (An article on the automotive "aftermarket" appears in the March, 1962, issue of *Fortune*.)

Why Philco?

The electronics industry was naturally high on the list of growth opportunities. Ford looked into "scores" of electronics companies. Why did it pick Philco? Certainly Philco's posture in the defense business—about 50 percent of its gross is government sales—was a major consideration. Philco is the prime contractor, for example, for the Sidewinder-missile program (30,000 units), and Philco set up and maintains vast space detection and tracking systems for NASA and for the North American Air Defense Command. Ford naturally likes the feel of a lot of hardware in the works, and Philco supplies this as Aeronutronic, as yet, cannot.

But there is also a significant reason why Philco was picked over other electronics companies that might have qualified almost as well from a defense standpoint. There were several well-managed companies available, making around 10 percent on net worth, which Ford could have had for a premium. But to buy such a company at the premium asked could bring the purchaser's return down to 3 or 4 percent on his investment, and this Ford considered unacceptable.

Philco, on the other hand, had over $400 million in annual sales (and was growing fairly well) on which it earned only $2,300,000. It was not, in the Ford company's view, a well-managed outfit, and it needed working capital. Ford thinks it can supply better management. It has already installed its own administrative team in Philco with business planner Beck as the company's president.

This, then, is the apparent pattern of Ford's future: (1) To wring all the growth that is yet possible in the U.S. automobile market by battling hard for a small increase in penetration each year; (2) to achieve a substantial increase in penetration of the faster-growing overseas market in automobiles; (3) to press for a position of substance in the defense industry; and (4) to remain on the alert for nonautomotive opportunities, here and abroad, where it can put its two most abundant resources, capital and management, profitably to work. It is an ambitious program, but not an impatient one. Finance Chairman Ted Yntema's current assignment from Henry Ford II is merely to prepare a study of what's ahead for U.S. transportation in the next forty years.

How General Motors Did It*_____

BY ROBERT SHEEHAN

Among U.S. industrial companies, General Motors Corp., of course, is the perennial leader in sales and earnings, but the figures it came up with in 1962—sales of $14,640,241,000, profits after taxes of $1,459,077,000—were of a magnitude to benumb the mind. Never in history has a private corporation made so much money. Once before, in the record car year of 1955, G.M. broke the billion-dollar barrier in earnings with a net of $1,189,477,000. Apart from G.M., only the vast A. T. & T. network is in the range (the utility's profits were $1,432,952,000 in 1962). Indeed, most journalists and analysts, in an attempt to make the G.M. figures understandable, compared them not with the results of other corporations—they simply didn't relate vividly enough—but with the statistics of various countries around the world. Thus readers have been informed that G.M.'s sales topped the national budget of France, that its net income was roughly equal to the national income of Ireland, that G.M.'s employees, together with their families, outnumber the population of New Zealand.

Admiration of those awesome figures is accompanied by recurrent rumblings in Washington and elsewhere that General Motors is "too big." The Justice Department, for one, keeps a team of eight antitrust attorneys busy pondering and probing G.M. Thus far, most of the antitrust court action has been aimed at the company's peripheral or non-automotive activities, though "peripheral" is a pretty weak word in this instance. G.M.'s "other" businesses—in diesel locomotives, earthmoving equipment, aircraft engines, Frigidaire, etc.—added up to something just short of $1.9 billion in sales in 1962. If G.M. didn't sell the public a single car, truck, automotive part or accessory, it would still rank eighteenth in size among U.S. industrial companies.

* June 1963

It is the company's preponderant position in the U.S. passenger-car market, however, that raises the most controversial questions. The atmosphere becomes tense whenever G.M.'s penetration of the domestic car market approaches or exceeds the 50 percent mark. It is probably no coincidence that when the company first went over the mark, in 1954-55, it was promptly called down to Washington for a session with the late Senator Joseph C. O'Mahoney and the Subcommittee on Antitrust and Monopoly. In 1962, after a considerable lull, G.M. sales ran to 51.9 percent of car registrations. And for the first quarter of 1963, G.M.'s share of the market, as measured by factory sales, was 56 percent (the highest recorded share was Ford's 61.6 percent in 1921).

Inevitably, such a record sharpens the debate about the significance of G.M.'s size and power. But before such questions can even be reasonably discussed, it is essential to understand how G.M. achieved its success. It is a fact of business life, of course, that when the demand in any industry expands rapidly—as it did in the auto industry in 1962—certain advantages naturally accrue to the largest, front-running company. General Motors has the largest ownership—i.e., G.M. cars on the road—to draw on, and the largest number of retail outlets, or dealers. Assuming other things to be equal, G.M. could be expected to enjoy a somewhat greater leverage in a strong car year. But this is not the whole story by any means. For this has been not only a growing market; it was a changing market characterized by a whole new rash of consumer preferences. The past few years have been a time of challenge, and of extraordinary opportunity for all the car companies to break out of their historic patterns and forage vigorously for conquest sales. It was a competitive free-for-all, and the way things turned out, it simply must be concluded that General Motors prejudged the market considerably more accurately than anybody else, adjusted more nimbly to the sudden changes in consumer tastes, maintained an edge in the quality and styling of its products, and sold them as hard as it knew how—and it does know how.

Size, in short, is not the answer to G.M.'s glittering success in the car market, nor for that matter in other markets. What is? Many earnest and able attempts have been made to explain this matter, and many theories new and old have been advanced.

"*It is organization that has done it,*" some say, and once again eighty-eight-year-old Alfred P. Sloan, Jr., now honorary chairman of G.M., is being justly canonized for the system he conceived, back in the early Twenties, of "decentralized operations and responsibilities with coordinated control," for which read, "Give a man a clear-cut job and let him do it." Unquestionably, it is due to the Sloan system that huge General Motors is able to remain so wonderfully lithe. Here is a balance of two apparently conflicting concepts—centralization and decentralization—that preserves the best elements of both. On the one hand, it permits the maximum exercise of initiative by the relatively autonomous division managers, thus fostering, throughout the units of G.M., all the beastly aggressiveness you would expect of a small, hungry company. On the other hand, the system provides, through the subtle ministrations of the G.M. governing committees and general staff, the centralized planning, policy direction, specialized services—and all the considerable economies that go with them—so necessary to a large-scale enterprise.

"It is G.M.'s depth of management that has done it," others say—an impression that may well be affirmed as one considers G.M.'s administrative committee. And remember that this select pride of lions (the administration committee) represents less than a third of G.M.'s top-ranking company officers and divisional general managers. Moreover, for a true picture of G.M.'s bench strength, one would have to encompass the so-called "Greenbrier group," a complement of over 700 "top executives" who are invited about every three years to White Sulphur Springs, West Virginia, for a three-day comprehensive review and forecast of G.M.'s place in the world. These men have worked with and around each other for most of their business lives—the average length of service with the company is twenty-five years. No group of executives is more handsomely paid (of the ten highest-paid executives in the U.S. in 1961, eight were G.M. men), and thanks to the company's combination bonus-and-stock-option plan, it is probable that a very high percentage of the personal estate of each is in G.M. stock. They don't have to be wheedled to work hard.

"The people in G.M.," says Chairman Frederic G. Donner, "add up to the greatest single asset G.M. has," and he believes that his most important single responsibility as chairman is to see that he has the right people in the right jobs and good men coming up under them. Yet in another context Donner remarks, "G.M. people are ordinary folks," and this also is true. From a tour of the G.M. executive phalanx, one comes away vastly impressed by the solid competence of every man jack of them—it is difficult to conceive of a surface-slick pretender even penetrating, let alone surviving in, this realistic assembly. On the other hand, they certainly do not dazzle, nor man for man exhibit any patent supe-

riority over their opposite numbers in industry. But one can say of G.M., as a Victorian sage once said of the House of Commons: "It has more sense than everyone in it." G.M.'s corporate or collective judgment—and it lives by collective judgments—adds up to something far sounder and more sensitive than the individual judgments of any or all of its executives.

The fact is that all these things—organization, depth of management, and just the ordinary people of G.M.—do serve to explain in part at least its record. But in this article *Fortune* is less concerned with the universals of G.M.'s structure and philosophy than with the particulars of its accomplishments and more specifically with the hard-nosed facts of the company's conquest of the booming U.S. car market of 1962-63; for if these particulars are known, the universals will fall into perspective. In thus focusing on cars it is not meant lightly to dismiss the importance to the company of its large and booming truck and coach business (484,835 units produced in the U.S. in 1962). And G.M.'s close to $2 billion in business abroad will be looked at a little later. But, of course, the U.S. passenger-car business is the heart and pulse of the G.M. operation. In 1962 it represented an estimated 65 percent of G.M.'s total dollar sales, or a cool $9.5 billion and, as noted, G.M. is still far out in front in 1963.

In explaining its commanding position, it is significant that though many forecasters grossly underestimated the size of the 1962-63 auto market, G.M. did not. In the fall of 1961, Fred Donner was estimating a 7,200,000 car year for 1962, Ford thought the figure would be around 6,750,000, and other estimates were lower still. The final tally was 7,092,079. As early as August of 1962, Chevrolet's General Manager Semon E. Knudsen was forecasting an equally good market for 1963, but it was the critics' consensus that, in the light of history, it was most unlikely that the auto industry could put two such years together "back to back." Some suggested that sales-minded General Motors was being consciously overoptimistic (it overestimated the 1961 market, for instance). But G.M.'s Executive Vice President James E. Goodman says, "We believed our forecasts and we were prepared. If you based all your plans on history, you would find some new history in the making, and part of that new history could be that you weren't prepared for the change."

Perhaps the difference was that G.M. had a little more confidence in the general U.S. economy than some other people did. Given a stable economy, and a reasonably good figure for consumers' disposable income, there was no mistaking the forces at work that augured for a sharp rise in unit auto sales in 1962, 1963, and beyond. The most compelling factor, as everyone now realizes, was the prospective steep rise in replacement sales as measured by the scrappage rate. As cars purchased in the large-volume years of 1954, 1955, 1956 began to approach their eighth birthday—the age of heavy scrappage—a big bulge in replacement sales was inevitable. At the low point in the auto market in early 1961, the annual scrappage rate was 4,800,000 units. It has since increased by more than 200,000 units a year, and for 1963 General Motors estimates the replacement demand at 5,200,000 cars. Thus only 1,800,000 "growth" sales will be needed to roll up a seven-million-car year. The forces stimulating these additional sales are several. A major one is that the wartime population explosion is now getting into family formation. Not only are new households forming at the rate of around one million per year, but there is a relative increase also in the number of families with sufficient income to buy a new car. There is, morever, this interesting fact about the millions of war babies now coming into the auto market at eighteen to twenty-two: they have been heavy buyers of used cars, and a tremendous factor in sustaining the strength of the used-car market, which is, in turn, a powerful stimulus to new-car buying. Finally, there has been a continuation of suburban growth, and with it an acceleration in the number of two-, three-, and four-car families.

In view of all this, it is not surprising that all U.S. companies increased their unit sales in 1962. Ford was up 9.2 percent; Chrysler, 5.6 percent; American Motors, 14.1 percent; Studebaker, 7.9 percent. But only General Motors, up 32.1 percent in units, increased its penetration, a rise of nearly five and a half points to 51.9 percent. Ford fell two points to 26.3 percent; Chrysler a point to 9.6 percent; and American Motors was fractionally off at 6.1 percent. Now, of course, there were almost as many factors, of one degree of importance or another, involved in this outcome as there were cars produced. It is possible, however, to describe rather briefly and explicitly the *anatomy*, at least, of G.M.'s triumphant increase in penetration over its competitors. The bare bones of the story are as follows:

Since about 1959, the great new dynamic in the market had been the small car. (And for simplicity's sake, let's call it—as the customers do—the "compact" car, ignoring for the moment such industry subclassifications as *small economy, intermediate, medium-priced small*, etc.) In 1958 the imported small cars, plus American Motors' Ramblers, took 10.8 percent of the total U.S.

car market. When the U.S. Big Three began building compacts in 1959, the share of this class of car rose to 18.6 percent, then soared to 31 percent in 1960, and to 38.6 percent in 1961. This was a new ball game, and for the competitors, obviously, a critical test of over-all strategy and all-round skills. For this was not simply a slugging match of compact vs. compact and may the better car win. More important, in a sense, than the quality and attractiveness of the product itself were such considerations as the timing of the introduction of each particular car, its impact on the vital used-car market, and the degree of its incursion on the sales of the corporation's own line of standard-sized cars.

Indeed, if one regarded the competition as strictly a horse race among compacts, G.M., in the early stages, looked astonishingly laggard. In the fall of 1959, G.M. entered the field with the Chevrolet Division's Corvair, a novel, highly specialized little car with an aluminum rear engine. At the same time, Ford introduced the Falcon, a conventionally built small economy car, and early in 1960, the Comet, a slightly larger sister compact, which was marketed by the Lincoln-Mercury Division. Chrysler Corp.'s compact entry was the Plymouth Division's Valiant, and later the Dodge Division's Lancer. In calendar 1960, sales of compacts in the U.S. divided up as follows:

Ford .... 29.9 percent
Rambler 20.7
Imports 20.4
G.M. 13.5
Chrysler 10.3
Studebaker 5.2

In 1961, Ford led again with 30.6 percent of the compacts sold. But G.M., now strengthened by the introduction of its three "B-O-P" compacts—Buick Special, Oldsmobile F-85, and Pontiac Tempest—boosted its compact penetration to 27.6 percent. Chrysler dropped off to an 8.1 percent share.

Meanwhile, hearken to what was happening to the G.M.-Ford competition in the low-price, standard-size car field. In 1959 the standard Ford and the standard Chevrolet had fought to a neck-and-neck finish, each of them taking a fraction over 22 percent of the total car market. But in 1960, while the Ford compacts were mopping up the small-car field, the standard Ford's share of the total car market fell precipitously to 13.5 percent. The standard Chevrolet, in contrast, held firm at 22 percent. In 1961 the standard Ford's decline was substantially checked—it fell a little less than a point to 12.7 percent. The standard Chevrolet was off a point to 21 percent of the market.

Now the stage is set for G.M.'s decisive breakaway, across the board, in booming 1962. In the small-car field, which rose to almost 42 percent of the total market, Ford had added the Fairlane, a so-called "intermediate" car placed between the Falcon and the lowest-priced standard Ford, and the Meteor, which fitted in between the Comet and the lowest-priced Mercury. With this added punch, Ford increased its share of the compact market to 31.4 percent. This was not good enough, however, to fend off G.M. First of all, G.M. had a hot new compact in the Chevy II, a conventionally built car that squarely opposed Ford's Falcon. Second, it had sharply jacked up Corvair sales by adding the sporty, bucket-seat Monza model to the Corvair line. Finally, all the B-O-P compacts registered some gains in penetration, and G.M. swept past Ford to capture 35 percent of the compact business.

While this was going on, Ford again lost out in its race with Chevrolet. The sales of the successful new Fairlane, like the Falcon before it, seemingly ate into the sales of the standard Ford, which fell from 12.7 to 10.1 percent of the total market. The standard Chevrolet, despite the great forward thrust of the G.M. compacts, held doggedly to 20 percent of the total car market.

For the clincher, let us turn to the medium-price field. Since 1958, when it accounted for around 47 percent of total car sales, this class of car had steadily declined in penetration. In 1961 medium-price cars accounted for only 32 percent of all the cars sold (and that figure includes the top-of-the-line Chevrolet, Ford, and Plymouth models, which had pushed up into the medium-price range). Along the way, all the companies except G.M. had practically given up on the classic medium-price makes. Ford had surrendered on the ill-fated Edsel, and sharply reduced the number of its medium-price Mercury models. Chrysler dumped the DeSoto, and shifted most of its Dodge production over to the smaller Dart. But though G.M.'s medium-price makes slumped in total market penetration and in absolute numbers, the corporation never compromised the essential concepts of the Buick, Pontiac, and Oldsmobile, and these divisions never ceased to work full pitch at improving the performance, styling, and distribution of their products.

In 1962 this persistence paid off, for public taste turned toward more variety and luxury in automobiles. Unit sales of medium-price cars increased 27 percent over 1961, and their share

of the total market rose from 32 to 34.5 percent—a highly significant shift, in such a great car year, in terms of dollar sales and
profits. G.M., of course, had most of the desirable merchandise in
this class, and captured 66 percent of the market. Meanwhile, in
the high-price class (e.g., Cadillac, Continental, Imperial, Thunderbird, Corvette, etc.), which accounted for about 7 percent of
the total market, G.M.'s share in 1962 was 71 percent.

Deep Are the Roots

From this outline it is logical to deduce that G.M.'s ultimate
success was rooted in the fact that (1) it so timed and positioned
its small cars as to achieve a maximum amount of "plus" business
from the new lines, while at the same time (2) it worked very
aggressively to strengthen its position in the standard-size cars.
No other company had a comparable balance and spread when
the turn in the market came.

All of which would seem to prove, prima facie, that it was
superior planning that "did it" for G.M., though it is not to be
doubted that in some areas G.M. simply fattened on the mistakes
and misfortunes of its competitors, and that at least one triumph—
the Corvair Monza—was a stroke of sheer luck. But at least we
know that what we are looking at in the current G.M. showcase
is not something that was conceived today, or yesterday, nor is it
something that can be traced to any single dramatic circumstance
or any one hero-type man. The story goes back through many
years and involves many people. In the main, however, G.M.'s
current success is based on decisions made no later than the fall
of 1958.

Start of the Cycle

As it happens, this is the point in time when the current management team of Frederic G. Donner as chairman and chief executive officer and John F. Gordon as president took over the leadership from retiring president and chief executive officer Harlow H.
Curtice. As *Fortune* then observed ("G.M.'s Remodeled Management," November, 1958), this was a significant rearrangement of
the power lines: it transferred the top executive authority from
the president in Detroit back to the chairman in New York. But
the change in command was only coincidental to the changes in
essential strategy and product planning that were evolving in
G.M. at the time. To be sure, there are quite some differences in

temperament and style between Fred Donner and the late Harlow Curtice. As a former car-division manager, with many solid successes to his credit, Curtice was naturally inclined to rely rather strongly on his intuition at times, particularly in respect to product decisions. As a former G.M. chief staff officer for finance, Donner is naturally of a more analytical bent of mind. Though he definitely does not lack confidence in his own ideas, he is skilled at synthesizing the ideas of others in the group. But on the thread of G.M. thinking on the small car, for example, there is no telling where Curtice leaves off and Donner takes over. It was a collective judgment all the way.

It is worth recalling, however, that the skies were far from sunny at the start of the Donner-Gordon regime. The economy was severely depressed in 1958; G.M. had to report a 22 percent decline in its domestic car and truck production that year and a drop in earnings of 25 percent. What's more, the public mood was distressingly scornful of Detroit and all its works. Writers were writing vitriolic pieces about the "insolent chariots" and the "two-tone jukeboxes on wheels," and everyone was asking why Detroit couldn't make a small, simple, sensible car like the foreign cars that were selling so well in the U.S. Against these attacks G.M. stood stonily silent or else responded with that irritating blandness that is so often characteristic of the corporation's reaction to criticism. "You take out quality much faster than you can take out cost," G.M. executives would solemnly explain. Or, again, "We have yet to find a way to make a small car larger and more comfortable."

But all the time executives were saying these things they were in fact working like hell behind the scenes to de-emphasize the bulk and blatancy of their standard cars and to develop a line of compact cars. By 1958 the Corvair was already designed, prototyped, and practically tooled up for production. G.M.'s inscrutability went beyond security reasons, though everybody in Detroit guards against, and practices, espionage. There was serious doubt and extended debate throughout the company in the years 1957-59 as to just what the small-car market was going to be worth, and as to what kind of U.S small car would be most acceptable. Though it dutifully consumer-researched the market, G.M. is not overly trustful of such surveys on an untried product, and never uses them as gospel. Recalling his own cogitation at the time, Fred Donner says, "I hadn't seen a small car costed out. You can't really research a thing that the customer can't see, feel, ride in, and watch his neighbor buy." Furthermore, G.M. had the most to lose, of all companies, if there was a mass defection from large to small cars. It had to be prepared for the eventuality, but it wasn't of a mind to lead the stampede. It certainly didn't intend to do it with the Corvair.

Cole's Car

The Corvair was aborning before there was a known market for a small car, and its biography tells a lot about the pliability of G.M.'s renowned "system." It was the brainchild of Edward N. Cole, now group executive in charge of all car and truck divisions. Cole first began fooling around with the rear-engine concept, more or less as an academic exercise, when he was chief engineer of Cadillac back in 1946. In 1952 he was made chief engineer of Chevrolet, where his first major task was to design a new light-weight V-8 engine for the all-new 1955 passenger car that was such a smashing success; shortly afterward, Cole was promoted to general manager of the huge Chevrolet Division. Through it all, Cole persisted in the development of his rear-engine idea, and of a car that was now shaping up in his mind as a sort of American Volkswagen. He reached over to G.M.'s Vauxhall Division in Great Britain for the services of its star engineer, Maurice Olley, and made him chief of research and development for Chevrolet. Under Cole's eye, Olley purchased a variety of little foreign cars, tore them down, ran costs, and explored new manufacturing processes.

All this work was carried on without so much as a do-you-mind to anybody in the G.M. hierarchy. A G.M. division manager works under a broad yearly budget with allocations for advertising, engineering, research, and so on, and is not questioned on the things he may choose to do within those limits. What he *is* called to account for is the last line on his profit-and-loss report, and the position of his products in the market. If he has been spending excessively on futures, to the neglect of his salable merchandise, it will show up there. Cole and Chevrolet, needless to say, had no worries on that score. With Corvair, Cole even had the G.M. styling staff secretly working on possible configurations for several years before there was any "official" awareness, at the committee level, of the project. It was not until the fall of 1957 that Cole formally displayed first the clay mock-up and then the camouflaged test model to President Curtice, who liked what he saw and threw it open to the engineering policy group for discussion.

This group—and other policy groups like it—is another heritage from Alfred P. Sloan. Aware that his grand design for the company might in time harden into a stultifying bureaucracy, Sloan encouraged the formation of informal groups, the membership of which cut across lines of authority, to review and project plans and policies in such particular categories as engineering, distribution, overseas operations, etc. Under Donner, the engineering policy group has become, in effect, the spade-working subcommittee of the G.M. executive committee in the area of automotive programs. Though the chief of staff for engineering is chairman of the group, the staff heads of research, manufacturing, styling, and distribution are also members, as are all nine members of the executive committee. The meetings, held regularly once a month, are long and frequently controversial. Thus, when the executive committee later sits to decide on policy, it doesn't have to engage in the tedious review of written reports, or in a lot of feckless discussion. The problem is already in focus and the decision is made promptly.

It was the consensus of the engineering policy group, and of the governing committees, back in 1957-58, that G.M.'s first move in the small-car field should be to compete directly with the foreign imports. The Corvair, being more European than American in concept, seemed to be the vehicle to do it. What's more, it was ready. So it was approved, and laid down early in 1958. There remained, however, the question as to how the Corvair should be merchandised within the company. There was some feeling that the Corvair ought to be handed around to all the divisions to sell: G.M. dealers everywhere needed a product to entice the growing number of compact shoppers into their showrooms. This problem, as the deadline approached, fell mainly to Donner and Gordon for solution. But since plans were now afoot to introduce a line of B-O-P compacts in 1960, it was decided that Chevrolet's Corvair should be Chevrolet's alone.

When the Corvair first hit the market it was far from a success, except in the backhanded sense that it did not cannibalize its Chevrolet big brothers to any visible extent. It was deliberately designed not to, of course, and in that respect it represented a plus for G.M. But it would be naive to think that General Motors anticipated, or accepted without gall, the extent to which Ford's Falcon exceeded the Corvair in sales. From the time they left the post, Falcon was outselling Corvair by nearly two to one (the actual numbers in calendar year 1960 were Falcon 451,158, Corvair 229,525). No doubt the Falcon was taking some sales from the standard Ford, but it was also clear that the Falcon was satisfying a segment of the market—people in search of low-cost family transportation—that the cute little Corvair package, with its smaller interior dimensions, was unable to reach. General Motors moved awfully fast to plug that gap with the introduction, in the fall of 1961, of the Chevy II compact.

But in the meantime a funny thing happened to the Corvair. As a stunt for the Chicago Auto Show in February, 1960, William Mitchell, G.M. vice president for styling, dolled up a couple of Corvairs—in "His and Hers" versions—with bucket seats and other sporty accouterments. The car was named Monza, after the famous racecourse in Italy. The Monza was the surprise hit of the show. G.M. quickly decided to put it into production—Monzas began coming off the line in May of 1960—and total Corvair sales picked up sharply. In 1962 about 290,000 Corvairs were sold, of which more than 75 percent were Monza models. What's more, the Monza experience gave the rest of General Motors an early tip on the bucket-seat fad, and Buick, Oldsmobile, and Pontiac went in for them in a big way. In 1962 nearly a million of the cars sold in the U.S. had bucket seats, and of these approximately 60 percent were G.M. cars. Ironically, just when automotive engineers have finally begun to master the problem of reducing the transmission hump so that three passengers can ride comfortably in front, the buyers are clamoring for cars that can seat only two, with a big, flashy console in between.

The proposal for the Chevy II originated with the engineering policy group, though the division was by no means caught off guard. Donner says, "From the time the Corvair was introduced, Jack [Gordon] and I were getting at each other that we weren't covering the waterfront in this market." But there were no directives issued. To Donner's best recollection, he first broached the subject to Ed Cole as they were "coming down the stairs" together after a meeting in the fall of 1959. Cole, as it happens, had some fears that a conventional compact might bite into the sales of the Chevrolet, but he was able to say to Donner, in all truth, "Well, I've been doing some work on it." Chevrolet engineering had long since been working on the development of a lighter-weight cast-iron engine, a lighter-weight power-glide transmission, and on single-plate springs as a substitution for multiplate springs. So much was on the shelf that the Chevy II, begun in the winter of 1959-60, was on the pilot line by June 1, 1961, and into production in August, 1961.

By now G.M. was fully alive to the new character of the market, with its marked emphasis on variety, and in an unusual move for a new car, Chevy II was brought out in a complete line of models—sedan, coupe, hard-top, convertible, and station wagon. In 1962 it captured 5 percent of the total market with sales of 343,693 units, and it stood off the Falcon, which dropped three points in penetration. (This fall Chevrolet will introduce an intermediate car, reportedly named the Chevelle, to oppose the Fairlane.)

So Chevrolet likes to think its new cars were perfectly timed: that Corvair helped stem the foreign tide, then went on to find its own niche; that Chevy II, brought out in an expanding market, filled the needs of buyers shopping for a second car, or for a good used car, of which there was a shortage in 1962; and therefore that neither of its compacts, in contrast to the Ford experience, hurt its standard-size car. At Ford Motor Co., however, it is not conceded that there was anything wrong with the company's small-car strategy. The tendency in Dearborn, rather, is to attribute the decline of the standard Ford's penetration to a styling failure in the 1960 car—it had a sloping front end that bothered buyers inordinately—and to an insufficiency of models and of change, which has since been redressed.

Whether Chevrolet outwitted Ford or not in the small-car maneuvering, there is no question that its concomitant effort to keep the standard Chevrolet at peak quality and style is what won the over-all competition. For several years running the resale value of a regular Chevrolet, across the line, has been around $100 higher than that of a used Ford or Plymouth. This, above all, has accounted for Chevrolet's relative invulnerability to the low-priced, small-car competition. And so long as this trade-in advantage obtains, there is a great mass of Chevrolet owners that will not defect, including, notably, the big company fleet buyers and the rental outfits, like Hertz and Avis. In 1962, 1,428,212 standard Chevrolets were sold; 52 percent of them were the highest-price Impala models. With the compacts and the Corvette, total sales came to 2,078,029 units. This is more than Chevrolet sold in the record car year of 1955, and is a world record for sales of a single make of car. With 30 percent of the total U.S. car market, the Chevrolet Division was a bigger factor than the whole of the Ford Motor Co. This is the legacy Ed Cole left when he moved up to the group executive post in November, 1961. Taking no chances on a change in pace, G.M. brought in, as his successor at Chevrolet, Semon E. (Bunkie) Knudsen, fresh off a remarkable record of his own at Pontiac, which he had raised to the third-largest-selling car (the Ford is second) in the U.S.

The Little Bopeeps

About the time the Corvair was finalized in the spring of 1958, work was begun on the medium-price Buick-Oldsmobile-Pontiac small-car concept. The idea for this class of car was developed in the central planning groups, and the central engineering staff, then headed by Charles A. Chayne, was assigned the task of performing the preliminary aluminum-engine work and the development of lightweight components. Central engineering ultimately built several prototypes, then turned the program over to the divisions so that each could build its own distinctive car. To coordinate the B-O-P program, a special group was set up consisting of the general manager, chief engineer, and chief financial officer of each division involved. They met once a month for two years. Their responsibility was to see that, without sacrifice of the performance and individuality of the cars, everything was being done to effect the greatest possible economies in costs through the sharing of common parts.

The best way to follow the progress of the B-O-P compacts is to look at them in their divisional context. There is no denying the strength and flexibility General Motors derives from its semi-autonomous divisional system of operation. Think of all that individual inventiveness and ambition it gives rein to—and all that concentrated competitive fire it stokes up—one against the other, and then all against the field. But just how do the G.M. car divisions, and their products and customers, differ from one another? Back in the Twenties, when General Motors was just being pulled together, there used to be a saying: "Chevrolet is for the hoi polloi, Pontiac for the poor but proud, Oldsmobile for the comfortable but discreet, Buick for the striving, and Cadillac for the rich." Today it would be pretty hazardous to attempt any such pat characterization. There is considerable overlapping in price and position among the divisions, and the "identity" of any one division with a particular segment of the market, or a particular style and quality of car, is a very fluid thing from one three-year cycle to another. Often it depends largely on the division manager's evaluation of the way he wants to approach the market. He asks himself: "What can I do to be different?" Different enough, that is, to capture the share of the market he is set up to supply. A good case in point is the transformation and turnabout in Pontiac that took place under the regime of Bunkie Knudsen.

Prescription for Pontiac

Semon Knudsen is the son of the late General William S. Knudsen, president of General Motors, 1937-40. Young Knudsen took his engineering degree at M.I.T. in 1936, worked for two other companies before joining the Pontiac Division of G.M. in 1939 as a tool engineer. He spent ten years with Pontiac, and was assistant general master mechanic there when he was appointed director, in 1949, of G.M.'s Process Development Section in Detroit. In 1953 he was transferred to the Allison aircraft-engine division, where he was manufacturing manager, and in 1955 he was named general manager of the Detroit Diesel Engine Division. A year later he was brought back to Pontiac to succeed the retiring general manager, Robert Critchfield. At forty-four, Knudsen was G.M.'s youngest car-division manager.

Pontiac's malady at the time was a peculiar one. There was nothing outstandingly wrong with the car in any single respect. It simply seemed to have been drained of its personality—it was a "nothing" type car, competitors were saying. It was low man on the B-O-P totem pole, and sixth in the industry rankings. Knudsen set out to recast Pontiac for more youthful tastes. "You can sell older people a young car," he said, "but you can't sell young people an older car." To help him do it, he brought in a number of younger men from other divisions of the company. A major catch was his new chief engineer, Elliott M. (Pete) Estes, just turned forty, who was assistant chief engineer at the flourishing Oldsmobile Division. Estes is now general manager of Pontiac.

Pontiac quickly did three things that the public could see to change its image. Knudsen at once stripped the Pontiac of the traditional "silver streaks" that dominated the hood (the legend is that they had been put on the car at the express order of his father twenty years earlier) and effected many other spirited styling changes. Estes came through with the new "wide-track" wheel principle that gave the car better looks and better balance, and was a feature that Pontiac merchandised to the hilt. Third, in a practice that G.M. officially frowns on today, Pontiacs popped up as the winners of an awful lot of highly publicized stock-car races, a factor of considerable weight with the youthful clientele.

By 1960, Pontiac had overtaken Buick, Oldsmobile, and Chrysler's Plymouth in the sales standings. It was very conscious and very proud of its "identity," and when the division was shown central engineering's prototypes for the proposed medium-price compacts, it was ready with some definite and original ideas of its own for harmonizing the concept with Pontiac's needs and aims.

Tuning Up the Tempest

One of its aims was to maintain a lower price position on its compact, as against the Buick and Oldsmobile compacts. Pontiac felt that the Buick V-8 aluminum engine, designed for use in the other compacts, was too expensive. Accordingly, its engineers set to work developing a four-cylinder iron engine for the Tempest: they simply cut their standard V-8 engine in half, bored four holes in it instead of eight, and were able to use the same assembly line. A four-cylinder engine, however, has always been stigmatized by a certain roughness, and something had to be done about that. Pontiac's advance design group had already developed a rear transmission, for use in the big cars, and it now came up with a new flexible torsional drive. These two features, in the words of Pete Estes, "made a lady out of the four-cylinder engine." In case competitors started reviving the old slurs against the four-cylinder, however, the Tempest offered a V-8 engine as an option.

Sales of the Tempest have been satisfactory, rather than sensational, running to just short of 140,000 units last year. But most important, they have been 80 percent plus business. And for the Pontiac Division, taken as a whole, its success has, indeed, been sensational. Pontiac sold over 528,000 units in calendar 1962, an increase of 42 percent over the previous year, and first-quarter sales in 1963 were running 20 percent ahead of 1962. Behind this rise is a little story which shows that G.M. is not infallible, though quick to adjust. In laying down its 1961 model-year standard-size cars, Pontiac listened to what it now regards as a siren song: that the public was yearning for shorter, simpler cars. Sitting today as Chevrolet's manager, Bunkie Knudsen wryly recalls that when he was Pontiac's manager, "I pulled back Pontiac's wheelbase three inches, and sweated out 1961 with the same wheelbase as Chevrolet, 119 inches. When you give 6,800 Chevrolet dealers a talking point like that to use against you, believe me, you sweat blood." But the next year Pontiac returned to a longer wheelbase, and made a special effort to improve the appeal of its top-of-the-line Bonneville series of luxury cars. Where once the Bonneville was merely window dressing for the Pontiac line, and accounted for less than 6 percent of the division's standard-size car sales, it rose to 27 percent of such sales in 1962. And beyond that, Pete Estes, with little additional tooling cost, developed a sports coupe, with bucket seats and console, called the Grand Prix. It is aimed, of course, at the market the Ford Thunderbird once had all to itself. The Grand Prix is currently accounting for 18 percent of Pontiac sales.

These cars—and almost all G.M. luxury cars—are, for all their gadgetry and rich appointments, notably subdued in their exterior styling. At G.M. today everyone is striving for what they call "the clean, expensive look." The "brightwork" is vastly less obtrusive than it was several years ago. Not only is there less chrome used in the appliqué; it is more tastefully distributed. In the Bonneville, for instance, a thin strip of chrome runs around the bottom of the body instead of across the middle; and on the Grand Prix and the Buick Riviera there is no chrome or molding of any kind—merely a slightly sculptured indentation along the beltline. "Five years ago," says Pete Estes, "none of us would have had the guts to try it."

This is a rather revealing remark. It suggests that G.M. executives themselves had some reservations about the gaudy cars they were building in the Fifties. Certainly they were stung by the criticisms, particularly those that charged them with inflicting their own insular, midwestern standards of taste upon the rest of the American public. The answer from Detroit was that they were businessmen, dedicated to giving the public what it wanted. In the view of Styling's Bill Mitchell, there has been a vast improvement—almost a renaissance—in American taste in recent years; people everywhere are developing a more subtle sense of color, line, and form, and this is reflected in such things as clothing and furniture as well as cars. "Today," says Mitchell, "a good design sells, and we can do a lot of things we always wanted to do but didn't dare gamble on with the sales of a million cars at stake."

Buick Bounds Back

As with Pontiac, both the Buick and the Oldsmobile divisions managed to launch their compacts without harm to the sales of their standard-size cars, though in each case the story has its unique twist. The dramatic ups and downs in Buick's history are indicative of both (*a*) the great deeds a G.M. division can do on the strength of its own initiative, and (*b*) how necessary it is to have the help of the central staff when things go wrong. The Buick

experience suggests that in G.M., in the last analysis, the strength
of the wolf is the pack, and perhaps it offers a hint of what could
happen if, by government order, a division was sheared off from
the corporation and made to shift for itself.

In the days when Red Curtice was running the division, Buick
rose from near-failure to the fourth-ranking position in the industry. In 1955, Buick sold 737,859 units, more than any car in its
price range ever sold before or since. From there, sales declined
headlong to only 245,508 in 1959. One of the troubles was that
when Curtice and a number of his top aides moved on to the
G.M. executive suite in Detroit, Buick's management was denuded
in depth. Buick cars were plagued by mechanical troubles and
styling blunders, and of Buick's fine dealer force, nearly half were
operating in the red. By 1959 the worried G.M. hierarchy decided
it had to intervene. It put in a new team at Buick, headed by burly
Edward Dumas Rollert as general manager.

Rollert had handled a number of troubleshooting assignments
for G.M., including, in 1951, the organization of the company's
first "dual-purpose" assembly plant at Kansas City, which simultaneously turned out automobiles and jet fighter-bombers. In
taking over Buick in May of 1959 there was little that Rollert
could do about the basic design and look of the Buick that would
show up before 1962. But he did effect an almost immediate transformation in the mechanical quality of the cars. Drawing on his
experience in jet-aircraft production, Rollert thoroughly revised
Buick's testing and reliability procedures all along the line. And
once the quality of the cars was re-established, Buick, through
its energetic new general sales manager, Roland Withers, em-
barked on a comprehensive program of selling the dealers on
Buick's new virtues, and of retraining them, from the ground up,
in service and sales techniques.

And when the new compact, called the Special after an old
Buick favorite, came along in the fall of 1960, it gave a big lift
to many a Buick dealer. It developed into the best-seller of all
the B-O-P compacts, especially after it began offering, as an
option to its aluminum V-8 engine, a new iron V-6 that was
about $100 cheaper. The Special now runs to 35 percent of the
Buick Division's output, but 73 percent of it is plus business and
sales of the regular cars in the Buick line have gone ahead handsomely. In 1962, Buick sold 400,267 cars, an increase of 37.7
percent over 1961. The comeback of Buick has been a big factor
in G.M.s share-of-market triumph. Back in 1960, when the execu-

tive committee decided to enter a G.M. car in the luxury sports-car market, Buick was assigned to build it. The car, called the Riviera, made an exciting debut in the fall of 1962, and Rollert expects it will sell between 40,000 and 50,000 units for the model year. With this extra lift, Buick could very well snuggle up close to Oldsmobile in 1963 sales standings.

The Elegant Olds

Under the steady hand of Jack F. Wolfram, longest in tenure of any car-division manager, Oldsmobile has been consistently successful. And of all the B-O-P's, Oldsmobile has perhaps most consistently maintained its image, which is one of elegance on the outside, and high performance under the hood. Thus, when Oldsmobile took aboard a compact, Wolfram felt that it, too, should bespeak "power and elegance," however contradictory that may seem in a small car. The F-85 was rather costly for a compact, and it was offered only with the aluminum V-8 engine (though an iron engine is in the works for the 1964 models). The best-selling model has been the bucket-seated Cutlass, which costs close to $3,000.

To be sure, the unit sales of the F-85 have been considerably below those of the other B-O-P compacts (its sales in 1962 were 94,983, as against 152,312 for the Special, and 138,144 for the Tempest). But Oldsmobile had fat increases in 1962 in the sales of its big cars, all of which were given a longer and sportier look. Oldsmobile's entry in the so-called Thunderbird market is the Starfire, which it brought out in a convertible in model year 1961, and in a hard-top in 1962. In this case Wolfram beat the Riviera to the market by glamorizing and sporting up the basic shell of the Super 88. Around 40,000 Starfires were sold in 1962, and that just about represented the margin of Oldsmobile's lead over Buick in total sales. At 440,995 units, Oldsmobile's total sales were up 34.2 percent in 1962.

In Wolfram's thinking, the big virtue of the F-85 was that it enabled Oldsmobile to get representation in the low-price market, something Oldsmobile couldn't do with a standard-size car without hurting its traditional image. It puts Oldsmobile in a position to jump in whatever direction the market takes. It is his hope that, in time, the new customers coming in by way of the F-85 will begin to grade-up: "We'll get people into Olds earlier in their careers."

Calm and Classic Cadillac

The one G.M. division that didn't have to agonize over the compact question was, of course, Cadillac. Even so, Cadillac had an amusing if rather expensive brush with the problem of size. Along about 1960, dealers began reporting to the factory that customers, especially in the big cities, were clamoring for shorter Cadillacs: they had trouble squeezing them into the garage. Cadillac's General Manager Harold Warner ordered a survey run in seventeen large cities and, sure enough, 30 percent of the sedan buyers expressed a preference for a shorter car. So Cadillac tooled up for and produced a "short-deck" model to appease these people. The wheelbase was the same as in the regular car, but seven inches was sliced off the trunk. The model was a flop. It accounted for less than 4 percent of sales, and at that volume lost money for Cadillac. But Chairman Donner never chided Warner for the experiment. "It served an important purpose," Donner said. "It left the customer in the right frame of mind when he bought the big one because he had a chance to turn the small one down. And it put an end to the talk about the Cadillac being too big."

"I think fundamentally that everybody wants a Cadillac," says Harold Warner, and it is on that pleasant supposition that the division is run, the object being to make sure that when a customer is finally able to buy one he won't be disappointed, and won't ever desert. Cadillac has the highest owner-loyalty rating of any G.M. car, and it depreciates, percentagewise, less than any other car. Consequently, Cadillac never pushes the panic button in styling—for three years now, it has been gracefully retreating from the big fin, inch by inch. Cadillac dominates its price class, and its pattern is one of steady but gradual growth. Its sales of 151,528 cars in 1962 were about 10,000 units ahead of 1961. But though its problems are rather distinctive, Cadillac is integrally G.M. The division is a great hatchery of G.M. engineering firsts— the Hydra-Matic transmission, the overhead-valve, high-compression V-8 engine—and of top-rung G.M. talent: President Gordon, Executive Vice President James Roche, and Group Executive Ed Cole are Cadillac graduates.

The Show Behind the Scenes

Thus far, in tracing G.M.'s success, division by division and car by car, we have been looking mainly at those plain-to-see elements that have been basic to the company's superior competitive thrust—its high marks in over-all market strategy, product selection, and styling. And needless to say, for its final thrust, G.M.'s success depends on its great strength in distribution and sales. It has long been pretty much beyond dispute that G.M. has not only the largest but the financially strongest and most effective dealer organization in the industry. These are the elements, in any given year, that sell automobiles.

But behind all this is, first of all, a vast internal business in parts and accessories that is of itself one of the largest manufacturing complexes in the U.S. Supervised by one of G.M.'s ablest administrators, Group Vice President Roger M. Kyes, this complex includes AC Spark Plug, Delco-Remy, Delco Radio, Harrison Radiator, Hyatt Bearings, Detroit Transmission, and six other divisions. Their products are basic to the structure and performance of all G.M. cars and, of course, through the internal economies effected, this whole operation is a vital factor in G.M.'s profit performance. And in addition to supplying G.M. car divisions with original and replacement parts, this group sells well over $1 billion in parts to the independent aftermarket.

One has to go behind the scenes, also, to see what G.M. is doing to keep its cars sold, which is largely a question of quality, and to keep these hordes of cars coming off the line at the right time, the right place, and in a fantastic number of expressly ordered combinations of color, equipment, and trim. Underlying and sustaining General Motors' remarkable record of sales and profits is its performance in these two areas: the job it does on reliability control; the job it does on scheduling and logistics.

It is rather striking that at a time when its cars are selling with such effortless ease G.M. should be straining so hard to improve quality. Of course, now that the whole industry has extended its new-car warranties to two years everybody is quality-conscious. But this is not the principal motivation. At G.M. it is simply recognized that, the replacement factor being what it is, repeat sales are terribly important. G.M. believes it is the quality of the car, beyond all other factors, that enhances its trade-in value. If that value turns down in any one year, as in the case of the 1960 Ford, it may take several years to turn it back up.

Building in Reliability

G.M. has always rigorously carried on physical inspection and has long engaged in quality control, which is a statistical or

sampling approach to inspection. But these practices, as Oldsmobile's Jack Wolfram puts it, are essentially police actions that
catch mistakes after they have been committed. The big pitch at
G.M. now is the preventive concept of "systems reliability control," adapted from the military and introduced throughout the
divisions some four years ago. Each division has a well-staffed
reliability department, which usually works independently of the
inspection and quality-control forces. The director of reliability
reports to the general manager. Reliability's job is not to check
the work against the blueprints, but to begin with a study of the
initial design of each component, determine all probabilities, and
see that the utmost reliability is engineered into the product at
the design stage. Reliability then follows through with the same
kind of study of the manufacturing stage, and after that it runs
a series of reliability tests on the product prototypes that are the
equivalent of a year's operation.

Among other records or near-records broken by G.M. in 1962
was its percentage of net income to sales. At a neat 10 cents on
the dollar, it was the company's highest profit-to-sales ratio in
a dozen years. It is a characteristic of the automobile industry,
where such a high proportion of the costs are fixed costs, for the
profits to rise sharply in a high-volume year after the breakeven point has been passed. But General Motors had something
more than that going for it in 1962. Partly because of its accurate
forecast of what the total market would be, and partly because
the rise in sales, though spectacular, was remarkably steady, G.M.
was able to avoid peaks and valleys in its production scheduling.
The fact that the company did not have to go through the usual
process of putting on extra workers, then laying them off, saved
substantial sums in supplemental unemployment benefits required
under the union contract. The even flow of its line rate also had
a beneficial effect on quality. When an assembly-line rate is increased from forty to forty-three cars per hour, it not only means
an addition of 100 people on the line but it changes the job
content of every man on the line, and workers have a tendency to
be less productive and to make more mistakes.

Nevertheless, the proliferation of models, options, and varieties of color and trim has enormously complicated G.M.'s problems in logistics and inventory control. There are now a total of
136 models of passenger cars offered by G.M. compared with
eighty-five models eight years ago. But that doesn't begin to
suggest the problem—the options on engines alone run to almost
unbelievable figures. The standard Chevrolet, for instance, has

four basic engine options, and with the different carburetor combinations offered, the number of engines is, in effect, raised to twelve. But when the power requirements of all the optional equipment are taken into consideration, it means that Chevrolet has to be prepared to furnish no fewer than 106 varieties of power plants for its standard-size passenger cars alone.

Yet Chevrolet delivered over two million cars in 1962, with an actual reduction, in the averages throughout the year, of dealers' stocks on hand. Where it used to take about four weeks to deliver a Chevrolet on a sold order, the time has now been cut to an average of sixteen days from the date of the order to the date of delivery anywhere in the U.S. This flexibility has been achieved largely by virtue of the computer. Chevrolet production, procurement, and sales reports are now on a complete electronic data-processing system. In the past, schedules were reviewed and revised on the basis of the dealers' ten-day reports. Today the dealer reports his sales daily to the zone office, and the complete information is fed into the EDP equipment for instant transmission to Detroit. Thus Knudsen, his sales manager, and his manufacturing manager do not have to wait ten days to know what is going on in the market. Changing customer preferences in models, options, color, and styles can be instantly sized up, and the production schedules and the mix can be adjusted within a week's time. Chevrolet manufactures on the replacement theory rather than on order. If the rate of depletion on red trim, say—or any other buyers' choice—is faster than originally projected in the schedules, the factory immediately starts replacing at the higher rate. It is by such techniques that G.M. has been able to adjust so rapidly to the public's rapidly changing tastes.

Concurrent Growth Abroad

G.M.'s galvanic performance in the American market puts the corporation's foreign operations in a new perspective. A few years back, when there was so much talk about the U.S. car market's approaching maturity, there was a tendency to regard the overseas operation as a compensatory factor. Perhaps there was a dead end just up the road in the U.S., but in the faster-growing car market abroad G.M. had a chance to make up the deficiency. Well, the foreign potential is as bright as ever, and G.M. is driving hard to exploit it. But with the domestic market expanding as it is, the situation now shapes up as one of growth-on-growth.

In 1962, G.M.'s capital expenditures abroad of $220 million were a little more than half of what it spent in the U.S. In 1963, G.M. is stepping up U.S. spending to $530 million, and foreign spending will decline to $150 million. But the reason for this is that G.M. has now completed its major expansion program for the Opel operation in West Germany, and is about winding up the construction of new facilities for Vauxhall in Great Britain. These programs were for the launching of two new cars, both in the low-price class, that may strikingly improve G.M.'s competitive position in Europe. Opel's new car is the Kadett, a mite smaller than the Volkswagen, with which it will compete. Opel's other cars are the Rekord, considered a medium-price car in Germany, and the top-of-the-line Kapitan, which does its best to buck the dominant Mercedes-Benz. Before the Kadett came along this year, Opel had an 18 percent share of the West German market.

The new Vauxhall, yet to be named, will start up this fall. It is a one-liter car (slightly bigger than the Mini-Minor) and will give Vauxhall its first crack at the low-price class, which accounts for 49 percent of the market in Great Britain. Last year Vauxhall's penetration of the British car market was 9.9 percent.

The exclusion of Britain from the Common Market affected G.M.'s forward thinking somewhat; it had some ideas for interchange of operations between Vauxhall and Opel. But G.M.'s expansion in Europe was by no means contingent on Britain's participation, and its business has not been hurt by the de Gaulle freeze-out. Unlike some of its competitors, G.M. did not allow Vauxhall to absorb tariff charges and sell its cars at a loss in France and in other Common Market countries in order to get a foothold there. Fred Donner takes care to hold G.M. to the standards of Caesar's wife abroad as well as at home. A little over half of Vauxhall's production is exported; a little less than half of Opel's output is shipped out of Germany. Their combined output makes G.M. the fifth-largest producer in Europe. In Australia, where G.M. pioneered auto manufacturing in 1948 with its Holden operation, the company's margin of leadership is more in line with its U.S. performance. Over 40 percent of the cars sold in Australia are Holdens.

General Motors' net investment overseas is in excess of a half-billion dollars, and on its overseas sales of nearly $2 billion last year it earned over $102 million. Substantial as these figures are, they don't begin to measure the intense interest that G.M.

people, from Donner down, take in the international aspect of the business. Last fall, in a talk to the International Congress of Accountants on "The Worldwide Corporation in a Modern Economy," Donner offered some striking proposals for increasing worldwide participation in the ownership of international industrial corporations—ownership, that is, in the shares of the parent corporation, not just in the local subsidiaries. One suggestion was that the stock certificates and the annual reports be printed in the languages of the various countries in which the corporation operates.

Sunlight and Shadow

In its pursuit of business abroad, G.M. is always consciously the preacher and practitioner of free trade, and of free, competitive enterprise. In the U.S., G.M. is, by all measurable standards, a mighty impressive monument to the American economic system. But the monument casts a shadow—a giant shadow of the giant's sheer success. Has G.M. now grown so big as to threaten the health of the very system that made its success possible?

The pending government antitrust actions against G.M. are a somewhat mixed bag of suits principally aimed at G.M.'s non-automotive activities, although one of them challenges G.M.'s bus business, and another relates to the distribution of Chevrolet cars. The suits now total five:

• A criminal suit charging the company with unfairly using its power as the largest railroad shipper to capture over 80 percent of the diesel-locomotive market. A related civil suit seeks divestiture of the Electro-Motive Division that builds the locomotives.

• A civil suit charging the company with incipient monopoly in the off-highway, earthmoving-equipment field, and seeking to nullify G.M.'s acquisition, back in 1953, of the Euclid Road Machinery Co.

• A civil suit alleging that G.M. monopolizes 80 percent of the sales of city- and intercity-type buses.

• In a criminal suit a federal judge in Los Angeles, in March, 1963, entered a judgment of acquittal to charges that G.M. had conspired to prevent its dealers from selling new Chevrolets through discount houses. G.M. still faces a related civil suit, however, in which the government seeks injunctive relief.

Finally, since 1959, a federal grand jury in New York, fortified by voluminous documents subpoenaed from G.M., has been conducting a broad investigation of possible violations of the antitrust laws in the automotive industry.

The Billion-dollar Question

Of the pending lawsuits Chairman Donner simply says: "We expect to defend them one by one. We happen to think that what we've been doing is the right thing to do in a competitive market. We have done nothing to be ashamed of." This is straight-forward reaction to the specific charges, but the ultimate question of G.M.'s size will continue to be a matter of debate. Indeed, what the business world is forever wondering about is whether, one fine day, the government will go for the big one—a frontal attack on G.M.'s size, its better-than-50 percent share of the U.S. passenger-car market, and perhaps, after the pattern of the diesel-locomotive case, ask for the divestiture of a major car division, such as Chevrolet.

All this is pure speculation, of course, and is not based on anything the Department of Justice has publicly said, and certainly not on anything strange or circuitous that General Motors has done. As far as the passenger-car business is concerned, the questions raised by G.M.'s spectacular success appear to be concerned not so much with behavior as with structure, not with business morality but with economic philosophy, not with practice but with theory. Is bigness, of itself, bad? Should power be dismantled because of its capabilities for uncommitted abuses? These are legitimate questions that jurists and economists have wrestled with in the past, and they will continue to do so as long as the American economic system endures. Discussion of these abstract problems, however, should never get too far away from what a company did or did not do to achieve its success and eminence.

This report on what G.M. has accomplished of recent years at least makes plain that it has in its way served the consumer. G.M. never offered him more choice or better quality, and all at prices that have remained virtually unchanged since the fall of 1958. These prices, moreover, were certainly free of collusion, discrimination, exclusive deals, or below-cost subsidies. To be sure, G.M. was hard on the competition—all of it—but did it "oppress" any competitor? There's a difference. The best answer to that comes from a high executive of a rival auto company. "They beat us last year," he said, "on product and not with monopolistic power plays. If G.M. is going to be cut down to size, we want to be the party that does it."

Montgomery Ward:

*Prosperity Is Still around the Corner** _____

The news at Montgomery Ward in 1960 has been a bit spooky, as if the ghost of Sewell Avery's administration were clanking its chains in the old halls on the east bank of the Chicago River above the Loop. Anyway, something has happened not easily explained by plain business reasoning. On August 25, Chairman John A. Barr announced that for the first half of the year sales had climbed to $567,308,000, or 3.7 percent above the first half of 1959, but that after-tax earnings had fallen by more than 50 percent, and that the standing quarterly dividend would be cut from 50 cents to 25 cents. Furthermore, in a statement made on the occasion of the opening of a spanking new Ward store in a new shopping center in Santa Ana, California, Barr said that the earnings prospects for the full fiscal year 1960 (to the end of January, 1961) were for a new low in the company's postwar history.

This news, bad as it was, would not have been quite so startling but for an awkward circumstance. Not too many weeks before, at the annual stockholders' meeting in May, Barr had confidently set forth very different expectations. In 1959, Ward earned $30,700,000 on sales of $1.2 billion, and Barr said: "Our short-term profit planning is predicated on showing an improvement in earnings in 1960 over 1959, an improvement in 1961 over 1960, and so on. We believe that we touched the low point in earnings in 1958, and that, with normal business conditions, each succeeding year will show an improvement." And he concluded with emphasis: "Barring a marked weakness in our economy, we expect our merchandising plans, backed by a well-integrated and determined staff, to produce an improvement in earnings this year over last year, despite the disappointing first-quarter results."

The failure of Montgomery Ward to live up to this optimistic forecast is doubly disappointing because in recent years, and in 1959 in particular, great hopes have been based on its rejuvenation. As everybody knows, Ward in postwar years made a

* *November 1960*

wretched showing because its erstwhile head, Sewell Avery (now in retirement), refused to bet on American expansion, hoarded cash, and as the saying goes, turned Ward into a "bank with a store front." As a result Ward's sales remained static around the $1-billion mark while those of its archrival, Sears, Roebuck, soared from $1 billion in 1945 to over $4 billion today. But when Avery was ousted in 1955 and Chairman Barr took over, much was expected since Barr was committed to renovating, expanding, and indeed remaking the old company. In fact, sales if not profits did improve considerably and in 1959 security analysts were expressing the opinion that Montgomery Ward, the country's No. 3 nonfood merchandiser after Sears and Penney, had really turned the corner.

Now these expectations have received a rude shock with the announcement that Ward earned only $5,037,000 after taxes in the first half of 1960. Full-year earnings will be better than this figure indicates, since Ward normally does 60 percent of its business in the second half; but profits will certainly be far lower than last year, and Wall Street has duly reflected this prospect. In 1959 Ward's stock ranged between $40.50 and $53.50. It sold off in 1960 with the general market and then slumped from $40 to $30 as the bad news came out (it was around $28 as of late September). Such a bump in the evaluation of the new Montgomery Ward, whose shareholders are largely a group of conservative investors with old and deep loyalties to the company, reflects a sharp questioning of the promise of resurgence. What really happened in the short space of three months to bring about such a drastic failure of expectations? And what does this event portend for a great organization that employs 63,000 people and whose fortunes are important not just to its shareholders but to the whole U.S. business community?

It could be, of course, on the extreme, pessimistic view, that all the new faith in Montgomery Ward has been misplaced. It could be that this big organization will just never really "turn the corner" into a strong, growing, and increasingly profitable enterprise. The competitive system does not guarantee that a company with a long and famous tradition like Ward's will survive and prosper. On the other hand, it is also possible that present pessimism about Ward has been overdone, and that in fact the company has strength and prospects much better than recent appearances would indicate. It is at least plausible that in 1959, in particular, security analysts, if not the Ward management itself, greatly overestimated the immediate prospects of the company, and underestimated the time needed to turn it around into a really vigorous concern. If in 1955, when he took over its management, Barr had painted a gloomier picture of conditions and if he had made no forecast early this year, he might be in a far happier position today. For short-term expectations were raised that have now been sharply disappointed. But such disappointment does not necessarily endanger Ward's long-term future; and on the evidence the company is still potentially in an interesting come-back situation. This estimate could be wrong but it cannot be proved so until 1962 at the earliest, when present management policies will have had time to mature.

A Hefty Heritage

At any rate, it will pay to take a closer look at what shape Ward is in today, and how it got that way. It is still, to say the least, a pretty hefty organization. While its sales last year of $1.2 billion were only about one-fourth of those of Sears, they still represent about 1.5 percent of the $80 billion the U.S. consumer spends on the types of merchandise sold by Ward—domestic goods, clothing, small wares, etc. Unlike Sears, Ward manufactures relatively little of the goods it sells, but rather purchases them from some 20,000 suppliers, drawing on sources as far away as Hong Kong and Sweden. It sells in two ways. About one-third of its sales—$350 million last year—is catalogue business. This includes its traditional mail-order business, and also sales made through some 600 catalogue stores, where purchasers can sample Ward goods and place orders for them. The bulk of its business, however, is done through some 540 retail stores. Most of these are old stores inherited from the past; thirty are new full-line stores that have been opened up since 1958 under Ward's policy of renovation and expansion. The new stores have high-volume businesses with an average annual gross per store of $7,500,000. The older stores are far smaller, less well located than the new, and have suffered sharp competition from newer sub-urban developments.

The great bulk of Ward's stores, particularly the old ones, are located in the Middle West, as might be expected of a company that got its start in Chicago back in 1872. In that rural pre-automobile age, Ward was for a good many years a mail-order house, pure and simple, rendering a unique service to the American farmer. With the growth of the towns and cities, Ward in the late Twenties began to supplement its catalogue business by opening up retail stores in the farm belt. Scarcely had this logical move begun, however, when the U.S. economy, and Ward with it, was engulfed by the great depression. It was then, in November, 1931, that Sewell Avery, of U.S. Gypsum, was sent in to save the company, and save it he did. (See *Fortune*, January, 1935.) In a dramatic reorganization he cut costs, fired personnel, and in general shortened sail. As the economy began to recover as the result of or despite New Deal policies, of which Avery disapproved, Ward recovered with it. And Avery, in the Thirties at least, did not pursue purely defensive policies. While he closed about 100 old stores, he opened about 175 new ones in the latter part of the decade.

In the Forties, however, and particularly in the postwar years, Avery proved that he was not a brilliant pilot. While Sears confidently bet on a new and expanding America, Avery developed an *idée fixe* that postwar inflation would end in a crash no less serious than that of 1929. Following this idea, he opened no new stores but rather piled up cash to the ceiling in preparation for an economic debacle that never came. In these years, Ward's balance sheet gave a somewhat misleading picture of its prospects. Net earnings remained respectably high, and were generally higher than those of Sears as a percentage of sales. In 1946 earnings after taxes were $52 million. They rose to $74 million in 1950 and then declined to $35 million in 1954. Meanwhile, however, sales remained static, and in Avery's administration profits and liquidity were maintained at the expense of growth. In 1954, Ward had $327 million in cash and securities, $147 million in receivables, and $216 million in inventory, giving it a total current-asset position of $690 million and net worth of $639 million. It was liquid, all right, but it was also the shell of a once great company.

Chairman Barr Plays It Cozy

It was this shell that Barr took over in 1955 after Louis E. Wolfson of Jacksonville, Florida, started his proxy fight against the Avery management (see *Fortune*, May, 1956). Wolfson was unable to capture the company, and in the end succeeded only in getting three directors on the board. But his fight finished off Avery, whose policies were recognized as mistaken, and brought in Barr, a lawyer who had been a vice president and secretary of the company for many years. Barr at this juncture stood in a peculiar position. On the one hand, he had been part of the

Avery team, and indeed had coolly led the Avery forces in the fight with Wolfson. On the other hand, he was convinced that the company had to be renovated from top to bottom; he quietly went about doing so. Unfortunately, if understandably in the circumstances, he did not come right out and say that Ward was in a state of crisis. Having come to power in one of the ways men come to power—that is, in defense of previous power—he began a course of verbal courtesy toward his old mentor, Avery. His first report as chairman began with the soporific: "For Montgomery Ward & Co., 1955 was a year of progress." A more forthright statement would have been, "After fifteen years of inaction this company is in a tough spot, which for your new management is a challenging position."

Now, of course, only in a business fable could realities have been stated thus flatly. But had Barr thus stated them there might have been fewer illusions bred that Ward could be rapidly turned around, and some of the high expectations of recent years, and particularly of 1959, might never have gained credence. Moreover, Barr would have been facing the stark realities. For in 1955, Montgomery Ward was a very sick cat. To be sure, Barr inherited a mountainous pile of cash and the company's reputation for quality and service, but that was about all. Ward's top command had been shot by Avery's dictatorial one-man methods. Barr had only one vice president. He also lacked middle-management manpower, and a research department to provide intelligence as to where and how to invest the cash he had inherited. Besides its catalogue business, Ward had in 1955 some 568 stores, few of which had been rehabilitated since the Thirties, and there were no new stores whatever, the company's youngest being fourteen years old.

Barr's most important task was to build back management, and it took him some years to do so. In effect, he has had to weld a whole new team together—a team that today includes Paul M. Hammaker, president, Charles J. Kushell Jr., financial vice president, and Edmund P. Platt, executive vice president of regional operations. He rebuilt and reshuffled much of middle management. He set up a new training program for store personnel. He also called in consultants, notably Robert Heller & Associates, and within two years got a workable organization structure far more decentralized than in the Avery days. Ward's gigantic buying operations are, of course, supervised by the home office, and it maintains some forty-five merchandising departments, each specializing in a particular set of products; the home office also provides promotional plans and advertising material for displays in the field. On the other hand, individual store managers are given latitude in their merchandising, and it is a cardinal principle of Barr's that a manager should run his store as if it were his own business. Says Barr: "He's the most important man in the whole organization."

The Store's the Thing

While recasting management and procedures, Barr also struck out along other lines. He took special pains to tailor Ward's prices and products to middle-class customers in the $5,000-to-$15,000 family income group. He completely revamped the look of Ward's catalogues, and the company now gets out 45 million catalogues per year, 12 million copies of which catalogue the full line; the rest are specialized. Barr also expanded catalogue stores, where customers can sample products, from 278 as of August, 1955, to approximately 600 today. In 1957 he bought up the Fair chain of four department stores in Chicago for $9 million, but he discovered that department stores and Ward-type chain stores don't mix. Today the Fair is operated independently.

But Barr's big and critical problem was to lay down programs for Ward's retail stores, one for the old stores and one for opening up new ones. All of the 500-odd old stores had to be studied in order to decide whether to modernize them or give them up. In general Barr made the decision to close down non-paying stores selectively, and has closed sixty of them in the past five years. Meanwhile he systematically tackled the much more important problem of opening up new retail stores. He brought in Howard Green, a young man whose head contained a large amount of what is known in universities as location theory. At the end of 1957, Howard Green established a Store Research and Development Department, staffed with several highly trained intellectuals who spend their time making detailed studies of population movements, markets for Ward-type merchandise, transportation, the competition in relation to location, shopping habits and desires, capital costs, sales and profits for periods ahead equal to the length of leases, and a return-on-investment analysis. They come up with specific recommendations for stores by type, location, and size. Executive decision makers with these recommendations in front of them are in a much better position than their predecessors who located stores by "instinct."

Working with this new kind of brain trust, Barr opened his first five new stores in 1958, another twelve in 1959, and will add twenty-one more in 1960. His long-term program calls for an expansion of Ward's sales from new stores of $150 million per year. This requires opening about twenty new stores per year with an average sales volume of $7,500,000 per store per year. This is an aggressive competitive plan, which envisions an increasing share of the U.S. retail market. It is also, however, a plan that will not mature for some time to come, and Barr's general strategy was not likely to show sudden and spectacular results. What he has done over the past five years is to swap a large part of Avery's hoarded cash for an increase in receivables and inventories, and for general expansion. Given this heavy investment program, profits have not been spectacular. They were about $35 million in 1955, somewhat above that in 1957, and about $30,700,000 in 1959. Sales, however, increased from $887 million in 1954 to their $1.2 billion last year, and on the record it seemed reasonable to expect they would continue to increase, and that as the new-store program bore fruit, profits would finally increase.

What Went Wrong?

These expectations, as we have seen, have been disappointed by the sharp drop in profits in the first half of 1960, and at first glance this drop seems to call Barr's whole strategy into question. Yet on closer examination of what happened early this year, the reverse conclusion may well be justified. For what happened was this. On the basis of 1959 predictions for a continued business upturn, Ward's management figured that the new stores it had in actual operation would do well, and that meanwhile there would be a $16,500,000 increase in the sales of its old stores, which are still the overwhelming majority of its retail outlets. Instead, in the first half sales of the old stores actually slumped by $14 million under those of the previous year. This meant that old-store sales were $30,500,000 under the expectations for which the company had budgeted. The effect of this reversal was a reduction of about $12 million in pretax earnings. In addition, earnings from the catalogued business were down $637,000 owing to the fact that large expenditures were made on promotion and advertising that did not pay off in sales. The result of all this was the precipitous fall in after-tax earnings in the first half of 1960 to only $5 million. At the moment the company will give no estimate of earnings for the full year. Outsiders put them in the range of $18 million to $22 million.

This is certainly discouraging, the more so because Sears's earnings in the first half went off only 5 percent (although Sears is not strictly comparable because of inside factory sales and insurance income). Yet the point to grasp is that Ward's troubles centered not in its program for new stores but in its *old* stores. What this means is that the company has to race in replacing old stores with new. Barr has been trying to do just that; the question is whether he is doing it fast enough. The 1960 downturn does not so much indict Barr's strategy as emphasize that Ward must hasten to carry it out and shake off the last vestiges of the Avery legacy of inaction.

This conclusion is confirmed by a closer look at the troubles of the old stores. While their number is large, their actual volume per store is relatively low. As we have seen, the average new store does a business of $7,500,000 per year, but the business of the old stores ranges far below that. Of stores operating in the first halves of 1959 and 1960, seventy-five of the old stores had a volume of under $500,000 per year; 214 had a volume of $500,000 to $1 million; 115 had between $1 million and $1,500,000; eighty had a business of between $1,500,000 and $3 million, and thirty-five do over $3 million. Because of their small size, the cost structure of the smaller stores is much less flexible than the newer big stores. It takes a minimum number of people to run a small store regardless of volume, whereas the big stores can expand and contract their payroll with varying business conditions through use of part-time employees. Finally, most of the older stores are badly located in non-growth areas of the Midwest, and in many instances, even where business is good, they are in downtown districts, lack parking space, and suffer from suburban competition. This does not mean that Ward's old stores cannot make a profit in good times. But it does mean that their earnings will fluctuate sharply with market conditions, and that Ward has not yet weeded out enough of the really bad actors.

Simonetta in Santa Ana

To do so, however, is at best a defensive operation. Ward's offensive operation obviously lies in building new stores on new locations. Here Barr is pursuing an aggressive and imaginative policy, and Ward's new stores, while still few in number, have the bright new look of middle-class America. Typical of Ward's new merchandising efforts is the store opened last August in Santa Ana, California, Ward's fourth new one in the state. It sparkles in the midst of a huge parking lot two miles from downtown Santa Ana, the center of Orange County, one of the fastest-growing counties in the U.S. It has about 90,000 square feet of net selling space and expects to achieve a normal sales volume of about $8 million, and is part of a shopping-center development known as Honer Plaza. In opening it, Ward invited stockholders to a gala preview ceremony, and as they arrived, they had white gardenias pinned on them by local belles, and were later dazzled by a fashion display collected in France, Italy, and the U.S. by Rita Perna, Ward's fashion coordinator. The new Ward fashions ran the gamut from tartan culottes for the back-to-school set to mink-trimmed cashmere sweaters and originals from Simonetta of Rome. All this was a far cry from Avery's austere type of merchandising.

This particular store was opened at an unfortunate time since it happened to coincide with Barr's first warnings that profits in 1960 were not going to be what they were in 1959. Nevertheless, the new merchandising techniques duly impressed even the most skeptical stockholder. Said one: "I've never seen anything like this at Ward before . . . It's so sophisticated." Said another: "My husband was on the point of selling the stock yesterday, but I told him we should come down here and see what they have to say. Of course retail business has not been good this year. They have put the money into expansion . . . they are just good, honest people. I don't think I have ever seen such a sparkling fashion show as this."

Ward's new store program has followed a pattern of clusters, that is, an intensive cultivation of a limited number of areas. There are two good reasons for this. First, in starting to look for locations, it is not possible to make a detailed study of all the principal elements of the problem in every market in the U.S. Second, by locating stores in groups, a more economical system for feeding these stores from a distribution center can be devised. The areas chosen of recent years were Detroit, Kansas City, San Francisco, San Diego, Phoenix, St. Petersburg–Tampa, Houston, Dallas–Fort Worth. A few new stores are "free standing" (i.e., stand alone), but most of them are in shopping centers. Often a new Ward store is made the nucleus of a new shopping center as the result of a deal with a real-estate developer. In general, Ward chooses a location that involves leapfrogging over the competition (Sears, Penney, local stores, etc.), which made outgoing moves in the past fifteen years. The leap generally is made to the rim of a community with a present population "inboard" and an expected population movement "outboard."

From the time a new-store site is chosen to the time the store opens can take from one to three years. Thereafter it takes another year or so for the store to reach its normal sales volume and somewhat longer for it to achieve its expected earnings. This time lag accounts for the fact that, while Barr has been strenuously pushing his new-store program, returns are still comparatively small. In 1959, sales from new stores ran to only $62 million. This year it is expected that such sales will run to $158 million (of which $60 million was realized in the first half), in 1961 the target is $280 million; and by the fall of 1963, on some projections, sales of new stores will reach as much as $500 million. Meanwhile, of course, some deduction must be made for older and smaller stores that will be going out of business. Nevertheless, if all goes well, Ward's total sales—$1.2 billion last year—should be substantially rising and the increased profitability of new stores should give Ward insurance against the kind of disappointment it suffered this year.

The Wherewithal

All this, however, is only a projection, and the qualification *if all goes well* is critically important. In the first place, Ward must find the money to finance this expansion, and in the second place much depends on the course of general business from here on out. On the first point, expansion entails much more than opening new stores; it also entails an increase in receivables and inventories. Investment expenditures from now to 1965 are scheduled to run to $500 million, of which $100 million will go into the increase of inventories; $200 million will go into receivables, and another $200 million will go into real-estate operations.

This is a substantial program, but Ward is in a strong position to meet it—thanks, ironically enough, to Sewell Avery's policies in the postwar years. Since 1955, Ward has reduced his mountainous pile of cash and securities from $327 million to $34 million as of early this year; but the decrease in cash has largely gone into an increase in liquid receivables, and Ward's working-capital position remains satisfactory. Equally important, and again in part thanks to Avery, Ward is not burdened, as are so many other corporations, with a long-term funded debt.

In addition, Ward has recently taken two procedural steps

that will facilitate its expansion of receivables and its real-estate operations. In the past the parent company financed receivables directly, and between 1954 and 1959 they rose from $147 million or about 17 percent of sales to $357 million or about 30 percent of sales. As new stores are opened there will be need of extending still more credit to customers. To meet this need, the Montgomery Ward Credit Corp. has been set up with an equity of $25 million on which it can borrow in the market at a ratio of about four to one. It has already borrowed about $100 million and used this to absorb a like amount of receivables from the parent company. This reduced Ward's receivables to about $240 million as of September 1, and the Credit Corp. will now take care of future expansion requirements.

Ward has taken a somewhat similar step for swinging its new-store program. Until recently it used its own capital to buy property in some cases, or in others to lease store sites from real-estate entrepreneurs. In February, 1960, its net property account was $105 million, and its lease obligations to maturity ran to $187 million. Some months ago it set up the Montgomery Ward Real Estate Corp., which will probably handle all future real-estate expansion involving store ownership. The new corporation will buy land and own the bricks and mortar of the new stores. It will then give a lease on the store to the parent company, and assign the lease as collateral for its own borrowing in the market. By this device Ward shifts its long-term borrowing to its subsidiary; its own debt will be the commitment to pay rent. By the end of this year the Real Estate Corp. will have taken on only $20 million in property, but in the future this is likely to increase considerably.

What's Ahead?

The ultimate test of a capital program, however, is earnings, and the question remains whether and when these will recover from their present unsatisfactory condition. This in turn ramifies into the question of where the U.S. economy is headed. The mild turndown of early 1960, sometimes called "high-level stagnation," was enough to undermine profits in Ward's old stores and to disappoint all expectations. If the economy doesn't pick up, prospects for 1961 earnings are also poor, the more so because Ward will be facing heavy pre-opening expenses in the fall of that year as it opens up new stores, which will not immediately show maximum profits. And should there be a real recession, then Ward's earnings would really be knocked to pieces.

Yet even on this most pessimistic assumption, Ward would still have an ace in the hole, owing to its present liquidity, and specifically to the fact that the parent company still has about $240 million in receivables on its books. If worse came to worse, Ward could negotiate these receivables and carry on. Hence, even if we assume that earnings dip to zero in a real recession the company could continue to open up the new stores on which its future sales and earnings depend. Dividends would, of course, be omitted in this kind of situation, but the basic expansion program would go forward.

But this is the gloomiest of assumptions. What Ward's management, no less than its shareholders, are obviously hoping is that the economy will not slide off much further and that in fact the major part of the 1960 recession or stagnation is over. In this case, while earnings prospects may not be bright for the rest of 1960, and even for 1961, still the company would make enough money to maintain its present restricted quarterly dividend of 25 cents per share, as well as go forward with its renovation and expansion program. In any case, completion of that program seems assured, come foul or fairer weather, and that is the important thing for the future. Ward's setback this year was certainly painful in terms of psychological expectations but, to repeat, disappointment of short-term expectations is not the same thing as defeat of long-term aims. Ward remains an interesting company in an interesting situation, increasingly well prepared to ride with the economy. It is a new company with a destiny date, say, early in 1963.

Magowan's Way with Safeway*_____

BY ROBERT SHEEHAN

It might almost be called "the classic situation" of modern American business. It is the case of a corporation that has been built to greatness by the fierce competitiveness and individuality

* October 1958

of a single leader, and then suddenly finds itself held back by that leader's principles and unwillingness to conform to the realities of a more dispassionate, more up-to-date philosophy of management. The old warrior is unhorsed and a crisp young master of compromise, committees, and delegation-of-authority succeeds him and rides off in another direction.

The giant Safeway corporation, under crisp Robert A. Magowan, has been trotting along in such a new direction since the fall of 1955, and the consequences of the changeover can now be reported in some perspective.

Magowan was fifty-two when he was plucked from his partnership in Wall Street's Merrill Lynch, Pierce, Fenner & Beane (now Smith), and hustled into the chairmanship of Safeway Stores, Inc., of Oakland, California, the grocery chain that ranks (after A & P and Sears, Roebuck) as the world's third-largest retail organization. He replaced the then sixty-six-year-old Lingan A. Warren, who wasn't wringing a satisfactory profit out of Safeway's nearly $2 billion of sales. The profit margins of all food-store chains are extremely narrow, but Safeway's was notoriously so: the company was earning only seven-tenths of a cent, after taxes, on each dollar of sales.

Magowan, who is five feet seven inches tall, weighs 140 pounds, and is catlike quick in mind and movement, proceeded to turn Safeway inside out. He promptly put a stop order on Warren's costly crusades against such of his pet hates as trading stamps, manufacturers' advertising allowances, and direct deliveries to individual stores. No more wars; no more lawsuits. Where Warren's organization was monolithic, as in its merchandising operation, Magowan decentralized drastically; where it sprawled, as in its manufacturing operation, he consolidated equally drastically. At the top level he fired liberally, hired sparingly, and shuffled the talent around like a Casey Stengel: the company controller abruptly became vice president in charge of supply; a former chief accountant shortly found himself heading up advertising, research, and personnel.

The sum of all this manipulation was that Safeway almost doubled its net in Magowan's first year. On a gain of 3 percent in sales, Safeway's net income soared 87 percent. Last year sales increased 6.4 percent to a record $2.1 billion, but Magowan was still paring away at overhead, and profits rose 21.7 percent to almost $31 million.

In November of last year, Safeway stockholders were treated to a three-for-one split, followed by an increase in the dividend.

Based on the shares outstanding before the split, Safeway's 1957 earnings were $7.44 per share compared with earnings of $3.25 per share in 1955, when Magowan took over. And at midpoint in 1958, Safeway was one of that small band of U.S. firms that could flout recession talk with hard figures and a dividend increase. Profits for the first half were $15 million, up 7 percent. Safeway is now earning 1.5 cents, after taxes, on each dollar of sales, the best showing by far among the industry's five largest chains, and better even than the industry median for all chains, which is about 1.3 cents.

The Scientific Innovator

On the other hand, Safeway's sales under Magowan have shown extremely modest gains. Lingan Warren, now watching silently from the sidelines, has doubtless been observing this point with extreme interest. For Warren was a brilliant innovator who built Safeway to sales eminence on the strength of a basic policy that is still to be discredited. He believed unequivocally in meeting all competitors' prices at all times, and held that in the grocery business, once you begin to take more than a very modest profit on your goods, you leave yourself vulnerable to the competition.

Warren, who is wry-minded, dry-spoken, and rustic-looking, was born on a Virginia farm and quit school after the seventh grade. He was running a lumber business in Jacksonville, Florida, in 1926, when he encountered and impressed Charles E. Merrill, who later hired him to handle the new-business department of Merrill Lynch. It was through the underwriting services of Merrill Lynch that the present Safeway company was formed in 1926, by the merger of Safeway Stores of southern California with the slightly smaller chain of Skaggs's stores, which operated in northern California, the Rocky Mountain states, and the Pacific Northwest. In 1928 Merrill sent Warren out to the Coast to organize still another string of stores known as the MacMarr chain. In 1931 MacMarr was put together with Safeway, and in 1934 Warren took over the presidency of the whole works.

As a student of chain-store economics, Lingan Warren probably had no peer. He regarded Safeway as an instrument for the scientific distribution of food, and through his innovations in manufacturing, warehousing, transportation, and inventory handling and control, he made Safeway second only to A & P in its ability to reduce the spread between producer and consumer. As a merchandiser, he stressed cleanliness, service, and rock-bottom prices. He originated Safeway's distinctive and tremendously successful meat program, whereby only U.S. Choice meats were purchased, were trimmed and aged to rigid specifications in Safeway plants and sold with a money-back guarantee. As an expansionist, Warren was cautious but shrewd. In acquiring new locations, he was the first man in the food-store business to use the "buy-build-sell-lease-back" technique, thus keeping his capital free for operating purposes. He pursued a policy of replacement, rather than spectacular expansion, and actually reduced the number of stores by 1,200 units during his twenty years in the presidency, while building Safeway's sales from less than $300 million to upwards of $1.9 billion.

Where Warren erred—if such a magnificent obsession can rightly be called an error—was in clothing his business beliefs and principles in the robes of a cause for which he was prepared to fight to the death. For instance, many grocerymen dislike trading stamps, but most swing over to them as a necessary nuisance. Warren regarded stamps as practically immoral: a gimmick that raised the price of food to the consumer. He spent millions in advertising to excoriate trading stamps, and finally, in trying to beat them by naked price cutting, ran afoul of the Antitrust Division of the Department of Justice.

In his fight against the retail milk price laws that exist in several western states, Warren wanted to break the *floor* price, offering to sell at 1.5 cents a quart cheaper to the consumer. Warren succeeded only in stirring up the wrath of the farmers, and of his competitors. The consumers were confused and relatively apathetic. For all the expensive and futile wrangling, Safeway never managed to put itself over to the public as a public benefactor. In the mind of the average citizen, Safeway in this controversy was just another big corporation with an "angle."

Battle of the Brands

Similarly with national brands: virtue may have been on Warren's side, but he was again tilting at windmills. Lots of retail grocers resent, but few defy, the pressures exerted by national manufacturers. Warren went right to the mat with them. He didn't want their "advertising allowances," a discount contingent on the retailer's agreement to plug the brand product in his weekly advertising. Warren preferred to buy at fair prices, advertise as he pleased. Moreover, he didn't want the manufacturers delivering rack goods—soft drinks, and the like—directly to his stores. He didn't like the idea of the delivery salesmen poking around his stores, setting up their own displays. Let the goods simply be shipped, he said, to the Safeway distribution center and, for a price concession based on the savings to the supplier, Safeway would deliver the merchandise to the stores. (When one California Coca-Cola distributor balked, Coca-Cola disappeared from Safeway shelves in the area.)

Meanwhile, Safeway's own brands (consisting of 200 different products, 600 different labels) were pushed mightily by Warren. But when Safeway division managers anywhere in the U.S. wanted to stock national brands, they had to send the order to the Safeway central buying offices in the San Francisco Bay area. There the order was scrutinized and processed, and when the division, in turn, was billed for it, the central office added an "up charge" for handling. Obviously, the system wasn't calculated to encourage division managers, or store managers, to promote the popular national brands.

To be sure, the traffic in Safeway brands was producing good profits; item for item, private brands will almost always outearn nationally advertised brands. The trouble was that the manufacture of these private brands nearly constituted Safeway's sole source of profit. In the retail operation Safeway stores were missing out on the volume of earnings it is possible to roll up on the faster-moving, though lower-profit, national brands. More important, retail profits were held down by Warren's well-policed ukase that no Safeway store could permit itself to be underpriced by a competitor on any item whatsoever, even a loss leader.

In the minds of some stockholders, the cumulative effect of Warren's pet policies added up to inadequate profits. Among the dissatisfied shareholders was Warren's sponsor and mentor, Charles Merrill, who owned the largest singly held (6 percent) block of stock. There were many earnest discussions between the two old friends, with Warren contending that if you ran a retail food business to please the stockholders rather than the customers, the stockholders in the long run wouldn't get anything. Suddenly, in August, 1955, Warren asked to be relieved (so the story goes) of the arduous duties of the Safeway presidency, and agreed to remain as "consultant and adviser" (at 0.9 percent of the company's net income, though not to exceed $150,000 a year) for the ensuing five years.

Macy's or J. P. Morgan?

Magowan was Charles Merrill's son-in-law, which helps to explain the how, but has little to do with the why, of his being chairman and president of Safeway. Nobody doubts Magowan's ability to succeed handsomely on his own, in any kind of business situation.

Magowan was born in Chester, Pennsylvania, the son of a railroad stationmaster. He went to Kent School in Connecticut, and to Harvard, where he was an editor of the *Crimson*, and helped pay his way through by reporting college news for the Boston *Globe*, the New York *Times*, and other newspapers.

When Magowan graduated from Harvard in 1927 he had a chance to go either with J. P. Morgan & Co. at $15 a week, or R. H. Macy & Co. at $30 a week. He chose Macy's, quickly became a buyer (which involved yearly trips to Paris), and at thirty-one was made merchandise manager of Macy's inexpensive ready-to-wear departments. In 1934 he left Macy's to become vice president and an account executive for the advertising firm of N. W. Ayer & Son, in Philadelphia. In 1935 he married Doris Merrill. On the weekend following their honeymoon, the Magowans visited Mr. Merrill on Long Island, where Lingan Warren also happened to be a guest. Warren offered Magowan a job with Safeway, at $2,000 a year more than Ayer was paying him. Magowan accepted and moved out to Oakland.

At Safeway, Magowan went through a trainee program worked out especially for him by Warren. He began as a store clerk, progressed through various jobs in the bakery, produce, meats, real-estate, and accounting departments before becoming, after three years, an administrative assistant in Warren's office. Magowan would have stayed on at Safeway except for the fact that after Edmund C. Lynch, Merrill's close friend and partner, died in 1938, Merrill invited his son-in-law to come into the firm. (Magowan has a modest explanation for this: "I think Mr. Merrill was lonesome for his daughter.")

Magowan was director of advertising and sales promotion for Merrill Lynch, later became senior partner in charge of sales. Less the two years he spent in the South Pacific as an officer in Naval Air Combat Intelligence, Magowan served at Merrill Lynch for seventeen years until the day in 1955 when he replaced his old mentor. How did he rate there? Perhaps the best answer is found in the fact that when he took the Safeway chairmanship, numerous Merrill Lynch partners and employees promptly loaded up for their own accounts on Safeway stock. They did well: in Magowan's three years the market value of the shares has risen roughly 100 percent.

Peace at a Price

Magowan took over Safeway at a moment of great crisis. The company was in deep trouble with the Department of Justice, which had brought an ominous antitrust action against Safeway, and Lingan Warren personally, in the Texas courts.

Warren had been fighting the bloodiest of all his wars in Texas, where Safeway has 151 stores. When Safeway would cut prices to meet stamp competition, the competition would cut prices to match and still issue stamps, so Safeway would cut still further. But the competitors, having the initiative, were able to use hit-and-run tactics: they'd strike suddenly with deep cuts on coffee, say, over a two-to-three-day period, then pull back. To meet this kind of attack, Safeway finally lowered prices on a number of items, and held them down for a period of time. Thereupon, several competitors in the summer of 1954 complained to Anti-trust that Safeway was violating the Sherman Act and the Robin-son-Patman Act. In July, 1955, a federal grand jury in Fort Worth returned an indictment, and later the government filed criminal and civil suits against Safeway.

In one of his first and most fateful decisions, Magowan moved to file a *nolo contendere* plea in the criminal case, and sign a consent decree in the civil case. In the first instance the judge imposed fines of $187,500, and suspended jail sentences on Lingan Warren and on Earl Cliff, then Safeway division manager in Dallas. Under the terms of the consent decree, Safeway, among other things, is enjoined from selling items at prices below cost, and from operating below cost any store or department thereof, anywhere in the U.S.

For a retail grocer this is not any easy situation to live with. Warren would certainly have gone to trial, and carried it to the Supreme Court if necessary. But Magowan was thinking not only of the expense—to fight further would have cost at least $1 million in legal outlays, and as much again in the cost of officers' time—but also of the price Safeway was paying in terms of the distraction and uncertainty created by its involvement in litigation and quarrels.

Having given up the fight against stamps, Safeway today has a small interest, along with several other chains, in the Blue Chip Stamp Co., and in communities where Safeway can't lick the stamp competition, it joins 'em.

Magowan also ordered a three-year fight dropped that Warren had been waging in the courts, at legislative hearings, and in the newspapers against the retail minimum-price milk laws of California. He simply felt it was unrealistic to think Safeway's pious plea that it was being forced to make "too much profit" on its milk would be taken at face value by the public. (Safeway is the only big chain on the Coast that owns its own milk plants. Without state-maintained retail prices, it could easily undersell its competitors on milk, still make a reasonable profit, and attract a whale of a lot of traffic to Safeway stores.)

By pulling out of Warren's legal battles, Magowan in his first year cut Safeway's legal costs by one-half, and its bill for public relations by 25 percent.

"Your Own Business"

Far more dramatic, however, was Magowan's reversal of Warren's cherished pricing and buying policies, and his sweeping reorganization of the central command.

In September, 1955, Magowan called a meeting in Atlantic City of the eighteen retail-division managers (since increased to twenty-four) who supervise Safeway's 2,000 stores in twenty-five states, the District of Columbia, and five Canadian provinces. It was the first meeting of division managers in over twenty years. It was the first time, for many of them, that they made one another's acquaintance. Under the old regime if one Safeway manager wanted to exchange information with another, he had to get clearance from Warren.

Without any preliminaries, Magowan told them, "I don't know anything about the grocery business, but you fellows do. From now on, you're running your division as if it were your own business. You don't take orders from anyone but me and I'm not going to give you orders. I'm just going to hold you responsible."

He then announced that Safeway units no longer had to meet every single price along the street but had to meet only legitimate competition; that they could stock Safeway's private brands or not as they pleased—just so long as the customer was able to get what she wanted; and finally, that division managers would henceforth buy their national brands through regular trade channels, rather than through the central buying offices.

Magowan might have gradually replaced Warren's dogma, item for item, with his own dogma. Instead, he made the magnanimous and flattering gesture of empowering the division managers to make the decisions, though he knew full well what their decisions were likely to be. After all, the Safeway incentive-compensation system could enable some of these men to make up to $115,000 a year. All Magowan had to do was put them on their own, and retail profits, as we have seen, began to turn up sharply. When managers didn't respond to the challenge, Magowan had no hesitancy in replacing them. It wasn't long before new managers took over a number of major divisions.

Magowan now proceeded to cut deeply into the cumbersome central-office system for supply, services, and supervision. Suddenly, the need for some 400 to 500 jobs evaporated, a couple of high-priced vice-presidencies among them.

The most extensive surgery took place in the supply division, which was responsible for the manufacture and promotion of Safeway-brand products, and the purchasing of all meat, fish, and produce. William S. Mitchell, forty-four, was shifted from controller to this operation.

Under Warren, the department of supply had consisted of fourteen divisions, all with separately located offices and separate accounting divisions. Mitchell reduced the number of divisions to seven. Within the divisions there were fifty separate "companies" for the manufacture, processing, and buying of various products. Mitchell consolidated these to twenty-nine. He disposed of three slaughtering plants (in San Francisco, Los Angeles, and Nampa, Idaho), a soft-drink plant in Seattle, a wine-bottling plant in Fresno, a wholesale meat house in Kansas City, and several other scattered small plants.

Amalgamating the Brands

There was also a vast consolidation of the 225 Safeway brand names. Mitchell got them down to 100, by taking the best-known names and putting them on a broader line of products. In canned goods alone there were forty brands. These have been cut to six, and those six, through concentrated advertising and promotion, now enjoy greater customer recognition.

The reduction in administrative overhead in the supply division alone runs to over $2 million annually. And another $1 million has been cut out of central services in advertising, research, and personnel since the divisions themselves are now largely responsible for these functions. There used to be fifty people engaged in market research in Oakland; now there are nine. Under Warren, division and district managers had to stock a library of more than fifty manuals, which spelled out every operation and problem down to the admonition that butchers must keep their hands washed, their hair combed, and their faces freshly shaven (no mustaches). A staff of seventeen writers was engaged in helping Warren codify and update these manuals. Since 1955 no addenda to the manuals have been issued. When Magowan has an idea for a division manager, he bats out a memo on his typewriter and ships it off, and to the dismay of the bureaucratic-minded, he rarely makes a carbon.

Perhaps the biggest source of cash savings has been in the decentralization of the store-construction program. Now Warren, as noted, was a very canny operator in a real-estate deal, and he pioneered the buy-build-sell-lease-back program. But when shopping centers came along, Warren didn't cotton to them. He preferred individual, free-standing locations, selected and financed by Safeway exclusively. And though Warren permitted his division managers to participate in the selection of sites and the planning of the stores, he felt the problem was primarily one for the home office. Magowan, on the other hand, favors shopping-center locations, and he likes the "owner-built" deals, in which Safeway merely signs a fifteen-to-twenty-year lease, because such deals conserve time and capital. In the last two years Safeway has reduced the capital tied up in real estate by over $18 million.

Today the real-estate department in Oakland acts principally as a consultant and service office for the division managers. For Safeway-built stores it furnishes the basic blueprints for five standard sizes, and leaves the details and adaptations up to the design departments of the various divisions. Where Safeway formerly required an average of twenty-six months to buy, build, and open a new location, it now takes twelve. With this faster action, Safeway opened 186 stores last year, and expects to open over 200 more this year.

Front and Backstage

Safeway stores rarely try for stunning effects in layout and display, as some Grand Union stores do, nor do they often run to impressive size, as Food Fair's vast marts do. Warren was never much for razzle-dazzle merchandising, and in this particular policy Magowan does not appear inclined to reverse him. Safeway stores attempt to fit the neighborhood they serve. In humble neighborhoods one finds humble, but clean, Safeway stores. However, in New York City's silk-stocking district (on Fifty-eighth Street near Park Avenue), it has just opened a store that is quite high fashion, offers phone service, deliveries, charge accounts.

Like Warren before him, Magowan is reinforcing his coverage in territories already occupied, rather than expanding geographically. Safeway's present sales distribution runs: Pacific Coast, 37 percent; east coast (New York and Washington, D.C.), 17 percent; Midwest, 15 percent; Rocky Mountains, 12 percent; Southwest, 10 percent; and Canada, 9 percent.

That Fearsome Cloud

Remembering Magowan's mission—to boost profits—it is difficult to imagine any executive in or out of the grocery business accomplishing it with more precision, or with such celerity. But as stockholders cheer, it is prudent to ask: What has he left undone?

Magowan himself is frankly dissatisfied with Safeway's rate of sales increase this year. At the six months' point, sales were 4 percent ahead as compared with an 8 percent gain for the industry at large. Magowan wonders if this deficiency can be traced to the division managers' fear of the antitrust cloud. The language of the consent decree is, after all, rather fearsome, e.g.: "enjoined from selling any items at an unreasonably low price . . . setting or maintaining a low gross profit . . . or low retail prices in any store or department, knowing that such profit or prices . . . will cause such store or department to operate below the cost of doing business . . ."

Of course, in reducing prices Safeway has nothing to fear unless evil or immoral intent can be proved, such as to destroy a competitor. But it's easy to see how Safeway managers could become overcautious in meeting competition. Magowan's decision to take the consent decree was not a unilateral one; the outside directors, and other advisers, were in full agreement with him. But he remembers that the meat packers took a consent decree over twenty-five years ago "and have been sorry ever since," and he hopes that twenty-five years from now, Safeway people won't be saying, "Why did that little s.o.b. saddle us with this thing?" He is seeking further legal opinion to clarify the issues, and reassure Safeway managers that they can live with the decree.

Magowan's peace policy has its limits: he won't allow himself to be walked on. In a case in Oklahoma, brought by the Retail Grocers Association, the courts ruled, in effect, that Safeway couldn't sell below cost regardless of intent. Magowan is carrying the case to the U.S. Supreme Court. Also, in San Francisco, Safeway itself recently filed antitrust charges against certain brewers and beer wholesalers for alleged conspiracy to prevent Safeway from procuring beer through Beverage Distributors, Inc., a former subsidiary that supplies Safeway's California, Nevada, and Arizona stores with most of their beer.

Stamps vs. Stamps

About trading stamps, Magowan is not altogether happy. He says that where stamps bring a store a 15 to 20 percent increase in sales, enough profit from that increase carries down to the net to cover the 2 percent cost of the stamps; in communities where everybody gives stamps, the effect is neutralized. But where he has to, he'll go on fighting stamps with stamps.

On his private-brands policy, Magowan genially admits that his professed indifference as to whether Safeway managers stocked them or not was grossly exaggerated. His initial maneuver was to rid Safeway of the stigma of being predominantly a private-brand house. If a store doesn't carry a fairly full line of national brands, or if it fails to display them properly, it's bound to lose sales in the long run. Actually, of course, he was anxious to see Safeway increase its private-brand sales, since they earn, on the average, probably three times as much profit as national brands. Under the new policy, Mitchell rebates the profits from his manufacturing operations in the form of a check to each division (it's hooked into their bonuses). Now Magowan is worried that Mitchell will make the managers so enthusiastic about the system that Safeway will get that old house-brand reputation back. (Private brands currently run about 20 percent of total volume.)

There is such a thing, of course, as too much decentralization. In other chains, where decentralization has been carried to the extreme, division managers have been known to take the short-term view, fudge a bit on quality, and raise prices out of line for the sake of quick profits. Magowan is confident that this is not happening in Safeway. It appears, rather, that the remarkable rise in profits has come about from Magowan's intelligent pruning and sensible pricing, and from the general improvement in the initiative and morale of the managers. Nevertheless, Magowan may find it necessary to modify his decentralization at least to the point of setting up some machinery to maintain control over basic price policies and quality standards throughout the divisions.

It is also the opinion of many knowledgeable grocerymen that a profit ratio of 1.5 percent for a chain of Safeway's size is close to the top if the company is to continue to grow. (However, Safeway's profit on U.S. operations is only slightly more than 1.3 percent; Canadian profits are running above 2.6 percent.) After all, A & P, with sales approaching $5 billion, deliberately holds its profit margin at about 1 percent. Obviously no competitor of A & P can get too far above A & P's margin without risking loss of sales.

Is He There to Stay?

One of the minor irritations that Magowan has had to put up with is the persistent belief among many people, in and out of the company, that he is in Oakland solely for the purpose of pulling Safeway's profits up to par in fast order, and with that done, will take off to other pastures in the East. The Magowans own, and still maintain, a house in Manhattan, and a summer place at Southampton. Somehow it was difficult for their friends to think the Magowans would dedicate the rest of their lives to the grocery business in California.

Magowan swears they will. The New York house, he says, is kept for the convenience of the four oldest boys (there are five, all told), who have been attending eastern schools. Not so long ago the Magowans purchased a spacious home high on a San Francisco hill. The view of the Bay is breath-taking, and they love it.

Every day, as he drives to his Oakland office, Magowan passes a small, privately owned store—what the trade calls a "Poppa and Momma" store—which he knows outsells the Safeway store in the area. "It just makes me sick to see this," he says, "but that's what we've got to do with our managers—make them as thorough and smart managers as the little guy who's got his own money in the business."

That Magowan should be so concerned with Safeway's sales is understandable. Most critics will agree that in most of the instances in which Magowan counteracted Warren's policies, Safeway benefited. But it is the consumer who will decide, over the long run, who was right and who was wrong on the basic issue of pricing.

Pinching 500,000,000,000 Pennies at A & P*

George L. Hartford—known to all the employees as "Mr. George"—was the last surviving son of the founder of the century-old Great Atlantic & Pacific Tea Co. As he lay dying in 1957, at ninety-two, he beckoned sixty-eight-year-old A & P President Ralph W. Burger to his bedside and whispered his final orders. "Ralph," he said, "take care of the organization." Now it may strike some readers that good Mr. George's last words, though touching, were somewhat less than unique or epigrammatic. Other dedicated businessmen have been known to expire with similar admonitions on their lips. But to Ralph Burger, the simple words carried a genuine message. What Mr. George was really saying, he felt, was "Carry on the organization in the way that Brother John (who died in 1951) and I would run it if we were still here." This Burger has done with complete fidelity, and with—on the whole—considerable success.

A & P's sales last year (the fiscal year ending February, 1963) were approximately $5.4 billion. At that rate A & P easily maintained its position as fifth largest in sales of all U.S. business firms. It is outranked only by General Motors, Jersey Standard, A.T.&T., and Ford, and it outsells such giants as General Electric and Sears, Roebuck by half a billion dollars or more. In its own category, groceries, A & P has been the undisputed champion since early in the century. Among food-store chains, the nearest, Safeway, at $2.5 billion in sales, is hardly within hollering distance. What principally sustains A & P's staggering volume of sales is its ability to take a microscopic markup on its products. Not forgetting the tremendous efficiency factor at work here, it is the simple principle of selling more goods for less that has put and kept A & P on top. A & P achieves, deliberately, a profit of only a fraction more than a penny on each dollar of sales (the margin in 1962 was about 1.1 percent). By way of comparison, G.M. makes upward of 7 cents (9.9 cents in 1962). This greater spread reflects, of course, G.M.'s much more intensive use of capital. But even Sears

* March 1963

runs a profit between 4 and 5 cents. Naturally, A & P's policy has anchored all food-chain profits at a low base, though some companies are making more than 1½ cents per dollar of sales. The late John Hartford ("Mr. John") used to say: "I have always been a volume man. I would rather sell two pounds of butter at a profit of 1 cent each than one pound at 2 cents profit." And Ralph Burger echoes these sentiments precisely.

Two Such Giants

Not that Burger doesn't have a mind of his own. He is, in fact, an extremely strong-willed man. But in mind and spirit he is the product of fifty years' total immersion in the peculiarly insulated world of "the Tea Company," as the old-timers call A & P, and in the forceful philosophy of the brothers Hartford. "Not many men," he says, "have had the fortunate privilege of working with two such giants." Like the vast majority of A & P executives, he has never worked anywhere else. He began as a store clerk, at $11 a week, in his home town of Glens Falls, New York, rose to bookkeeper, and was sent on to a job on the premium desk at the company headquarters, then located in Jersey City, in 1912. There he caught the eye of John Hartford. As personal secretary and aide to Mr. John, and from 1925 on as secretary of the corporation, it became his special function to act first as a sort of glorified messenger and ultimately as a mediator between the relatively ebullient and progressive Mr. John and the highly conservative Mr. George. He liked and admired them both with equal fervor, and in the process became a kind of blend that was more Hartford than the Hartfords. In 1949, Mr. John, at seventy-seven, stepped aside as president, and Executive Vice President David Bofinger was named to succeed him. But in less than a year Bofinger died of a heart attack. Burger, then sixty-two, was reluctant to take the presidency, but bowed ultimately, of course, to the earnest wishes of Mr. John and Mr. George.

Interestingly, after Mr. John died in 1951, Ralph Burger never moved into the semi-elegant office he had used. It now serves as a sort of reception and conference room for distinguished visitors. An oil painting of the "Old Gentleman," George Huntington Hartford, is set into the wood paneling, and standing on an easel is a large color photograph of Mr. John and Mr. George. Like all other top executives at the A & P headquarters in the Graybar Building, Ralph Burger still works out of a singularly drab and unadorned office. Austerity, indeed, pervades the headquarters.

One of the top executives recently worked for weeks in a busy bullpen while his office was being redecorated. Another had to explain that the wall-to-wall carpeting in his Chicago office hadn't cost the company a penny. Lush "expense-account living" hasn't corrupted A & P's New York officers, who are likely to be found lunching at Schrafft's. One other interesting footnote: Following the death of Mr. George, Ralph Burger assumed, in addition to the chairmanship of the board and the presidency, the responsibility for supervising the company's coffee operation. Why? Well, it seems that though his forte was finance, Mr. George, from his earliest years with the company, had been crazy over coffee. To his dying day, he was the official taste tester and selector of A & P's coffee blends. A & P, indeed, was woefully late in getting on the instant-coffee bandwagon because Mr. George simply couldn't stand the stuff. It is the belief throughout the company that Ralph Burger became the company coffee buyer because of a deathbed pledge to the ninety-two-year-old man. And they respect him for it—as who wouldn't?

The Somewhat Disgruntled Heirs

Burger, however, turned out to be a lot less solicitous of the wishes of the so-called "Hartford heirs," who made their presence felt in the ownership picture after Mr. George's death. The essentials of the rather complicated A & P ownership situation are as follows: Founder George Huntington Hartford had five children. In addition to George and John (who were both childless), there was another son, Edward, and two sisters; each of these three had two children each. Shortly before the Old Gentleman died in 1917, he put his stock in a trust vested equally (20 percent each) among his children, and the power to vote the trusteed stock was vested in brothers George and John as long as either lived. When Mr. John died, he left his 20 percent of A & P voting common stock to the John Hartford Foundation (for medical research), of which he named Ralph Burger head. When Mr. George died, he left his 20 percent to the foundation also. So Burger had the power to vote 40 percent of the common stock. But Mr. George's death also dissolved the voting trust, and gave the other Hartford heirs the power to vote their stock. By that time there were ten heirs all together, one of them being George Huntington Hartford II (10 percent), art patron, theatrical producer, and publisher. There was arranged, however, a secondary offer of stock to the public. At present roughly one-third of the stock is held by the family heirs, one-third by the foundation, and one-third by the public.

There never has been an open fight between the family and Ralph Burger for control, but the heirs have been badgering and pushing Burger on a number of issues. Early in the game, the heirs succeeded in enlarging the board with six outside directors (they are: Manning Brown of New York Life; John L. Burns, former R.C.A. president; Donald K. David, Ford Foundation; Jay E. Crane, former Standard Oil executive; Gwilym A. Price, chairman of Westinghouse; and John E. Slater, partner in Coverdale & Colpitts). Fourteen members drawn from the company's management make up the rest of the board. Some of the stockholders have been disenchanted with the traditional low-price, low-profit policy. There has also been pressure to replace the seventy-three-year-old Burger with a younger man as president. On this point they recently won a victory—of sorts. In January of this year Burger did indeed guide the board into electing a *younger man* as president. He was none other than sixty-seven-year-old John D. Ehrgott, long vice president and treasurer, and to all appearances a thorough-going John-George partisan (indeed, he is treasurer of the Hartford Foundation). Burger remains chairman and chief executive officer of the company. The six outside directors publicly protested the election of a man of Ehrgott's age as president. At the same meeting, however, the board created three executive vice presidencies. The men designated were Stephen W. Shea, fifty-eight, who supervises A & P's purchasing and sales; Melvin W. Alldredge, fifty-one, who headed the Pittsburgh (Central) division; and Francis H. Bucher, sixty-two, head of the Detroit (Central Western) division. If they are given enough rein, they may stir up the action a bit at the Graybar headquarters.

"Uneasy Lies the Head . . ."

Does A & P, with that astounding volume, need stirring up? Many informed outsiders think that it does. It's true that its sales are more than twice those of Safeway, and indeed are almost as big as the sales of its three nearest competitors (Safeway, Kroger, and Acme) combined. Nobody expects that a single competitor is going to knock A & P off the pinnacle in the near future, but when measured against the field it is clear that A & P's rate of growth is somewhat less than exhilarating. On its share of total grocery-store sales, A & P has held up pretty darn well: in ten years it yielded slightly more than one percentage point—11.6 to 10.5. But in the classification of total grocery-chain-store sales, A & P has lost nearly 10 percent of penetration. Its share went from 32 percent in 1952 to 24 percent in 1961.

In addition to the other big chains, A & P has been harassed by the gadfly competition of a host of small regional chains, and of independents that have entered into cooperative arrangements for mass buying and joint advertising. These little fellows can move fast. They will snap up a promising location into which A & P had been contemplating moving four or five years hence. Or they will set up a specialty store—say one that features sparkling fruits and produce—across the street from an A & P store, and feed handsomely on the heavy traffic generated by A & P's bargain prices on staples.

When it comes to purchasing, manufacturing, and shipping goods to market quickly and cheaply, A & P's efficiency is doubtless without peer in the industry. And this is not just because of its size. Says a division executive, "Actually, we can't buy any lower than our smaller competitors—our whole advantage is in the people who work for us. You take Tony Vogt in Milwaukee, for instance; I think he's the best man on peas and tomatoes in the U.S." No doubt he is, and A & P has an army of Tony Vogts in butter and cheese, and in produce, meat, and milk. Back in the Graybar Building, a vice president for manufacturing says significantly: "We were a purchasing organization before we were a merchandising organization—our growth really came through purchasing." A junior executive puts it more bluntly: "We are a buying organization that hasn't learned to sell."

But They Know Their Groceries

In today's affluent society, success in the supermarket business, granted prices are not blatantly out of line, turns more and more on merchandising skills and strategies. And A & P is not so much a poor merchandiser as a reluctant one. For example, many chains—notably Grand Union and First National—have in recent years put a tremendous emphasis on the design and decor of their stores, on the play of light and color on merchandise, and on a variety of customer conveniences. Most A & P stores, in contrast, are studies in austerity. Floors are clean but bare of covering of any kind. Display shelves and cases are sturdy and functional but innocent of enticements. An A & P divisional sales director, admitting the contrast, simply says, "Being practical about our accouterments is what gives us a competitive edge. We would rather pass the saving along to the consumer." But his competitor says, "We have conveniences that modern people want, and carry items that are only lately in demand. A & P doesn't, and we are slowly weaning the younger customers away from them."

Another major trend in food-store merchandising, of course, is the introduction of a wide variety of nonfood items—drugs, cosmetics, kitchenware, nylons, children's snowsuits, etc. If handled smartly, this kind of merchandise can bring substantially higher margins than most food lines. A & P has done some dabbling in this area but with extreme caution and considerable distaste. The attitude is summed up by a divisional president of the company who says: "I think our primary purpose is to sell food cheap, and tangents tend to hurt the food operation. There is a higher profit margin on nonfoods but it's *just not our business.*"

Those Damn Stamps

Finally, there is the matter of A & P's soul-searching struggle with the trading-stamp issue. Generally speaking, merchants everywhere would prefer a world without trading stamps. There is a saying in the food-store industry that "nobody likes them but the customers." To the A & P, understandably, trading stamps are particularly abhorrent. A gimmick of that kind is bound to be upsetting to their high-volume, low-profit-margin policy. And old Mr. George thought trading stamps were downright immoral. But along about 1954, A & P began to hurt rather severely from stamp competition. Stores were reporting to headquarters that shoppers were splitting their grocery purchases—going to other supermarkets for stamp "bargains," and coming to A & P only for staples. A & P tried to fight back with still lower prices, but it was limited in the lengths to which it could go. A & P labors under the shadow of an antitrust consent decree in 1954 that prohibits it from operating any one of its seven divisions at a loss for competitive purposes.

Then, in 1959, A & P's total sales fell back by $46 million, the first decline in any year since World War II. In 1960 sales rose 3.9 percent, but in 1961 they were off again by a knife edge—$6 million. So in 1962, A & P plunged into the stamp act. It didn't originate stamps in any area, but used them "defensively" in about 55 percent of its market. The results are still somewhat inconclusive. The company's sales did increase 3 percent in 1962, and perhaps about 1 percent of that increase can be attributed to the stamps. There was also some increase—3 or 4 percent—in A & P's

price index. Reluctant as he was to take the plunge, Ralph Burger
is confident that he has at least plugged the slippage in sales,
and that in due time A & P will be able to absorb more of the cost
and pull back its prices. But a competitor scoffs, "They should
have come in five years earlier or stayed out altogether."

Now it is entirely possible that in some or even all of these
merchandising decisions, time will prove A & P to have been right
as rain. The significant thing is that no current problem is decided
or even discussed without reference to company tradition. In an
almost literal sense, Mr. John and Mr. George have a strong voice
in the present-day councils of the company even though they are
occasionally, with deep apologies, voted down. But the phrase
that is heard with greatest frequency throughout the A & P is:
"Well, you can't quarrel with a hundred years of success."

Gilded-Age Beginnings

Clearly, therefore, to comprehend this company today one
must know something of its past. In the beginning, in 1859, George
Huntington Hartford, a solemn, full-bearded young man from
Maine, was a junior partner in the venture. The senior partner
was George Francis Gilman, an importer of hides and leathers.
They conceived the idea of buying tea at shipside in New York
Harbor and selling it by mail to consumers at a price considerably
below the prevailing retail rate of $1 a pound. It was in 1869 that
Gilman and Hartford decided to establish a number of retail
branches of the company under the grandiose name of the Great
Atlantic & Pacific Tea Co. The original stores were outrageously
flamboyant. The façade was done in Chinese vermilion and gold
leaf, and the cashier's booth was done up in a miniature Chinese
pagoda; customers received a premium with every purchase and
were treated to a free band concert on Saturday nights. In 1878,
Gilman withdrew from the active management, and under Hartford the stores took on a somewhat more conservative tone. There
were now one hundred of them, the major locations being in New
York, Philadelphia, Baltimore, Chicago, St. Louis, and St. Paul.

Hartford lived quietly in Orange, New Jersey, with his wife
and five children, commuting each day by ferry to the headquarters store on Vesey Street in New York. In 1880 his eldest son,
shy little George Ludlum Hartford, quit school at fifteen and went
to work in the business, squeezing his fat little frame into the
pagoda-shaped cashier's booth, where he had the assignment of
counting the money as it came pouring in from all the rest of the

stores. In 1888 the second son, fifteen-year-old John Augustine, came to work in the Vesey Street store. He was charming and outgoing, and immediately took an intense interest in the selling side of the business.

By 1900 the company had 200 stores around the country, and a series of wagon routes to cover the rural areas. And the stores now carried, in addition to coffee and tea, a line of spices, flavorings, and fundamental groceries. Even then the company was known for its low markup, but like most other storekeepers of the time, it also went in for S. & H. stamps, no less, and free deliveries, charge accounts, and premiums.

Mr. John's Brainstorm

But in 1912 the company underwent an explosive change. By then the price of groceries, and of all commodities, was a matter of great concern to a great many people. The "high cost of living" was a catchword of the day, and a lively campaign issue in the elections of 1912. In that year inquisitive John Hartford heard about a store in Jersey City that had no deliveries, no charge accounts, nor premiums, nor stamps, but was doing a bang-up business on the basis of its extremely low prices. John wanted to try out the idea but the Old Gentleman and Brother George strongly demurred. Finally, they grudgingly gave him a budget of $3,000 for the experiment. He set up his stand around the corner from one of A & P's most successful stores in Jersey City, and within six months the experimental store had run its neighbor out of business.

The secret of the new "economy store," as it came to be called, was not merely cash-and-carry, but availability. It had to be located where its price advantage would not be cancelled by inconvenience. Before the universal automobile had revolutionized shopping and living patterns, this meant a very large number of very small stores in neighborhood locations. Within the next three years John and George opened 7,500 stores—a rate of about seven a day—and closed about half of them: George refused to pay more than a week's rent on a store that would not carry itself. Years later, John, indulging in hyperbole to explain that hectic period, said, "We went so fast, hoboes hopping off trains got hired as managers."

From that single great merchandising concept of Mr. John's the A & P was launched on a surge of expansion that continued practically without abatement through the first world war, through the Twenties, and even into the early years of the great depression.

It wasn't until the supermarket revolution surprised an unwary A & P that the company faced a merchandising crisis, and curiously enough, John and George opposed each other just as they had in 1912. In the years between, Mr. George's thrifty mind had perceived the advantage to the company of manufacturing its own products, and it was largely through his guidance that A & P's great manufacturing complex was built up. And it was thanks to his almost ultra-prudent financial policies (except for some five-year debentures issued in 1916-17, he never permitted the company to assume any long-term debt, never allowed it to become loaded down with real estate) that A & P was able to come through the worst days of the depression with hardly a scar. But Mr. George, his nose buried in the company's books, was really rather innocent of what was transpiring in the marketplace. On his part, Mr. John had been preoccupied with a vast decentralization program undertaken in 1925. And like many another chainstore executive, he couldn't bring himself to believe that these upstart cut-raters with names like King Kullen and Big Bear were really going to get anywhere in the food business.

Supermarkets or Disaster

But by 1936, with his volume in a steep decline, and a number of his stores operating in the red, Mr. John knew he was in trouble, and proposed that the company begin to take the supermarket way. He was vigorously, almost bitterly opposed by Mr. George, who was horrified at the expense of such an undertaking. Finally, in 1936, John flatly stated that the choice was either to adopt supermarkets or face disaster. In 1938, A & P opened 500 supermarkets; in 1939, nearly 1,000 more. By the end of 1941 nearly 70 percent of the old stores had been closed out, and the A & P had regained its 1929 share of the market. Success, however, was the prelude to trouble: the very next year began the Justice Department's antitrust campaign against A & P on charges that the company exercised monopolistic control of processing, manufacturing, and distributing of food.

Finally, there is one other historical thread that has current relevancy. Throughout his stewardship John Hartford had to wage a constant struggle with his regional and unit managers to hold down markups in line with his high-volume philosophy. Though everyone was supposed to live by the policy, there was always the temptation to make a profitable showing over the short run. Even austere Mr. George, during the 1936 crisis, argued for higher markups to cover the rising overhead.

The brothers, according to Ralph Burger, had a genuine regard and affection for each other. It is not important to speculate on which brother scored more points in their rugged sparring matches; their clashes served to shape the organization and the men who ran it. Burger, who was closest to the fray between the brothers, was trusted by both and deeply influenced by both. Considering how long the Hartford brothers had dominated the company, the transition to Burger's regime was accomplished smoothly, and in the years of his successful stewardship the A & P was not torn or even strained by struggles between partisans of Mr. George's way and of Mr. John's way.

A Crack in the Monolith

It is unlikely that the new appointments foreshadow any basic changes in the organizational structure of the A & P, a structure built in the long decades of the joint dominance of Mr. John and Mr. George. Not only has it served A & P admirably, but it is a system that most other successful food chains have seen fit to imitate to a large extent. In theory, the A & P system aims to maintain tight central control over price and purchasing policy while permitting a certain latitude and flexibility in the operations of the divisions and units in the field. In practice, however, the right balance between the headquarters in the Graybar Building and the responsibilities of subordinate units has not been easy to maintain. There have been situations when the A & P seemed too monolithic, where local operators lacked the freedom and initiative needed to meet the aggressive and varied tactics of their local competitors. Perhaps the induction of the new executive vice presidents, two of whom are fresh from the firing line, will help the company in its unending effort to find and keep the balance. All three are interesting personalities—they are smart; they are tough—but first a word about the way things run in the world in which they were raised.

A vast part of the world of A & P is concerned, of course, with the buying, processing, packing, warehousing, and shipping operations of the food business. A & P's Quaker Maid Division, for example, processes, packs, and sells to A & P about $500 million worth of goods a year. A & P is one of the country's biggest coffee importers; the company maintains its own coffee-buying offices in

Colombia and Brazil, and operates twelve coffee-roasting plants in the U.S. For years A & P has ranked among the five largest commercial bakers in the U.S. The company also has five salmon canneries in Alaska and in the Puget Sound area, and it operates three cheese plants, two milk-processing plants, two French-fried-potato plants, and a printing plant that makes the labels for its private brands. In meat, which accounts for 26 percent of A & P's retail dollar sales, the company's meat-buying headquarters in Chicago maintains its own staff of inspectors to certify the quality. Its produce-buying division is the largest single factor in the market. Three teams of buyers—on the West Coast, in the Mississippi Valley, and on the East Coast—follow the crops northward as they ripen and keep in constant communication with the central office, and with one another, over a national teletype system.

The payoff in the grocery business, however, is rung up on the cash registers of the individual stores. A & P has nearly 4,500 of them (down from almost 16,000 in the days of the small "economy store"). The command of the retail operation lies with seven geographical divisions, each of which has its own president. Divisional headquarters are located at New York, Boston, Philadelphia, Detroit, Chicago, Pittsburgh, and Jacksonville. Each division is broken down into distribution units. There are thirty-five of these units throughout the U.S., each consisting of one or more warehouses and from sixty to 225 stores. The territory of a unit is limited by the distance the trucks can economically cover from the warehouse headquarters, and usually corresponds roughly to the circulation area of the metropolitan newspapers, in whose pages the battle of the grocery ads is fought. It is in the unit headquarters that, as a rule, goods are bought, prices set, advertisements laid out, and the thrust and parry of competitive selling carried on. But unit buyers and sales managers are in constant daily touch with their opposite numbers at divisional headquarters. And it is the divisional office that plans and selects new store locations.

The Rise of Pat Shea

Of the three new executive vice presidents, Stephen W. Shea has been the most potent. Indeed, a number of people in the company were surprised at the failure of the board to elect him president. For all his versatility, Shea's experience has been mainly in sales and, recently, in purchasing. As treasurer, Ehrgott has been closer to management functions that Shea has scarcely touched. It could be, as one friend suggests, that Shea actually was not bucking for the president's job; though he is intense and thoroughly aggressive in his work, he is not overweeningly ambitious. He is paid more than $100,000 a year, and is not one to seek status for its own sake.

Shea's is the classic A & P success story, slightly accelerated. Born and brought up on New York's lower West Side, he started clerking with A & P during high-school vacations, became a full-time worker in the Bronx unit after his graduation in 1922. He was transferred to the Brooklyn unit during a time when it was undergoing rapid expansion and as a result crowded in a heap of experience. He supervised the opening of several stores, relieved managers from time to time, and was a general trouble shooter for the unit. He was named assistant sales manager at Brooklyn, then moved up to sales manager of the Newark unit, and in 1928, when he was only twenty-four, was promoted to assistant sales and purchasing manager of the giant Eastern Division. Six years later he was made director of purchasing and sales and, ten years after that, vice president of the division. In 1950, Mr. John, in one of his last official acts, made Pat Shea sales director of the A & P company. In 1962, when Harry George, vice president in charge of purchasing, retired (at age sixty-nine), his job was combined with Shea's under the title of merchandise manager. Shea has been a director since 1953 and a vice president and an executive-committee member since 1958.

Shea is not an ivory-tower-type administrator. He has all the divisional sales and purchasing managers come into New York four times a year. In turn, Shea visits each division at least once a year. He is an inveterate prowler of A & P stores, and once, not so long ago, took some time away from the office to serve, anonymously, as a workaday clerk in one of the stores. He wanted, he said, to refresh his feeling of what it takes to sell an order of goods to a customer. Shea has a good deal of Mr. John's evangelism bred into him. "I sincerely believe that we in this business have a responsibility to do something about the cost and the standard of living," he says, and lists the consumer as A & P's first interest. Second is the interest of the employees, and third is the stockholders' right to a fair return. Shea is sure that if A & P increased its net to 2 percent, sales would decline substantially. "People do shop for price," he asserts, "and there are millions of families who have problems in making ends meet." A & P directs its sales at the medium-low income group, but this does not mean, Shea says, the exclusion of the upper-level customers: "If we do a good job on the medium-low, we attract the others." But Pat Shea is not crustily conservative. He has an instinctive interest in anything that's new in the business. He likes a fight and is quick to counter a rival's promotion with a promotion of his own, though not at the utter expense of his own best competitive weapon, which is price.

Changing the Signals

At this writing, A & P had yet to define the functions of the other two executive vice presidents—Bucher and Alldredge. Their names were included in the original "package" that management presented to the January board meeting, but the outside directors nevertheless resented the insiders' refusal to appoint a younger man than John Ehrgott to the presidency. Obviously, the appointments of Bucher and Alldredge indicate an intention to improve communication and the interchange of ideas between the Graybar Building and the field.

Though he had a smattering of college training, Francis Bucher, now sixty-two, didn't let it prevent him from starting at the lower depths, like all the other A & P luminaries. Bucher was a Rochester, New York, boy who attended the University of Detroit on a football scholarship. In 1924 he quit college to play professional football. He was a slashing end on the Pottsville (Pa.) Maroons when they beat the Chicago Cardinals, in 1925, for the championship of the National Football League. He came back to Detroit in 1927, worked in the construction business for a spell, and when the depression struck, took a job with A & P as a common laborer, unloading food from flatcars. "People had to eat, and as long as they did, I had a job." He worked his way up through the warehousing end of the business, becoming, in 1941, director of storage and transportation operations. In 1952 he was made vice president in charge of the Detroit unit of the Central Western Division; in 1956, president of the division.

Bucher's division, which covers Michigan, Indiana, Ohio, Kentucky, and Tennessee, has made an outstanding record. The 115 stores in the Detroit unit do a large percentage of all grocery business in the area. And this despite the fact that Bucher refuses to offer trading stamps, as his major competitors do. (He made an exception in Grand Rapids, however, where stamps are extremely popular.) Bucher makes a fetish of quality. "We want to sell the most food for the least amount of money without sacrificing quality." And he has run an ambitious store-expansion pro-

gram over the last five years to keep up with the population increase and the mass shift of 170,000 Detroit residents to the suburbs. A trim 200 pounds at five feet, 10½ inches (he's only ten
pounds above his football-playing weight), Bucher is a golfer,
hunter, skater, skier, and amateur chef. More of a mixer than
most A & P types, he is well known to and highly respected by the
competition.

Melvin W. Alldredge, a fledgling fifty-one, is by way of being
a protégé of Bucher. It was because of his fine record as manager
of the crack Detroit and Toledo units that Alldredge was promoted to the presidency of the Pittsburgh division, which he has
kept well ahead of the competition. Alldredge was a poor boy
in a small Indiana town, who started working part time in a grocery store at the age of ten to help out his widowed mother. The
little tyke brought home $4.50 a week. When his mother remar-
ried and the family moved to Detroit, Melvin worked after school
hours in an A & P store, and was given the managership of a
store at age eighteen. At nineteen, he started a premed course in
college, but ran out of funds and had to return to the A & P (his
daughter now has her M.D.). Alldredge is a modernist who believes in low prices *plus* all the conveniences that make shopping
in the A & P a "wonderful experience" for a woman. "There's a
generation that remembers the depression," he says, "and those
people never again can waste money. But my children, for example, know nothing about the depression, and youth is attracted
by glamour." So a number of his stores feature pastel colors,
murals, and rather elaborately designed showcases.

Though personally reluctant to take on nonfoods, Alldredge
has the courage to say, "Let's face it, we were a little slow." And
with Burger's blessing he is now experimenting with an A & P
discount-house–supermarket combination in Coraopolis, Pennsylvania. The results, carefully watched by the entire A & P organization, have been rather encouraging.

Tempest in a Tea Company

There are other experiments under way in other parts of
the organization. In New Jersey, for example, A & P has undertaken the pilot-plant operation of a chain of cut-rate, self-service,
drive-in restaurants called the Golden Key. They feature the return of the 15-cent hamburger and the 5-cent cup of coffee. And
in a number of new stores now springing up around the country,

one sees here and there a burst of elegance competing with economy.

All this is not to suggest that the A & P is in a ferment of innovation. And indeed it is not clear that it would be altogether wise for a company of A & P's character and basic strength to undertake, in an industry that is already "over-stored," a program of drastic innovation. What A & P seems to be doing, rather, is negotiating the transition from a great but rather quirkish family company to a great public company that feels the need of being a little more responsive to changing public taste. It is doubtful if Mr. John would quarrel very vehemently with that. And it is interesting to note that in the four years since A & P became a public company it has increased its cash dividend unfailingly. Mr. George, one fears, would at least purse his lips at that. But Ralph Burger could reassure him that there are still some prudent fellows around: in Burger's thirteen years the company's net worth doubled to $540 million.

How a Great Corporation
Got Out of Control

*The Story of General Dynamics: Part I**_____

BY RICHARD AUSTIN SMITH

Over a two-year period 1960-1962 General Dynamics has incurred the biggest product loss ever sustained by any company anywhere. The jet-transport program it built around the Convair 880 and 990 airliners has cost the corporation far more than the $121-million licking Lockheed took on the Electras and even overshadowed Ford's $200-million disaster with the Edsel. By the end of 1961, General Dynamics had to write off some $425 million of jet losses. Not only did this wipe out all profit on G.D.'s total sales of close to $2 billion a year—but, even with the tax credit, it put the company $27 million in the red for 1960, $40 million in the hole for the first nine months of 1961. And the

* January 1962

end is not yet. As long ago as September, 1960, General Dynamics was announcing it had written off "all anticipated future [jet] losses," only to have fresh losses make a mockery of its cost projections. Last November Chairman Frank Pace conceded his company still could not "fully identify all remaining costs of the jet-transport program." If it develops that the company has to make any more sizable write-offs in 1962, it may have to sell off a division.

As a consequence, General Dynamics is being run under the corporate equivalent of martial law. An executive committee of seven directors took charge of the crisis last July; the banks, alarmed because G.D.'s earned surplus had been nearly wiped out, moved in the next month with an armful of circumscriptions. These have included bank scrutiny of the company's divisional budgets, the pledging of its government accounts receivable, a bank veto on sale or leaseback arrangements, an end to further borrowing, and a two-year moratorium on dividends. The executive committee's hope now is that it can provide enough money to keep the healthy divisions of the company expanding, while it reviews budgets, reorganizes the management, and restores General Dynamics to the strong position it once was in. Divisions like Astronautics, Electric Boat, General Atomics, and Canadair give the committee a good deal to build on.

But meanwhile the Convair debacle has excited the close interest of the business community, the investing public, and Washington; G.D. is the biggest private manufacturer of weaponry in the world. And it had been a profitable one. Net earnings had risen from $599,000 on sales of $31 million in 1947, the year founder John Jay Hopkins made his first big acquisition, to the profit peak of $56 million on sales of $1.7 billion, the year Hopkins died (1957). What could have gone so spectacularly wrong?

The story has many episodes. They include the overriding episode of the jet-transport program—the "fantastic" underestimating of costs, to employ Chairman Pace's adjective, the gross miscalculation of the market, the entanglements with the capricious Howard Hughes; the tragic death at a critical moment of the company's founder, Jay Hopkins. Many people shared in the responsibility for the disaster: chiefs and subchiefs of the huge Convair plant, a number of whom have since resigned; General Dynamics' own board of directors; Jay Hopkins himself; and Frank Pace, who succeeded Hopkins in 1957 as chief executive officer and who will depart from the company in April ("if the company has turned the corner") and return to public life, which he now says "is my forte."

But the story has implications for American business beyond the errors that can be made in engineering or in negotiating a contract. General Dynamics is an example (probably the most extreme one) of a kind of corporation that has loomed on the industrial scene—a congeries of companies, decentralized, loosely directed by a small and remote group of financiers, lawyers, and (occasionally) professional managers. There is a certain rationality in the concept of such corporations, as there is in the structure of General Dynamics itself, which has been able to sustain losses of this magnitude and still, up to now, keep its head above water. All but one of General Dynamics' divisions is engaged in work requiring a high degree of engineering and technological skill; the exception, Material Service, deals in gravel and cement and thus provides a hedge against the uncertainties of defense business. There is a plausibility to the theory that such a corporation can supply its divisions with support when one of them gets in trouble, and that every one of the divisions is stronger by virtue of the association. But the question posed by the General Dynamics story is whether or not effective techniques have yet been developed to manage these aggregations. (There might also be a question whether American business is developing the managerial talent for such complex jobs. An observer gets the impression that in times of corporate trouble almost all any board can think of is to reach for Ernie Breech, which inspires the question, "Isn't there anybody around but Ernie Breech?")

Pace describes the quandary he has been in at General Dynamics in these terms: "When you have a company, employing 106,000 people, made up of nine different divisions, each a corporation really in its own right, most of which were separate enterprises before they joined the organization, and headed by men who were presidents of corporations, with their own separate legal staffs, financial staffs, etc., all of these highly competent men—the only way to succeed is to operate on a decentralized basis. Our total central office in New York City was something like 200 people, including stenographers. This group can only lay out broad policy. Your capacity to know specifically what is happening in each division just cannot exist. If you did try to know everything that was happening and controlled your men that tightly, your men would leave you or would lose their initiative which made them effective."

One is led to conclude that G.D.'s top management failed to

recognize that the new age of advanced technology demands advanced management techniques. It failed to establish the intelligence system that would have given accurate and timely warning of danger. It failed to limit divisional programs to those that would not imperil the whole enterprise and failed to call a halt on one such program even when it appeared to be in grave danger. Instead it pursued a "double-or-nothing" policy, risking greater and greater losses in the hope that one more commitment would square all accounts. This, in short, is the story of a great corporation that got out of control.

Jonah Swallows a Brace of Whales

The story begins with Jay Hopkins. He was a man of almost oppressive energy, with a bottomless capacity for alcohol, who could stay up all night drinking, then in the morning lucidly present a complicated program to his board of directors. Though trained as a lawyer (Harvard Law '21), he was best known for his brilliance and audacity in finance. The grand design he brought to fulfillment was the creation of a diversified defense empire; it was to be capable of turning out weapons for virtually all the armed services so that G.D. would prosper whatever the budgetary vicissitudes of any individual service. Thus he had almost singlehandedly parlayed a venerable builder of submarines, Electric Boat, into a company that could also make bombers and fighters and missiles. He went ahead with the acquisition of two major airframe manufacturers, Canadair in 1947, and Convair in 1954, undaunted by the fact that it was a case of Jonah swallowing a brace of whales. Hopkins' admirers insist that the sense of symmetry that compelled him to deliberate over the proper positioning of his socks in an overnight bag or to realign an ashtray when its use by a visitor altered the accustomed pattern of his desk top was decisive in the way he put General Dynamics together. But the truth of the matter seems to be that he built the company as much for size as for sense and ran it to suit himself. He kept posted on what went on in each division, questioning, admonishing, encouraging, vetoing with the red pencils he reserved as his exclusive trademark around G.D., at the same time managing to make each division head feel he was free to run his own show. In short, management control was a highly individualized affair at General Dynamics and worked reasonably well so long as Jay Hopkins was around to make it work. But unhappily he wasn't around very often, at least not at the headquarters office. Golf was a passion with him for one thing (he founded the International Golf Association); for another, he much preferred irregularly riding circuit through the divisions to keeping regular office hours.

An Association of Opposites

Thus, in 1953, Frank Pace was brought in as executive vice president and director of General Dynamics. Said a member of G.D.'s board, an old friend of Hopkins: "The truth was Jay was drinking too much and Washington had lost confidence in him. We had to get somebody in there who would restore that confidence." Commented Hopkins himself to a golfing companion in California. "Well, I just bought myself a show window. It cost me $75,000 complete with secretary. They give me hell because I'm never in the office, and I've got to have somebody there to answer the phone."

That was certainly not all the job meant to Pace, who had declined several other offers in order to accept it. Nor was this the way Hopkins represented it to him, Pace says. "Jay told me when he hired me, 'I'll turn over the operation to you. I will not second-guess you, but I will make the ultimate decisions.' He made broad policy and ultimate decisions of importance but left operations to me." If "answering the phone" meant handling General Dynamics' relations with Washington, few men then available were better equipped for that than Pace. He had a sharp mind, an excellent education (Princeton '33, Harvard Law '36), had served as Director of the Budget under Truman in 1949, became Secretary of the Army just before Korea and was responsible for that service's rapid wartime expansion. He was equally at home quoting Disraeli or some homespun philosopher of his native Arkansas, and he shot golf in the low seventies. But aside from golf, the law, and the high order of intelligence, Pace and Hopkins were complete opposites: Pace temperate in all things, oratorical, deliberate, anxious to be liked, a product of the federal staff system, prone to rely on his second-in-command in the making of decisions; Hopkins volatile, creative, earthy, intuitive, ingrowing, willing to listen but unwilling to share the making of decisions with anybody, a loner more likely to give the world the back of his hand than to extend the palm of it. "Hopkins thought he was both omnipotent and omniscient," said an admirer by way of emphasizing the ultimate difference. "He just exuded confidence in the correctness of his opinions. He believed there was nothing he couldn't do. Frank Pace does not in any way think he's either omnipotent or omniscient." Indeed, so far as Chairman Hopkins could see at the time he had not hired a potential successor but an able assistant for a specialized assignment: Hopkins considered the real drive of Pace's ambition to be political (he had his eye on the Democratic vice-presidential nomination) rather than corporate.

The Wayward Course of Empire

So in 1955, Hopkins was making the broad decisions when G.D. first considered going into the jet-transport program. The original idea, however, was not his. It came from Convair, the great California division that was separated from G.D.'s New York headquarters by roughly equal amounts of geography and autonomy. Convair spoke with a very loud voice in the councils of the corporation at that time, and for good reason. It was a virtual empire within an empire, making B-58 bombers at its Fort Worth plant; Terrier missiles at Pomona, California; the Atlas, jet-powered fighter planes, and propeller-driven transports at San Diego. Three dollars out of every four taken in by General Dynamics in 1956 (the total: $1 billion) came from Convair. The sprawling division was headed up by General Joseph T. McNarney with John V. Naish as executive vice president. Tough-minded Joe McNarney, ex-chief of U.S. forces in Europe, had always been pretty much a law unto himself, while Jack Naish wore his fifteen years' experience in the airframe industry like Killarney green on St. Patrick's Day. The division had already pulled off a successful commercial-transport program; the propeller-driven 240's, 340's, and 440's were world-famous. But what prompted Convair to consider making the formidable move into jet transport was a suggestion of Howard Hughes's.

It might be said that Convair should have been prepared for almost anything in any dealings with Hughes. The division had already gone through weird proceedings with Howard in trying to sell him some 340 transports back in 1950. To preserve the privacy Hughes habitually insisted on, negotiations for the aircraft had to be conducted by flashlight during the small hours of the night, out in the middle of the Palm Springs municipal dump. Then when Hughes and Convair's Sales Vice President Jack Zevely were writing the contract some days later in Pasadena, Ralph Damon of T.W.A. called up and told Hughes he had already committed T.W.A. to buying the Martin 404. That was that.

The memory of this episode was still fresh when Hughes asked Convair to build a jet—a big, long-range transport. Like most first customers, he insisted on taking a hand in the plane's design. By early 1955, Convair had gone through the preliminary design of two such aircraft—one with six engines and one with four. But Hughes, as Jack Zevely describes it, "kept us in a position where the plane was basically a T.W.A. design, and he could never make up his mind what the design was to be." Indeed, Hughes was still stalling and Convair still studying more than six months later when Boeing and Douglas came out with their preliminary designs for the 707 and DC-8. Boeing had already had a leg up on long-range jet transport—the 707 had been flight tested and sold to the Air Force as the KC-135 tanker—while Douglas had simply gone for broke with the DC-8, a "paper" plane. What this meant was embarrassingly simple. Convair had permitted Hughes's procrastinations to ruin its chances in the long-range market; confronted by the actuality of Boeing and Douglas models, it abandoned all plans for a competing long-range aircraft.

Now, still determined to get into jets, though the most lucrative market had gone glimmering, Convair had to choose between two alternatives. It could go for a short-distance aircraft (600 to 700 miles) or venture into the intermediate range (up to 1,800 miles). Since the division then held worldwide preeminence in the field of short-range propeller-driven transports with its 240's, 340's, and 440's, one might have supposed it would choose to make its play for the short-range jet market. General Dynamics' explanation of why it didn't is that it had no suitable engine at the time (all aircraft are designed around an engine) and that a poll of the airlines in 1956 showed no interest in a short-range jet. It could be argued, however—and subsequent events would bear out this point—that airlines have a way of changing their minds rapidly if offered something more tangible than a questionnaire: the opportunities Convair abandoned in the short-range market were capitalized on by the French who have sold 150 of their short-range Caravelles. As for a suitable engine, Convair would have had to wait, to be sure, but the wait would have made a lot of sense. No one could have beaten the division to it when it did become available, at least not in the opinion of experts like Arthur Raymond, designer of the DC-8 and Douglas' chief engineer until his retirement in 1960. "They would have had the

world by the tail," he says. "The short-range 727 Boeing now
has under construction would not have been built and the medium-range Boeing 720 would not have been competition for a
short-range plane. Boeing and Douglas, because of their commitments with the large planes, could not have come into the short-
range plane market." Boeing itself thinks it would have been
tough to compete against Convair if the latter had moved into the
short-range field. Richard Fitzsimmons of Boeing's preliminary
design group recalls: "Our biggest concern when we came out
offering the 707—because we were the first—was that the competition might come out with something revolutionary—like the
French Caravelle."

Forever Howard

In any event, Convair decided its best prospects lay in the
medium-range market, and the key elements in that decision
were three. First, its studies concluded the next market to open
would be the medium, mainly because it expected the new long-
range jets, the 707's and DC-8's, to downgrade piston planes
like the DC-6 into short-range use; second, the Air Force was
making a suitable engine available, the J-79 of the B-58 bomber
(which Convair makes); third, Convair's engineers believed that
with one and a half years' lead time in their favor neither Boeing's
big 707 nor Douglas' DC-8 could be economically transformed
into a plane able to go after the medium-range market.

When Convair had first proposed putting out a short-to-
medium-range jet the idea got an immediate and enthusiastic
response from Howard Hughes. "I'm your first customer," he said.
"I'll buy thirty planes." But the most consequential backer of the
venture was Joe McNarney. He was personally sold on the jet
program as a hedge against what the then emergent "peace offensive" might do to Convair's military business. Nevertheless, he
had gone through his usual procedure of calling the division's
key executives together for a final polling of opinion. Jack Zevely,
Engineering Vice President R. C. Sebold, and General Manager
B. F. Coggan of Convair's San Diego division had been for going
ahead with the medium-range jet. If their estimates were sound,
the prospects certainly looked great: 257 aircraft, over $1 billion
worth, could be sold within a ten-year period for a possible profit
of $250 million; at worst G.D. could lose only $30 million to
$50 million in the venture. But there were Convair men against
the program too. One of them was Thomas Lanphier, vice presi-

dent in charge of Convair's military business, who objected on grounds that the commercial program would crimp Convair's $650-million military program. Furthermore, in his experience the cost estimates and breakeven points of engineers and estimators just couldn't be relied upon: he had always had to double whatever estimates they gave him. Another who opposed the program was Jack Naish, Convair's executive vice president. Naish argued that it did not make sense for Convair to undertake a program which would increase sales only a modest 5 to 10 percent, while requiring 50 to 60 percent of McNarney's, Coggan's, and his own time. Moreover, he felt that the odds were against making money on commercial-transport ventures, particularly jet transports. But at the end of the discussion it was clear that McNarney was still solidly behind the venture. He smilingly remarked to everyone, "Well, we're going through with the program," and then took off for the March, 1956, executive-committee meeting in New York, where the final commitment still had to be made.[1]

How much of a gamble was the program the committee now had up for consideration? In the cold light of hundreds of millions of dollars worth of losses that eventually piled up, it was obviously a terrific gamble. But even if one foregoes "the advantages of 20-20 hindsight"—the phrase in current usage around General Dynamics—it was still a gamble. The following circumstances were all present at the time of the executive committee's final deliberations:

• Convair was well aware that its sole prime customer, Howard Hughes, again spelled trouble. That is indicated in a recent comment of Earl Johnson, General Dynamics president, about the Hughes deal ("We knew right along it was going to cost us a pile of jack")—but if G.D. was going to get into the jet business at all, it had to start the program with Hughes, or give up the whole thing. As an ex-Convair vice president put the predicament: "We were all worried as to whether Hughes would pay us [on schedule], even before the contract was signed, but at that late date in jet development, Hughes was Convair's only prime customer."

• Convair had itself done much to destroy the original premise

---

[1] The executive committee acted for the board of directors in approving many important ventures, as well as this one, which never came before the full thirty-two-man board. The committee, then made up of twelve members, was chaired by Jay Hopkins and included a banker, two investment bankers, two oilmen, and five lawyers.

that the 880 would get no competition from Boeing or Douglas. By the time the division's engineers finished with the design, the short-to-medium-range jet had become a medium-to-long-range one. It was now not much shorter in range than the 707 (3,400 miles vs. 3,600 miles) nor so much smaller in size that the Boeing 707 couldn't be chopped down to its dimensions and made highly competitive.

• Convair had limited the market possibilities of the 880 by making the fuselage too narrow to suit United, one of the three remaining prime customers for such an aircraft. United had already got Douglas to widen the fuselage of the DC-8 before ordering them in 1955, and throughout its discussions with Convair, United had insisted that for its purposes the proposed 880 should be wide enough to accommodate six seats abreast. But the aircraft Convair thereupon designed was too narrow to permit more than five-abreast seating. Such a seating arrangement, as Convair's Executive Vice President C. Rhoades MacBride explained it this fall, "was not based on passenger considerations, but was an aerodynamic decision to satisfy the antithetical requirements of transcontinental capability and short-field landing requirements." However this might be, the effect was to blight Convair's chances of selling United the forty 880's so hopefully listed in its market forecast.

The Sliding Breakeven Point

None of these discouraging considerations appears to have carried much weight with General Dynamics' directors. The executive committee to a man voted for the program on the assumption it would make money after sixty-eight planes were sold, that potential sales of 257 aircraft could be realized, that the maximum possible loss was only $30 million to $50 million.

By this time three airlines—T.W.A., Delta, and K.L.M.—had already taken options to buy the 880. Now the committee instructed Convair to go ahead and get letters of intent from them within the next fortnight. The committee laid down only three conditions in authorizing the program: first, that G.E. guarantee the 880's engine; second, that the ability of the airlines to pay for the jets be investigated by an *ad hoc* committee of Pace, Naish, and Financial Vice President Lambert Gross; third, that management was not to go ahead without orders in hand for 60 percent of the estimated sixty-eight-plane breakeven point.

The last proviso proved to be quite flexible. The breakeven

point on the 880 had been understated: after closer figuring, Convair raised it to seventy-four planes in May, up six planes in two months. Then when K.L.M. did not pick up its option, the executive committee indulgently dropped its 60 percent condition, allowing Convair to go ahead with only 50 percent of the break-even point assured. The new figure was made to fit the fact that by this time Convair had only forty firm orders (ten from Delta and thirty from Hughes).

These forty firm sales may seem on the surface to have been a reasonably strong beginning, but the circumstances under which they were made caused considerable anxiety in some offices at Convair. Because of an agreement with Hughes, Delta was virtually the only other airline G.D. was free to sell to for a whole year. One Convair executive says that "we were told if we sold the plane to anyone else but Delta, Hughes would get some of his money back. The 880 was an advanced plane with a better engine than any other at that time. Hughes wanted to keep it from T.W.A.'s competitors. So people who might have bought the 880 if we had been allowed to sell it to them, bought the DC-8 or the 707 instead."

Just who exercised the crucial influence in getting the jet program through was not too clear at the time, and it is certainly no clearer now when nobody wants to be singled out for fathering a failure. As a Convair vice president recalls it, Pace's role was more than passive: "When McNarney came back, he told us that one of the reasons, not the prime reason, but one of the reasons the company was going ahead with the program was because Pace felt this was his baby, whereas everything else Dynamics was doing was a Hopkins program." As Frank Pace remembers the circumstances, Joe McNarney made it plain he'd look on dis-approval of the venture as a vote of no confidence in his admin-istration at Convair. A Hopkins man declares that the program had Hopkins' active support. And what Hopkins wanted his directors unfailingly gave him.

A Dying Man's Vision

Unfortunately for General Dynamics, just about the time it was launching the greatest gamble in its history, the man who had made things work as well as they had for a decade was near-ing the end of his road. Jay Hopkins had been operated on for cancer in 1955, and understood the surgeons had "gotten it all," but now he suspected it might be incurable. In the late fall of

1956 he took a house at La Quinta, near Palm Springs, California, and there began to work on a five-year plan for the future of General Dynamics. His deliberations were necessarily colored by the fact that he always looked on the company and himself as one and the same thing, indeed, used his own name and the corporation's as synonyms. Hopkins had run General Dynamics out of himself, as an extension of his own personality, setting its standards and giving its people a sense of destiny. That destiny, as he saw it, was to be as big, or bigger, than the biggest corporation of them all, General Motors. But he was also aware that corporations, like trees, sometimes lose their foliage in the growth cycle, and he was determined that no winter would come to General Dynamics simply because one had come for him. More billions in sales must be added to the billion G.D. had attained for the first time that year (1956). At this point he made two decisions: to streamline the board of directors, cutting it from an unwieldy thirty-two to a compact fifteen. This meant risking his control of the company during his last days, for many of the men being dropped were his own old cronies. The second decision was to find someone to step into his shoes as chief executive officer.

He had some long and thoughtful discussions with his best friend and personal adviser, Ellsworth C. Alvord, brilliant lawyer and a General Dynamics director since 1954. Alvord was a large stockholder then, and he still controls 20,000 shares of G.D. Much of the discussion concerned what to do about Frank Pace—still executive vice president—whom Alvord had originally "sold" to Hopkins. Neither Alvord nor Hopkins, says Alvord, had any confidence in Pace's ability to do much more than take care of the Washington end of the business. In Hopkins' book his successor as chief executive officer should be an experienced businessman with a flair for finance and stockholder relations and the ability to talk shop—wages, salaries, programs, plans—with the divisional chiefs. Almost all these chiefs had been presidents of the companies that were now G.D. divisions, making it difficult for even the best top executives to ride herd on them.[2]

---

[2] Ironically Hopkins' difficulties in finding a suitable replacement in 1956 are the same that G.D.'s emergency executive committee is facing in the hunt it began last fall for a new chief executive to replace Pace. As committeeman Donald McDonnell of Blyth & Co. recently put it: "You just can't find the people of the national stature needed. You can't put Mickey Mantle over Carleton Shugg [of Electric Boat], Geoffrey Notman [of Canadair], Charles Horne [of Pomona], or James Dempsey [of Astronautics]. You can't put in a man they don't respect."

Beginning in 1955, when the jet program was first being considered, both Hopkins and Alvord, acting for Hopkins, had told Pace that if he wanted to become president—not chief executive officer—he should pick a good general vice president and a good financial vice president to make up for the business and financial experience he lacked. Alvord says: "I finally told Pace he had had plenty of time to look and that if he couldn't find the people he needed, I would." Pace had answered pleasantly and asked for more time.

Now as Alvord remembers it, Hopkins and he felt that time had run out and all they could see Pace had done by the fall of 1956 was to get in an old friend, Earl Johnson, comrade-in-arms from World War II, ex-Assistant Secretary of the Army (under Pace), ex-president of the Air Transport Association, a man whose business experience was fourteen years in the management of an investment-counseling firm. Alvord says that this wasn't enough to satisfy Hopkins, who decided not to promote Pace to the presidency but to keep him where he was and find someone else as his own successor in the top job. Alvord discussed three names with Hopkins that fall, and was actually negotiating with one candidate, an automobile executive. Then came an indication that Jay Hopkins in his sparring for time with Death and his board of directors might get crowded into a corner.

In February of 1957, General Dynamics' board met at the date ranch of Floyd Odlum, once owner of Convair. Odlum had offered his house in Indio, California, to spare his old friend and neighbor a trip east. Hopkins was then going through periods of great pain, but was as iron-willed as ever about carrying through his five-year plan for the corporation. Hopkins slipped into his seat early so no one could see the agony of his movements, and ran the meeting with his usual brilliance. He put through his personally selected slate of directors (cutting the board's membership from thirty-two to fifteen) and received from the survivors their promises of continued personal support for him in whatever he wished to do. Then, while everyone else was enjoying a steak fry on the front lawn, he quietly slipped away to his own place at La Quinta. But the plane that carried some of the board back east had hardly left the ground when director Clifton Miller mentioned to Alvord that Hopkins had looked very bad indeed and maybe the new board had a problem. Alvord dismissed the observation with "Jay knows what he's doing" and nothing further was said.

By late April, Hopkins, to the amazement of his doctors, was still alive. "I think that guy has invented something," said one of them, and in a way he had. Cancer patients characteristically are sustained right up to the end by the belief that the cure that will save them will turn up in time, but with Hopkins there was something more. It was almost as if he had managed by the terrible intensity he always put into everything to stand Death off. And so long as he was alive, he was going east just to show everybody he could. He would attend the annual stockholders' meeting on April 25. Then, as G.D.'s president, chairman, and chief executive, he would preside over the newly elected board— and the doctors be damned.

The evening of the twenty-fifth found him exhausted and in bed at his Washington apartment. In the end he had been too weak to make the annual stockholders' meeting at Dover, Delaware, which earlier that day had approved his hand-picked slate of directors, and was husbanding his strength for the morrow when his new board would meet to vote in the corporate officers. Nothing at all had occurred at the annual stockholders' meeting to arouse any suspicion that his grip on his company was not complete. Criticism of management at such meetings usually foreshadows bitter struggles for power within the board; but not a critical voice had been raised. That night, however, Clifton Miller, Donald McDonnell, and a third G.D. director paid a surprise call on Ellsworth Alvord in Washington.

Apparently word had got back to some directors that Hopkins was shopping around for a new chief executive, a situation that promised further unsettlement of a board that had just lost over half its membership at Hopkins' hands. Moreover, those directors who hadn't been aware of Hopkins' trouble before the Indio meeting had certainly become aware of it when they had seen him there. A number of them felt that the company was in urgent need of a new chief executive officer and that the only man available was Frank Pace. Alvord's three callers wanted him to persuade Hopkins to have Pace elected chief executive officer at the board meeting next day.

Alvord was completely taken by surprise. He indignantly refused the committee's request. Moreover, he expressed the belief that "this cabal," as he termed it, didn't have the votes to put Pace in. But the committee was insistent and he finally challenged them to muster all directors favoring the proposal at his offices next morning, before the board officially met. When he heard the news from Alvord, later that night, Hopkins was equally indignant and equally convinced the challenge to his power would come to nothing. "Hell," he growled, "that's *my* board. I picked every man on it."

On the morning of the twenty-sixth, however, a disturbingly large number of directors turned up in the law offices of Alvord & Alvord. The fight began then and there, went on into the meeting that day and next and carried over into the following week. After one of these stormy board meetings, Pace came to tell Alvord: "I want you to know I had nothing to do with this," and he has since declared that he held himself completely aloof from the whole procedure.

During the struggle, Alvord argued that the company was running well and every division was prospering. Why not let Hopkins die in peace, he asked; even the most optimistic doctors gave him only six months to live. Moreover, he insisted Pace was not qualified to run the company. Pace's supporters argued that from what they had observed of him as executive vice president he was well qualified and his succession should not be delayed: plenty of trouble could come to a company whose chief executive officer was under sedation. As Hopkins' slender support withered away, Alvord turned to parliamentary strategies to block the proceedings, but at the end of the final board meeting (April 29) Frank Pace was voted in overwhelmingly as president and chief executive officer.

When Hopkins, white as the pillow under his head, heard the news he couldn't believe it. He went down the list with Alvord, ticking off names of old friends and associates, men like Donald McDonnell to whom he said before the Indio meeting: "You're going to be kept on the new board as my personal friend." Then he gave a great sigh and said, "Well, after all, it's the board's responsibility. My usefulness is gone." The next day, April 30, Hopkins went to the hospital. "A man has to have a lot of fight to live with cancer," said Alvord, "and this took all the fight out of him." On May 1 it was officially announced that Frank Pace had been elected president and chief executive officer. On May 3, Jay Hopkins was dead.

End of an Era

Hopkins' death marked the end of an era for General Dynamics. The genius was gone and with him the inordinate attention to detail, the capacity to do everything himself that had made it possible for General Dynamics to get along with the same control system it had had as a company twenty-five times smaller.

The time had come to institute managerial reforms that would both compensate for the loss of Hopkins and finally do what he had failed to achieve in his lifetime: give the billion-dollar enterprise the degree of control and communication such a corporation required.

The huge, sprawling Convair Division needed to broken up into smaller, more manageable units, each reporting directly to New York instead of channeling everything first to divisional G.H.Q. at San Diego, which might or might not send it on east, depending on how it felt inclined. The surprise checkups Hopkins used to make on the division chiefs ("Expect me when you see me") needed to be augmented by an intelligence system that would give top management time and automatic warning of trouble. Some cross-fertilization of divisional personnel was needed so that General Dynamics would develop a top management with intimate knowledge of the workings of the most important divisions. G.D.'s entire budgeting system, a hodgepodge of procedures carried over by each division from the days when it was an independent enterprise, required an overhaul, divisional budgets needed to be standardized and subjected to point-by-point review from New York so no divisional manager could get off target.

All these problems faced Frank Pace, ex-Director of the Budget, and ex-Secretary of the Army. He believes today that he moved effectively to meet some of them. But Financial Vice President Richard Knight, who was brought into the company from General Electric in June, 1960, says a unified budgeting system was not established until September, 1961, which puts it four years from the time Pace took over the company, and not until the spring of 1961 did Pace finally move to split up Convair. Indeed, one of Pace's first acts was to permit the divisions, particularly Convair, more autonomy than they ever enjoyed under Hopkins. Convair, which used to occupy three-fifths of Hopkins' time, seldom saw the new chief executive officer. "Convair resisted all along any attempt by General Dynamics to do anything," said Pace recently. "There is not the slightest bit of doubt that the effort of General Dynamics to dominate Convair was completely resisted. The number of times I personally sat down with Jack Naish [McNarney's successor as chief of the division] did not exceed seven or eight in a period of three years."

Thus the stage was set for disaster. When costs began to get out of hand at Convair, when critical production delays developed, when key sales were lost, General Dynamics' management was unable to cope with the crisis. What then occurred, and how management is now trying to solve its problems, we shall see in Part II.

How a Great Corporation
Got Out of Control

*The Story of General Dynamics: Part II**_____

BY RICHARD AUSTIN SMITH

The year 1957 was a disquieting one within "the Rock," the huge concrete monolith in San Diego from which Convair's top management bossed the 880 jet-transport program, for it was then that the first glimmerings of disaster began to appear. No doubt most Convair executives had accepted the 880 venture with the same stoicism recently expressed by Rhoades MacBride, General Dynamics executive vice president: "No new-plane program is less than difficult and dangerous because of the amount of dough these poker games require. The 880 was a horrendous decision, but all new-plane programs are horrendous." Even such stoicism, however, did not prepare the company for what was to transpire.

Both the Convair assistant division manager, Allen Morgan, and B. F. Coggan, the division manager, had informed management back in 1956, at the time thirty planes were sold to Howard Hughes, that the 800 was underpriced. Their conclusions were ignored then because of the difficulty of substantiating their cost estimates at so early a date. But now a year had elapsed, the 880's design was frozen, and components had been ordered preparatory to starting up the production line. So the cost of the aircraft could be figured with precision; it was an amalgam of money that *had* been spent on research and development and money that *would* be spent on materials, fabrication, and assembly. Usually about 70 percent of the material costs of an aircraft is represented by items bought from outside suppliers—the engines, pods, stabilizers, ailerons, rudders, landing gear, autopilots,

* February 1962

instruments, and so on—with only 30 percent of the total material costs being allocated to the airframe manufacturer himself. The 880 ratios followed this general pattern. But when an engineer in Convair's purchasing division began totting up the various subcontracted components, he came to a startling conclusion: outlays for the vendor-supplied components of each 880 totaled more than the plane was being sold for (average price: $4,250,000). He took his figures up the line, pointing out that when research and development costs of the aircraft (they totaled some $75 million) were added in, along with the 25 to 30 percent of the material costs allocated to Convair itself, nothing could be expected of the 880 program but steadily mounting losses. He recommended that Convair abandon the whole venture, even though the loss, according to his estimates, would be about $50 million.

Whether the engineer's recommendation and his supporting data ever reached New York headquarters is something of a mystery. In any event, when the engineer persisted with his analyses, Convair decided he was a crank and fired him—he was reinstated two years later after time had confirmed the accuracy of his judgments.

Target No. 1: United Air Lines

The sales problems that confronted Convair in 1957, however, were something that couldn't be sloughed off with the firing of a critic. At the start of the 880 program in March, 1956, the potential market had been estimated at 257 planes. By June of that year Convair had raised the figure to 342, in September it was down to 150 after an on-the-spot appraisal had let the air out of the sales estimates for European airlines. These gyrations gave substance to an industry rumor that the division undertook a thoroughgoing market analysis only *after* commitment to the 880 program, but at least one point was clear about the "final" forecast of 150. The bulk of that number, as General Joseph McNarney, Convair's president, said at the time, had to be sold before July 1, 1957, or the 880's production line could not be economically maintained. The trouble was that an understanding with Howard Hughes (see Part I) had kept Convair from selling the 880 to anybody but T.W.A. and Delta for a whole year. This had already caused the loss of customers who preferred a 707 or DC-8 in the hand to an 880 twelve months down the road. So in the spring of 1957, when Convair was at last free of the commitment, it had still sold no more than the forty 880's (to T.W.A.

and Delta) that started off the program. The success of that program, with only a few months to go before McNarney's July 1 deadline, now hinged on selling the remaining major airlines, American and United.

Convair's first target was United, which it had listed as a prospect for thirty aircraft. For a time things seemed to be going Convair's way in its pursuit of this critical $120-million sale. Boeing, Douglas, and Convair were all in competition for the United contract, but Convair had the edge with its 880, for it was then the only true medium-to-long-range jet aircraft being offered. All Boeing could offer was essentially the long-range 707, too big and, for its seating capacity, 50,000 pounds too heavy to suit United. The size could be reduced, of course, and some of the weight chopped out, but not 50,000 pounds unless Pratt & Whitney could substantially lighten the engines, the JT3C-6's used on the 707 aircraft. With Pratt & Whitney unwilling to make this effort, United's board decided in favor of the 880 on September 27, 1957, subject to a final going-over by United's engineers.

Soon thereafter, United's President William Patterson called G.D.'s Executive Vice President Earl Johnson, whom Pace had put in over-all charge of the jet program, out of a board meeting to tell him Convair was "in." But perhaps the most consequential call was one Pratt & Whitney's Chairman H. Mansfield "Jack" Horner then made on Patterson himself. Spurred on by Boeing, Horner had been galvanized into action, and now he wanted to know whether something couldn't be done about getting Boeing back in the competition, if Pratt & Whitney could come up with a lighter engine. Patterson referred him to United's engineers, who made very encouraging noises. They themselves had been pushing Pratt & Whitney for just that. Both Boeing and Pratt & Whitney then went into a crash program, the former to scale down the 707, the latter to develop a lighter engine than the JT3C-6.

At around that time, G.D. director Ellsworth Alvord, who made it his business to keep watch over the 880 venture, happened to see a squad of United Air Lines executives in Seattle, where Boeing is located, and surmised something significant was going on with the airframe manufacturer. He promptly called Johnson and told him the United deal might not be so solid as they'd all thought. After all, there was a substantial amount of old-school tie between Pratt & Whitney and United Air Lines, left over from the days when both were divisions of United Aircraft. Johnson, however, was blandly reassuring. Just why he was is hard to understand since Horner had himself told Johnson that Pratt & Whitney had started working hard to lighten the JT3C-6 engine. But apparently neither Johnson nor anybody else in G.D. considered that Boeing could come up with a new medium-range aircraft before Convair signed United on the dotted line.

On or about October 10, 1957; Convair's Sales Vice President Jack Zevely and United's Financial Vice President Curtis Barkes had happily worked out eighteen articles of a nineteen-article contract and in fifteen minutes more would have finished the nineteenth, merely a statement of where the notices were to be sent, when a call came through for Barkes. As Zevely recalled this fall: "He came back, shaken, and said, 'Sorry, Boeing's back in the competition.'"

It was indeed. Pratt & Whitney engineers had managed to get 750 pounds out of the JT3C-6 engine by removing unneeded strength and using titanium. Boeing engineers had shortened the fuselage of the 707, reduced the weight of such heavy items as the landing gear, and improved its cost per mile. Within a few weeks Boeing had come up with a new medium-range aircraft— the 720—45,000 pounds lighter than the 707. United then invited Boeing and Convair to cut their prices and both did, though Convair refused to cut below what Pace recently described as "the bare minimum." In November, United's chief engineer John Herlihy compared Convair's 880 and Boeing's 720 and then strongly recommended the latter. His reasoning: the commercial performance of the G.E. engine was an unknown quantity, while "we had the Pratt & Whitney engines in our other jets and wanted to regularize our engines if we could"; moreover, the narrower fuselage of the Convair 880 permitted only five-abreast seating, a shortcoming United had vigorously protested back in 1956 when Convair had first solicited its opinion of the 880 design; the Boeing 720, on the other hand, was wide enough for six-abreast seating, a difference of as many as twenty-five passengers at full load in the tourist section of a combination first-class-tourist airliner. This meant, in Herlihy's view, that the 720 with its lower operating costs per passenger-mile was a better buy than the 880 with a $200,000 cheaper price tag. On November 28, 1957, United's board approved purchase of eleven Boeing 720's, with options for eighteen more.

"Merely a Modification"

The loss of United meant a sharp reduction in the market potential of the 880, dropping it from 110 to 80 planes. Worse than this, Convair had a powerful new competitor in what had been its private preserve, the medium-range field. That competitor was now going to make it tough for Convair to sign up American Airlines just at the time when Convair expected to sell the airline thirty planes, nearly half of the 880's dwindling market potential. Discussions with American had been going on for some months, though pressure had naturally increased after United chose the Boeing 720 in November. But in January, 1958, American notified Johnson, who was in over-all charge of the negotiations, that it too was going to pass up the 880 for twenty-five 720's.

In February, however, Convair was able to reopen discussions with American on the basis of a revolutionary new engine General Electric had just developed. Called a turbo fan-jet, it required 10 to 15 percent less fuel than a conventional jet to do the same job (under flight conditions) and provided 40 percent more power on take-off. The aircraft that Convair intended to use with these new engines, later designated the 990, was billed as "merely a modification" of the 880. It was a modification to end all modifications. The 990 had a bigger wing area than the 880, a fuselage ten and a half feet longer, weighed over 50,000 pounds more, required an enlarged empennage, a beefed-up landing gear, greater fuel capacity, stronger structural members, and was supposed to go 20 mph faster.

Many of these changes were imposed by American's hard-bargaining C. R. Smith, whose talent for getting what he wanted out of an airframe manufacturer was already visible in the DC-7. But Smith hadn't stopped with just designing the 990; he designed the contract too, using all the leverage Convair's plight afforded him. In it he demanded that Convair guarantee a low noise level for the plane, finance the 990's inventory of spare parts until American actually used them, and accept, for American's $25-million down payment, twenty-five DC-7's that had been in service on American's routes. The DC-7 was then widely regarded as an uneconomical airplane, 12 percent less efficient to operate than the DC-6, and, as Convair discovered, it could not be sold for even $500,000 in the open market. When General Dynamics reluctantly accepted this down payment, worth only half its face value, American signed up for twenty-five 990's with an option for twenty-five more.

"We Had to Go Ahead"

Looking back, director Alvord recently commented on the whole affair: "Earl Johnson brought back a contract written to

American specifications with an American delivery date but the plane was not even on paper. It was designed by American and sold to them at a fixed price. There was not even any competitive pricing." What is more, Alvord says, "the 990 was signed, sealed, and delivered without board approval. It was just a *fait accompli*. An announcement was made to the board that there would be a slight modification of the 880." Pace himself believed at the time that the 990 was only a slight modification. He now says, "If we had known at the outset that major changes would be needed, deeper consideration would have been given it."

The decision to go ahead on the 990 was an important turning point in the fortunes of Convair and of General Dynamics itself. The reasoning behind it has been stated by Pace: "When the Boeing 720 took away our sale to United, we found ourselves in competition with a plane just as good as ours. This is just what we wanted to avoid. The 880 seemed doomed. We had to go ahead with the 990 or get out of the jet business. American had not bought any medium-range jets . . . When the fan engine was developed, they told us, 'We will buy your plane if you produce a plane like the 990.' It was absolutely vital for us to follow American's wishes. We had to have another major transcontinental carrier. I thought I was taking less of a gamble then than I did entering into the 880 program."

But what this amounted to was that G.D. had now committed itself to a double-or-nothing policy, gambling that the success of the 990 (beginning with the American sale) would make up for the failures of the 880. The nature of this gamble is worth specifying, in view of the fiasco that eventuated:

• The plane had been sold at a price of approximately $4,700,000. Yet nobody knew how much it would cost because its costs were figured on those of the 880, which were still on the rise and unpredictable.

• The number of planes Convair must sell to put its jet-transport program in the black had gone up sharply. The breakeven point on the 880 had been sixty-eight planes at the start (March, 1956), a figure that by 1958 should have seemed impossible of fulfillment. Nothing but dribs and drabs of sales to lesser airlines could be expected of the 880, for the "majors" (T.W.A., United, American) had already been sold or refused to buy. Convair's commitment to the 990, which had a breakeven point of its own, meant the division must sell 200 of the 880's and 990's to keep out of the red.

• The success of the 990 depended largely on its being the sole

plane on the market with a fan-jet engine. When it built the plane around the G.E. engine, Convair was confident that Pratt & Whitney would not make a fan jet. Barred from making a *rear* fan jet—G.E.'s licensing agreement prevented this—Pratt & Whitney simply built a *front* fan engine. Boeing used this for the 720-B, which took away a good deal of the 990's potential market.
• The 990 was to be built without a prototype, or advance model. G.D. had "lucked out," to use President Earl Johnson's phrase, on the 880 without testing a prototype.[1] So now the company was again going to gamble that it could take a plane directly from the drawing board into production without any major hitches. Said Rhoades MacBride, by way of fuller explanation: "Our time for debugging the 990 was severely compressed because we wanted to take advantage of being first with the fan-jet engine. If we had built a prototype and flown it, we would have minimized our advantage in having the fan engine before Pratt & Whitney had it. We realized that if everything went right, we would be way ahead. If the 990 didn't fly as stated, we would be in terrific trouble."

"Our Basic Mistake"

Yet if ever a plane needed a prototype and plenty of time for testing, it was the 990. As Earl Johnson himself conceded recently: "Our basic mistake in judgment was that we did not produce a prototype to fly to virtual perfection. From a management standpoint we should have said, 'If you haven't the time to build a prototype then you shouldn't get into the program.'" The 990 was an extremely fast aircraft, with short-field characteristics and a brand-new engine. The decision to go it without a prototype meant that Convair had committed itself to attaining the very high speed demanded by C. R. Smith—635 mph—the first crack out of the box.

The odds against fulfilling these speed specifications right off the drawing board were recently assessed by a G.D. senior vice president. "In piston aircraft," he said, "it is perfectly simple to predict the performance. You just plot the power available and

---

[1] On one test flight over the Pacific late in 1958, however, a big chunk of the plane's tail fell off. Happily for G.D., a courageous pilot decided against ditching the aircraft and was able to fly it back to San Diego. There the trouble was remedied by beefing up the tail and installing yaw dampeners. The 880 is now considered a fine plane by Delta and other purchasers.

the power required and where they intersect you get your maximum speed. But with jets, trying to guess the intersection of these curves is very difficult, and missing by 40 or 50 mph is easy and makes a fantastic difference. One way to avoid this is to have a lot more wind-tunnel testing. But when you've already underpriced the plane, you're not willing to spend too much money on wind-tunnel testing. So you try to guess, and you make bad guesses." As it turned out, a lag of only six minutes in the 990's flying time on a transcontinental run of 2,500 miles was to result in C. R. Smith's canceling his contract because American wouldn't be able to bill the 990 as the "fastest airliner in the world."

"The Furnace Treatment"

Just before Convair undertook the 990 program, General Mc-Narney retired, and the division got a new president, hard-driving John Naish. Naish's succession clearly indicated that Convair was still an empire within G.D.'s empire and would likely remain so. Pace had wanted the Convair job for Earl Johnson, the old Army buddy he'd made his No. 2 man. McNarney wanted Naish; McNarney got Naish. And the new Convair chief had soon made plain his confidence he could handle anything that came along—if left strictly alone. As he said at the time: "The company has a great many people who like to solve their own problems. It believes in the furnace treatment—you throw people in the fire and you can separate the good metal from the dross very quickly."

Naish had already got a taste of the furnace treatment at Convair, for trouble was piling up on all sides. Total orders for the 990 were only thirty-two, while those for the 880 were still stuck at forty-four. Overhead on the jet venture had risen as production of the Convair-made F-106 fighter dwindled and the Atlas program, which also shared the San Diego facilities, had had to be moved to another plant, on orders from the Pentagon. But these were just first-degree burns in comparison to the furnace treatment Convair's new head was about to get from Howard Hughes over the 880.

Hughes's vagaries had already caused Convair plenty of lost sales and missed opportunities, as set forth in Part I, and the contract negotiations with him on the 880 had been bizarre. Sales Vice President Zevely even maintains the 880 was not named for its eighty-eight seats but for the eighty-eight conferences he had had to go through with Howard; on one that lasted until three in the morning, Hughes had brushed aside Zevely's plea of extreme fatigue and insisted a movie was all the Convair man needed to get him back in the pink. Hughes then made a few phone calls and, with the groggy Zevely in tow, went out to the R.K.O. lot. There they were treated to a showing of *Jet Pilot*, Hughes having thoughtfully got the movie's star, Janet Leigh, out of bed to provide a running commentary on the film.

When the 880 got to the production stage, the Hughes group —T.W.A. engineers and executives—had quietly set up shop in an abandoned lumberyard near Convair's San Diego headquarters and for a time Hughes caused more mystification than trouble. A Convair engineer would be told to appear for a conference with him at a Las Vegas nightclub, only to spend the evening sitting in solitary splendor at the huge table the erratic Howard had reserved; Hughes never did show up. As 1959 wore on, however, it became increasingly difficult to get Hughes to commit himself on the final configuration (styling and arrangements) of his 880's. Such a situation, of course, raised hob with the Convair production line, delaying the 880's and making it certain that overtime would have to be used to meet the tightly scheduled delivery dates of 990's—they'd been promised to American for the spring of 1961—if their dates could be met at all. As a matter of fact, in September (1959) Sales Vice President Zevely was already notifying the airlines the 990 would be late.

Convair let more precious months slip by trying to humor Hughes before it came to a shattering conclusion: all his stalling on the final configuration of his 880's had its roots in the fact that he hadn't the money to pay for them on delivery. Indeed, in the fall of 1959, when it came time for Convair to fly his first two 880's out for delivery, Hughes blocked the move. These and the next two planes, said a G.D. vice president, "were actually impounded by Hughes and placed under bailment, then moved off the Convair property, and put in a locked hangar guarded by his men."

Convair could have made an issue of this, but chose not to. Nevertheless, a fateful decision had to be made. The division could move Hughes's uncompleted planes into a boneyard and resume work on them when he solved his financial problems or it could finish the planes and sue him upon delivery. The latter course had been successfully followed by Boeing when Hughes made the same sort of difficulties with his 707's and it had got paid without even having to resort to the courts. But Convair chose to pull his 880's off the line and put them out on the field. What made this decision so fantastic was that thirteen of the planes were in different stages of completion. Now the economics of an aircraft production line are geared to "a learning curve," which simply means that labor costs go down as each production-line worker becomes familiar with his particular phase of putting the plane together. On the first 880 the learning curve was at its peak with labor costs of roughly $500,000, on the fortieth or fiftieth plane labor costs were designed to drop below $200,000. Thus removing Hughes's thirteen 880's from the line in *different stages* of completion meant that the learning curve for them would have to be begun again at the top—to the cost of Convair not of Hughes.

"It's Not a Baby Any More"

This disastrous decision was made by Jack Naish, with an o.k. from Frank Pace and Earl Johnson. But even then New York was far from on top of the situation. Pace maintains he never knew the 880 was in serious trouble until *after* the Hughes decision: "We knew we had problems, but there were no major difficulties as far as we knew. The information that came to us fiscally, in a routine fashion, through Naish and substantiated by Naish, would not have led us to believe the extent of the losses that were occurring." Earl Johnson is not even sure just when he himself became alarmed over the jet program. "It's difficult to answer that. It's like living with a child—when do you notice it's not a baby any more?"

The sad truth was simply that General Dynamics was still being run as a holding company with no real control from the top. Its headquarters staff had been kept at 200, and this, in Pace's view, "automatically recognizes that it is impossible to police the operation of the divisions." But even if there had been a will, the means of policing seem slender indeed. Pace had established no reporting system that could tell him quickly when a division was in trouble; the key figures were buried in pages of divisional operating statements. G.D.'s Financial Vice President Richard Knight is still overhauling the system of auditing the divisional books so as to prevent any doctoring of the figures to make a divisional president look good. In short, millions of dollars of publicly owned money could be on its way down the drain at Convair before New York was aware of it.

In a letter of May 10, 1960, addressed to General Dynamics' stockholders, Pace reported jet-transport charges of $91 million (as of March 31, 1960) but added "[We] have every reason to believe [the program] will be one of our most successful ventures." By mid-August, however, Pace's springtime optimism began to show the signs of an early frost. It will be remembered that from the very beginning the 880 had been grossly underpriced in relation to its material costs; now Convair had virtually given up trying to keep those heavy costs within the budgeted amounts. For almost a year San Siego had been abuzz with rumor that losses on the 880, "the sweet bird of our economy," as local citizens called the 880, might reach $150 million. Some 880 components had overrun their original estimates by as much as 300 percent.

On the 25th of August, G.D.'s worried board of directors met to decide (1) what should be done about Convair, (2) whether to cut the upcoming dividend. Director Henry Crown, the company's biggest stockholder, had been told the week before of Pace's "disappointment and surprise" at Convair's mounting losses, but Crown, an astute businessman, had an uneasy feeling that further bad news impended. If so, he reasoned that any dividend cut the board voted then might have to be repeated later on. "I told Pace not to take two bites of the cherry," he recollected last December. "If we did find further losses, and the dividend had to be eliminated entirely, then I thought it should be done all at once." Pace agreed to get in touch with Naish and satisfy himself that no further jet write-offs would be necessary.

This he did, and on his appraisal of Convair's situation the board halved the dividend at the September, 1960, meeting. On September 22, at the same time that Pace informed the stockholders of the dividend cut, he also released a special report on the jet program. With program charges up $34 million in six months, the directors had decided to write off all *anticipated future losses* (based on sales of ninety-four 880's and 990's, for which firm orders were then in hand). This write-off, $96,500,000 pretax, $46,300,000 after taxes, meant that the planes should now be on a breakeven basis, each new sale bringing in a profit.

It was a wise move, but General Dynamics was far from out of the woods. Four months later (January, 1961) Hughes got his financing and Convair was confronted with the problem of completing his aircraft. And some problem it was. Since no two planes were in exactly the same stage of completion, they couldn't be put back on the production line. They had to be hand-finished on the field, at costs many times those prevailing on the line. Moreover, engineering changes had to be made—some Convair's and some Hughes's.

"It took a real expert," explained a vice president of General Dynamics, "to diagnose the exact state of completion of each plane, plus what engineering changes should be made. For instance, he had to work with a stack of blueprints to decide whether the wiring was nearly finished, just begun, or had to be completely changed. Do you continue the wiring? Do you rip it out? Additionally, there was some water damage from the months the planes had been sitting out on the field. Since the production line had been cut back, some of the trained people had been let go, others had to be retrained, and all this was terribly expensive. Hughes did agree to pay for the excess completion costs on the four planes he impounded, but we had to pay for most of the others."

A $40-Million Discovery

By February of 1961, General Dynamics was beginning to reap the economic consequences of the disastrous Hughes decision. New York "discovered" that Convair had not only failed to write off all jet losses the previous September but had incurred additional ones. These, amounting to $40 million, spelled the end for Jack Naish and for August Esenwein, the executive vice president Pace had put under Naish to try and control costs. "I felt," said Pace recently, "that if I couldn't get more accurate judgments from Naish than I had gotten, he ought to go." Then he added, "Whether these problems were passed on and not properly interpreted by Esenwein and Naish, I can't tell. There are conflicting points of view now that we go back into the problem. But we in New York didn't know the magnitude of the problem."

Regardless of whether New York knew then or not, the whole business community was shortly to learn how profound was Convair's trouble. The risky decision to build the 990 without a prototype began to bear some even more expensive fruit. Seventeen of American's twenty-five 990's had to be delivered during 1961, the first one in March. A flight test of this particular airplane in late January, 1961, four months later than the date scheduled in a previous announcement of Pace's, disclosed wing flutter and other problems that required rebuilding the landing flaps, the leading edge of the wings, the outboard pylons. These were not too difficult to correct from an engineering point of view, but as a G.D. vice president sadly remarked, "If you get into production with a plane whose design has to be changed, the magnitude of the troubles you then encounter becomes exponential." Moreover, these corrections now had to be made on overtime because of the tight delivery schedule to American. Ultimately this was to burden G.D. with an additional $116-million jet write-off, a source

of concern to Frank Pace, not to say considerable personal em-
barrassment. For now "a second bite of the cherry" would have
to be taken and in June, after twenty-five years, the dividend
omitted. The burning question, of course, is why *didn't* New York
know the magnitude of the problem. Naish maintains he leaned
over backward, because of his initial opposition to the jet program, to clear important decisions with either Johnson or Pace.
Last fall a member of G.D.'s executive committee, still puzzling
over why New York had been so much in the dark, for so long,
pressed Pace on the point. He wanted to know why, even if
Naish's information had been suspect, Convair's controller hadn't
told Pace of the losses, or why he hadn't learned of them from
MacBride, whom Pace had sent out early in 1961 to investigate,
or from Earl Johnson, whom Pace had given over-all responsibility for the jet program and sent to Convair in late 1958 and
early 1959 when the division was plainly in trouble. Pace, at a
loss to explain, wondered whether he ought to resign. No, said the
director, and Pace needn't make any apologies. After all, he
wasn't trained as a businessman. He (the director) made no
apologies for not being able to walk into an operating room and
perform like a surgeon. So Pace shouldn't feel badly about not
being trained as a businessman.

Pace, of course, does feel badly. He recently remarked to
Fortune, "If you don't think it twists my insides to see what has
happened to General Dynamics, you are very wrong. You must
know what this kind of a defeat does to a man who has been
successful." But the enormity of his defeat would appear to have
been due to something more than a lack of business experience.
Pace himself has stated that his primary interest and, indeed, his
forte are in public service. Business has been of secondary importance.

The Wages of Sin

Unhappily for General Dynamics, the departures of Naish
and Esenwein did little to lighten the corporation's load of trouble.
Nor was Rhoades MacBride, G.D.'s No. 3 man whom Pace put
in as acting president of Convair, able to bring the division under
control (after ten months he too was to be washed out of office).
There had simply been too many sins of commission and omission
to be cured by chopping off heads in San Diego; a corporate reorganization was called for.

In May of 1961, General Dynamics was split into two grand

divisions: MacBride was put in charge of the Western Division, essentially the old Convair broken up into five parts, and Executive Vice President Werner Gullander was assigned the Eastern Division. Both reported to President Earl Johnson, who made San Diego his headquarters. But then the company's creditors began to talk of calling the $150 million in notes G.D. had outstanding. This new crisis called for redoubled efforts by the executive committee of the board of directors, set up in secret six months earlier to try to set things to rights. Under the chairmanship of Henry Crown, the committee had been reviewing all divisional budgets, trying to persuade Prudential and the banks to substitute a $200-million revolving credit for their prime rate loans, and scouting around for a new chief executive officer. By August the committee had obtained its $200-million credit under rigid conditions: no dividend declarations for two years, no unapproved incurment of debt or sale of assets, working capital to be kept above $140 million.

This was no sooner settled, however, than G.D. ran into trouble with American over the 990. The gamble, mentioned earlier, that Convair's engineers could guess the jet power needed to meet the speed and fuel requirements in the American contract had failed. In addition the 990 was already six months late, so in September, 1961, Smith canceled his order. Now the G.D. board was confronted by two choices, both bleak. It could turn back the uneconomical DC-7's Smith had induced them to accept in lieu of a $25-million down payment, then with the $25-million cash reimbursement as a cushion, cut the price of the 990 and try to sell it to other carriers; or it could try to get a new contract from Smith. A few audacious directors, including Crown, were for trying choice No. 1, but the opinion of the majority, as epitomized by one member of the board, was: "Now let's not get C.R. mad. Earl Johnson knows him. Let's go and appeal to him."

The upshot was that Pace, Johnson, and Henry Crown paid a call on Smith. There Colonel Crown related a little story about his having let a construction company off the hook even though, legally, he had had every right to hold them to a disastrous contract. Smith made no comment but when Pace and Johnson pursued the same thought he finally said: "I understand your problem, but I have stockholders. You told me, Earl, that the plane would go a certain speed." A new contract was signed with American and it was a tough one. The airline cut its order from twenty-five to fifteen planes, with an option to take five more if Convair could get the speed up to 621 mph. Upwards of $300,000 was knocked off the price of each aircraft. With wind-tunnel tests completed, chances are now good that Convair will be able to meet the 621 mph specification.

But even as this article goes to press in mid-January, the end of General Dynamics' jet travail is not in sight. Howard Hughes has just canceled his order for thirteen 990's, an order that, surprisingly enough, Convair had accepted during the period when Hughes couldn't even pay for his 880's. S.A.S. and Swiss Air have cut their original order from nine 990's to seven. Moreover, the market is just about saturated in so far as additional jet sales are concerned, even for a fine plane like the 880. As for the 990, it too has missed its market. To date only sixty-six 880's and twenty-three 990's have been sold, which puts Convair well behind Boeing's 120 sales in the medium-range market. Small wonder that when somebody suggests selling off Convair, a G.D. vice president ruefully remarks: "Would $5 be too much?"

"This Has Hurt Us in Washington"

The failure of General Dynamics' management has had some serious collateral effects. As a member of the executive committee remarked, "The public has lost confidence in us. This has hurt us in Washington. We have to inject people of stature into the management." The company recently lost out on two of the three big defense contracts (the $400 million Apollo spacecraft contract went to North American, Boeing got the $300 million Saturn S-1 booster system). Its executive committee has also failed to find a new chief executive officer, "a man forty years old with one hundred years of experience" as John McCone remarked in turning down the job, and this has further delayed G.D.'s much-needed reorganization. Indeed, with MacBride's departure, the company abolished General Dynamics East and General Dynamics West and reverted to its old regimen of having all divisions report to New York.

For the near term, however, G.D.'s financial prospects are somewhat brighter. Last year's losses did drop working capital below the $140 million minimum, a default on its banking agreement that technically could have started the company down the road to receivership. But the banks quietly assented to the establishment of a new working-capital minimum of $100 million. G.D. believes it will have no difficulty staying on the sunny side of this figure. Moreover, Colonel Crown expects that the company will earn $50 million pretax during 1962, a decided improvement over the $60 million loss estimated for 1961. The great imponderable, of course, is whether any more jet losses will have to be written off. Says Colonel Crown: "Jet write-offs for 1962 should not exceed $5 million to $10 million."

Though the great losses are now a matter of history, the subject of what went wrong with the company will no doubt be discussed for as long as there is a General Dynamics. "It's a grave question in my mind," said one of the company's senior vice presidents, "as to whether General Dynamics had the right to risk this kind of money belonging to the stockholders for the potential profit you could get out of it. All management has to take a certain risk for big gains. But I don't think it's right to risk so much for so small a gain."

There are, however, larger questions of management's responsibility for the well-being of the corporation. That responsibility, in the jet age, is to keep management techniques developing at the same pace as the technologies they must control. Moreover, G.D. and other decentralized companies need to understand fully the basic limitations of decentralization. No amount of decentralization can put the head of a corporate division in the same situation as the head of an independent company—no matter that he once headed such a company. The division head may be rightly encouraged to take initiative, but the ultimate responsibility for avoiding failure cannot rest with him. For under decentralization his inhibitions against risk have been weakened while his initiative has been sustained. Under these circumstances the top management of G.D. and other conglomerate corporations, have to assume the "watch your step" function that formerly balanced the decision of the independent company chief.

Frank Pace, of course, has his own ideas on the whole fiasco. "Nothing ever occurs without human error," he mused, looking from his Rockefeller Center window as the rush of the Hudson seemed to be carrying the twilight out to sea. "Disraeli said 'Circumstance is beyond us, conduct is within human control.' We have been subjected both to human error and a remarkable series of circumstances."

GENERAL DYNAMICS: ITS OTHER PARTS

The Convair plant in San Diego is one of twelve G.D. divisions, which all together do $2 billion worth of business. Here are estimates of how the other divisions are doing:

Astronautics Division (Atlas missile)—It is G.D.'s biggest, most profitable division (estimated pretax 1961 earnings: $15 million), but has recently lost out on contracts for Apollo and Saturn.

Canadair (aircraft)—Licensed manufacturer of the Lockheed F-104, which is its mainstay. High hopes had been pinned on CL-44, a turboprop cargo plane, but only thirty were sold over the past two years, which may lead to substantial cuts in Canadair's payroll of 10,000 workers. Probable pretax earnings: $10 million.

Electric Boat (submarines)—Didn't do too well on low-priced submarine contracts of 1961, has got better ones in 1962. Expected to earn $10 million pretax 1961, but capacity for future growth is limited by capital for new building ways.

Fort Worth (B-58 bomber)—This year's output will be a little over half of 1961's with B-58 scheduled to phase out in 1963. Unless it gets contract for joint Navy-Air Force fighter, will have to shut down facilities.

General Atomic (nuclear development)—Very promising future but no income expected for several years to come.

Liquid Carbonic (liquefied gases)—"It isn't losing money," says one G.D. director, "but it isn't ever going to make anything substantial." Estimated 1961 pretax earnings: $5 million.

Electrodynamics (electric motors)—"It's usually in the red, or a little in the black, but it never really makes a dime."

Pomona (electronics plus Terrier and other missiles)—"Doing very well," with 1961 earnings of approximately $7,500,000.

Stromberg-Carlson (telephones, electronics)—Under reorganization after disclosure of $17 million in excess inventory. "The telephone business is doing excellently [$8 million], the rest you can have."

General Aircraft and Leasing—Leases or sells used planes received as trade-ins for jets. Business is poor.

Material Service (building materials, coal mining)—Good, steady earner, though tied to building construction, which Henry Crown says will be off in 1962. Earnings for 1961: $9 million to $10 million pretax.

How Rathbone Runs Jersey Standard*__

BY WALTER GUZZARDI, JR.

The executives of the Standard Oil Co. (New Jersey) are waiting for a meeting to begin—or, more precisely, they are waiting for another man, whose appearance will mark the beginning of a meeting. The man they are waiting for is Monroe Jackson Rathbone, the president of Jersey Standard and its chief executive officer.

The executives present have spent many years with Jersey or one or another of Jersey's 100-odd affiliates that pump crude from the ground, transport, refine, or market it. But now the whole group belongs to Jersey, which strictly speaking is not an oil company at all, but a holding company that invests in the oil business —a kind of Roman Empire of the modern business world. Paramount in the minds of the men now gathered together—on the twenty-ninth floor of Jersey's New York offices at Rockefeller Center—is the aggregate prosperity of a great and sprawling mosaic of investment. An affiliate may importune from the heat of competitive struggle or the environment of a foreign country, but (as with the Roman Empire) Jersey can never accede to a major request from a family member without considering what the reverberations through the provinces will mean to the larger interest—that of the Jersey company itself.

How Jersey executives manage the affairs of empire makes a case study in American management. Over its eighty years, Jersey has developed a highly refined managerial philosophy, which puts primary emphasis on the committee system. Thorough staff work digs out and distills the mountains of facts needed by Jersey's committees. Decisions that reach beyond one committee's scope are passed up to another level of committee management. At the top of the chain sits a seven-man executive committee whose members also serve on Jersey's fifteen-man board of directors. Meeting every day, this committee looks to the general good of Jersey by two major means. First, it governs the finances of affiliates by a detailed review of budgets and contemplated new

January 1963

investments. Second, bearing a different formal designation, the executive committee passes on the selection and promotion of the top officers who run Jersey's companies around the world. On this day, the executive committee is about to hold discussions in both these broad areas of responsibility.

Now the side door opens, and Rathbone, a man with the husky frame of a roustabout and the craggy features of an amiable pugilist, steps from his office into the boardroom. As always, he sets in a chair close to his office door, in the middle of the oval's broad curve. There is no gavel-rapping. At a nod from Rathbone, the meeting begins. Every executive officer has his style of running things. Let's watch the carefully modulated style of the man who presides over a corporation with assets of almost $11 billion.

Refinements in Building a Refinery

The first matter to come up for decision is a proposal for the construction of a refinery in France. Once the executive committee's controls were so tight that it had to pass on many small purchases contemplated by affiliates. Controls were loosened as Jersey grew. Then, when Rathbone became Jersey's chief executive, he and the board delegated a great deal of financial authority to another Jersey committee, the board advisory committee on investments, headed by company director Marion Boyer; now the executive committee considers only those expenditures over $1 million.

This refinery at Marseille, if Rathbone and the committee approve it, will cost Jersey in the neighborhood of $35 million. Three times before, the committee has been informed of the progress of the plans for the refinery; this time the proposal, to be explained in detail by staff officers, comes to the committee for formal action. Following his usual technique, Rathbone first hears the proposal all the way through, with only an infrequent interruption to clarify a point. He tests the staff work by calling attention to staff studies showing that the excess refining capacity in France will diminish over the next ten years, and asking sharply: "What about the fact that the decrease in that excess capacity depends partly on export markets? Are we sure those markets will still be there in 1966, when the refinery will be finished?" Satisfied with the reply, Jersey's president lets the presentation of details about the refinery run on to its end.

Then he moves in heavily on a matter always foremost in his mind—costs. "What about the estimates of the cost of the refinery

—how good are they?" Told that while they were not yet detailed, they seemed good enough so that the cost would probably come within the 10 percent latitude that Jersey allows in such cases, the president bears down: "We allow that 10 percent to take care of emergencies or unforeseen situations. But we don't want to start a project of this size with the idea that cost can be allowed to go up $3 million or $4 million. It's bad psychology to start with the idea that you have that kind of leeway. We've had some horrible overruns on these refineries, and I don't want that to happen in this case. If there is an overrun, the size of the refinery may have to be reconsidered. What we are approving is this: a $35-million re-finery at Marseille. If it comes to more, you come back to us. The proposal is approved on that basis."

Chairs are pushed back. The staff men who presented the refinery proposal depart. Presently the executive committee, now sitting in its capacity as the compensation and executive-develop-ment committee, turns its attention to the careers and next assign-ments of top officers. Rathbone has spent forty-one years working for Jersey; he appears to know everyone who comes up for dis-cussion, and listens carefully. Occasionally he drops in a comment. Upon hearing of the good performance of a man on a new assign-ment, he remarks: "It has taken a long time, but it looks like he has finally found his niche in this company. It's nice to have him in the right place at last."

A Jersey affiliate abroad needs a top manager, and one of the executive-committee members knows just the right man. But the man cannot move into the job for a year. One officer comments: "We'll send him next year. He's the man we want." Nodding of heads. The president (sharply): "But what about leaving that job vacant for a whole year? Can we afford to do it?" There is a small shock, and more discussion; it is decided to keep the job open for the man. But Rathbone has left hanging in the air just a suspicion that so long a delay borders on being unwise.

There is a discussion of a slate of three names for another job. "Don't forget that this spot is a breeding ground for the board of directors," says Rathbone. "When we look over these names, let's keep that in mind. Let's look down the road a way. Which of these men is going to be best for the board?"

Rathbone (on still another Jersey man): "I know he's got three children. But they have a fine nurse who's just like a mother to those kids. The children will get along fine out there. He's making $25,000 a year now—below the minimum for his class. Even after this raise, he'll still be below the minimum. But we can leave him at that level for a while. He's been moved along very well."

The meeting breaks up. A few people drift off. One or two stay behind for a word with Jersey's president. Answering questions or giving curbstone opinions, Rathbone seems consciously to eschew the attributes popularly assigned to the boss: he has no tough bearing, he generates no tension, he affects no elegance. He gives the impression of a willingness to talk every problem through, no matter how long it takes. His language is not incisive; instead he often clothes his positive views in negative syntax: "I'm not sure I'd buy that," or "That may not be the best basis to put it on." Such replies seem to satisfy his interrogators, who hurry away. Rathbone steps back into his own office. His schedule has run late on this particular day and the afternoon is almost over. Rathbone flips through a few documents his secretary brings him. He remembers to give to her the $5.64 that he owes her from the day before. Around 5:30 P.M., with his correspondence signed and his desk cleared, Rathbone goes home. He takes a thick tan briefcase with him.

A Long Day's Journey

No day at Jersey is without its report of crisis or potential crisis from some quarter of the empire. Rathbone handles them all with imperturbability, and sometimes has disposed of quite a few before committee meetings get under way. On one recent typical morning, a company car picked him up around 8:00 A.M. at his home in Summit, New Jersey. Being chauffeured to his office, Rathbone laid out the thick tan briefcase's contents on the back seat and shuffled through his papers. By 9:00 A.M. he was settled in his comfortable office, seated in a green leather swivel chair behind a spacious, stubby-legged desk. Rathbone has none of the nervous mannerisms that often afflict smaller men; at work, he may occasionally finger the old leather case of his reading glasses, but more often, when his big bony hands are not wrapped around a telephone or a pencil, he keeps them folded and motionless on his desk.

The first man to enter his office that morning was John White, a member of the Jersey board and a top officer in charge of Latin-American affairs. Rathbone moved from behind his desk to sit in a straight-backed chair beside it. He rested his elbows on his knees, clasped his hands, began to listen. White had come to report on a crisis: transformers belonging to the Creole Petroleum

Corp., Jersey's huge producing company in Venezuela, had been blown up by saboteurs on Lake Maracaibo. Lots of the crude that Jersey pumps from Lake Maracaibo goes into distillates for the European market, much of it to be burned for a new European luxury—central heating. Other large amounts of heavy fuel oil go to the United Kingdom for British utility companies.

White: "It looks like we may lose about 40 percent of our production. Four transformer stations were blown up—and they are huge things. But we have some inventory on hand, and we are arranging to borrow some crude from other companies if necessary. We're not in as bad shape as I thought at first."

Rathbone: "Still, it isn't good. Sure we can borrow crude and use inventories. But all that means is that we are transferring the problem from November until January. We must think of the product consequences—I'm not sure that the products are going to balance out." He began to consider the cost to Jersey of transferring crude from other areas to satisfy Creole's big customers. But within a few hours—after hearing a couple of reports on the exact nature and extent of the damage—he could relax. Only about one-third of Creole's production was interrupted, and that would be resumed within a few days. Once he knew the crisis was contained, Rathbone left its management entirely in the hands of others. To be informed on such occasions, to hear the full details, to think ahead to possible action that may be necessary, are standard procedures with Jersey's president—even though, as in this case, circumstances may sometimes dissolve the need for his action.

A Preoccupation with Crises

A tragic crisis also troubled Rathbone that day. Early that morning Eger Murphree, Jersey's top research scientist and company vice president, had died suddenly of a heart attack. Murphree was an old friend and a golfing companion of Rathbone, who was shocked and depressed by Murphree's death. "It's a big loss to the company, and a loss to me of one of my oldest friends." But by 9:30 A.M., inevitably, Rathbone was deeply involved in the difficult business of finding a successor to Murphree. "I don't want our research activity going for long with nobody in charge of it."

There was also a tragedy of a less personal nature. Over the weekend Enrico Mattei, Italy's oil czar, had been killed in a private-plane crash. It was Mattei who had slammed the door to the Po Valley in the face of American oil companies some years before; who had introduced large quantities of Russian crude into Italy; and who had been upsetting oil's status quo in the Middle East. The big oil companies were declared by Mattei to be his enemies; he was a bone in their throats. Putting together what he heard with what he knew, Rathbone gave this informal estimate to the people who called for his opinion that morning:

"I think there may be some kind of power struggle in Italy after Mattei. Lots of people probably want to get that plum. But no matter who gets it, there may be some change in the authority that goes with the job. Mattei's empire may shrink some. A.G.I.P.'s invasion of England may end." Added Rathbone to a colleague, in a rare use of a figure of speech. "But let's be careful not to give the impression that we are dancing on anybody's grave."

By 10:00 A.M. Rathbone was busy with a speech to be given later in the week. He had received a draft the Saturday before. Over the weekend he had rewritten large portions of it, but still seemed faintly dissatisfied. An executive assistant came in.

Rathbone: "I rewrote lots of that speech."

Aide: "I knew you wouldn't like it." Pause. "It did seem to lack some luster."

Rathbone (with a sad smile): "It was dull as hell."

10:30 A.M. People were streaming in and out of the president's office. In came a group headed by William Stott, an executive vice president and Jersey's top marketing man, to report on the pending purchase of a refinery in Denmark. The refinery, owned by Getty's Tidewater Oil Co., looked as if it might have special appeal for Jersey, since a Jersey affiliate has the lion's share of the Danish petroleum market. Getty's representatives wanted to keep a minority interest in the refinery, which has a capacity of 25,000 barrels a day. Jersey's position from the beginning was that it was interested in buying only the whole thing.

Stott: "It looks like the deal for the Danish refinery is all set. We're going to get 100 percent ownership. We think the refinery's capacity can easily be stretched to 33,000 barrels a day. We'll solve Getty's problems by reserving for him one-third of the refinery's productive capacity. On this basis, we're getting a good deal."

Rathbone: "What about refining all that crude for Getty? What is he going to do with it?" Told that Getty already had customers for the refined products, and could reduce substantially at any time the amount he had agreed to take from the refinery, Rathbone noted: "That's good. We don't want to force him to take big amounts from the refinery." Rathbone gave his approval: "It's a good deal for both parties. Sometimes we have to consider building refineries in response to local pressures, rather than just to the economics of the thing. Here we can get into a refinery in a sensible way. I don't think we are going to need 152 people in a refinery of this capacity, but we can work that out. The deal sounds O.K. to me." Rathbone's response to Stott's enthusiastic comment that "We've saved money on this deal," and to Stott's ebullient encomiums of his negotiating team, was a simple and amiable silence. Even on less busy mornings, Rathbone does not slather around his praise.

A Special Strain of Manager

Whether in board meetings, in the privacy of his office, or even at home, Rathbone has come almost automatically to think of Jersey first. Like Frederick Kappel of A.T.&T., Lawrence Litchfield Jr. of Alcoa, and Frederic Donner of General Motors, Rathbone belongs to a distinct managerial strain—men who mature in one company with the conviction that they or someone else going through the same maturation process eventually will be in charge of it. Rathbone was brought up in the Jersey system, shaped by it and at the same time shaping it. Virtually every Jersey board member has spent most of his working life with Jersey. None has worked for any other oil company. On an average, each board member has served thirty-one years with Jersey or its affiliates. The total time spent in the company by present members of the board comes to over four hundred and fifty years. The company believes that the place to learn the oil business is inside Jersey's family—a belief supported by the performance of system-made men like Rathbone.

The son of a Jersey Standard man, Rathbone studied chemical engineering at Lehigh, and joined Standard Oil Co. of Louisiana after graduation in 1921. He went to work in the big refinery at Baton Rouge. "Rathbone was the first man of a new wave," recalls Henry Voorhies, general manager of the refinery. "Refining oil was a combination of guesswork and art in those days. Jack was the first of a group of educated men who made refining into a science." Rathbone worked "in that old hellhole, the acid plant." Then he went into thermal cracking. "The first time I saw Jack, he was climbing up the ladder of one of the first big cracking units," recollects David Shepard, now an executive vice president of Jersey. "He seemed to be practically running up the ladder. I'll never forget the sight—there went Rathbone, climbing, climbing."

As Jersey measures time, the climb was quick. Rathbone became general superintendent of the refinery at thirty-one, and five years later was president of Standard Oil of Louisiana, the Jersey affiliate whose chief asset was the refinery. In an early test of his diplomacy, Rathbone staved off predatory attacks by Huey Long, who "customarily ran for office against Standard Oil of Louisiana." Then, in 1944, Rathbone took a big step. He left Baton Rouge, to which he now occasionally returns for a vacation at his camp on the Amite River. Taking with him a whiff of the bayous in his accent, Rathbone moved to New York to become president of Esso Standard. Five years later, he became a member of Jersey's board of directors. That took him another long stride forward—out of an operational oil company, and into the broader business of management of the empire. Five years afterward, Rathbone became the president of Jersey. Then, in May, 1960, he succeeded the late Eugene Holman as Jersey's chief executive. By then Rathbone was sixty years old.

Rathbone's accession meant many changes for Jersey. As a colleague says: "Rathbone and Holman worked closely and in harmony for many years. But it was natural that Jack should change some things—he would have been less than human if he hadn't." The first important change lay deep in the psyches of the two men. A friend who knew them both recollects that "Gene was shy and reserved. Jack is outgoing and enthusiastic. Holman solved tough problems by making the partners to the dispute work them out—he kept them coming back to him until they arrived at a compromise. Rathbone's procedure is different. He looks the situation over, figures out what's best, and proposes his solution to both parties. He may adjust it to meet their objections, and like Holman he may end up with everyone satisfied. But the solution comes initially from Rathbone." Another friend who once worked for Jersey adds: "Holman was a softer and a gentler man. He did well at stockholders' meetings, but I think they were an ordeal for him. Jack actually seems to enjoy them."

The Reorganization Man

Since becoming chief executive, Rathbone has changed Jersey's organization in various ways. Like his predecessors, he believes in the wisdom of an inside board of directors, all of whose members are full-time executives of the company. As it did before, the board still delegates most of its executive functions to the smaller executive committee. But soon after he became chief executive Rathbone changed the board's organization and direction. Before his accession, executive responsibilities were parceled out along functional lines. One director, for example, was charged with overseeing marketing, or refining, or transportation. As a collateral responsibility, the same man would oversee a group of affiliates, usually the ones whose principal activity lay within his functional province. But the system had serious deficiencies. At the joints, where the various functions dovetailed—as they did with the big integrated affiliates—Jersey's top-level responsibility tended to blur. Some directors were carrying enormously heavy loads. Others, to relieve the burden, took responsibility for some affiliates on the basis of expediency: the transportation director, for example, supervised the Scandinavian affiliates. Further, no one was looking at areas broadly enough: people thought about Brazil or Argentina, but no one was encouraged to consider the total problem of Latin America. To give a director experience in more than one function, says a Jersey man, "every couple of years we threw all the papers in the air and sat different men down at different piles. The result of it all was a dilution of the abilities and time of our top executives."

The time of dilution corresponded with a time of deluge. For Jersey was then being caught up in the flood tide of international oil surpluses, which threatened to bring down the whole fancy price structure of international oil. And, abroad, Jersey had never faced bigger or more difficult political complications. In seeking to meet those challenges, Jersey had to move swiftly in two areas. It had to search out and exploit new markets. And it had to bear down hard to reduce the per-barrel cost of oil everywhere in the world. But just when it needed most to move swiftly, Jersey found itself hamstrung by its old organizational patterns.

After he took over in May of 1960, Rathbone made some quick repairs. Atop Jersey's functional groupings Rathbone superimposed a regional grouping—"like an overlay of diagonal streets imposed upon a grid." In addition to their functional assignments, Rathbone gave some board members responsibilities as contact directors of geographic regions. Where two or more functions dovetailed, the new regional contact director now took responsibility for their coordination. The problems of new or difficult areas, like the Common Market or Latin America, could be considered as a whole. By thus breaking up the old compartmentalized approach, Rathbone did a good deal to prepare Jersey for combat in its new and tougher world. "After reorganization," explains David Shepard, "we couldn't point to a new chair or a new job title and say 'There's the answer to our need for new markets or for new economies.' It wasn't that simple. But the emphasis on regional thinking in fact enabled us to do just that."

Labors of Hercules

Other organizational changes also jelled under Rathbone. Abroad, the Standard-Vacuum Oil Co., owned 50 percent by Jersey and 50 percent by Socony Mobil Oil Co. Inc., was split up in the course of carrying out a Department of Justice consent decree late in 1960. But Jersey had been giving thought to breaking up Stan-Vac since the mid-1950's. The breakup already promises to be a blessing for Jersey, since the successor company to what was Jersey's part of Stan-Vac (Esso Standard Eastern Inc.) is proving to be more alert at exploiting new markets than was Stan-Vac, just at a time when new markets mean so much to Jersey. The dissolution of Stan-Vac called for a series of actions: the division of assets of more than $800 million; an evaluation of the worth of widely diverse markets: ("Is Laos worth more than New Zealand?"); a consideration of the tax laws of fifty countries and territories; negotiations between Jersey and Socony for the bodies of various officers. And the end result had to be satisfactory to the U.S. Justice Department. This truly Herculean job was carried out by Lloyd Elliott, a Hercules-sized executive vice president who was given wide powers by the Jersey board to get the job done. "When it came to deciding who got Thailand, and who got East Africa, I worked that out myself," says "Shorty" Elliott calmly. "I couldn't consult the board on such matters—it was just too complicated."

Rathbone himself was far more closely involved with the reorganization of the domestic companies of Jersey. In a vast maneuver, one of the biggest corporate reorganizations in history, Rathbone integrated Jersey's major regional subsidiaries (Carter, Oklahoma, Pate, Esso Standard, Humble Oil, and the chemical company Enjay) into a new Humble Oil & Refining Co.—an integrated company that has become the nation's biggest supplier of energy. This reorganization had long been close to Rathbone's heart. The result so far is summed up by Mike Wright, Jersey executive vice president who is contact director for Humble: "Putting domestic operations under one management has improved our competitive position. Individual deals by single affiliates that didn't help the general interest very much have ended. We don't have men from different companies showing up in Washington on conflicting missions. And big investment decisions, such as where to spend most of our exploration dollars, can be made with a clearer view of the total result than we ever had before." Further, sales can be made anywhere in the U.S. under one company name—Humble is already marketing in forty-five states.

These organizational moves were made with the full participation and approval of the executive committee and the board, supported by the extensive staff work of other committees. It is sometimes argued that the company is overcommitted to committees; and occasionally even its own officers feel that way: "To make a decision isn't so hard," snapped one of them recently. "After I get the facts, I can make up my mind fast. But then I have to spend more time in committee meetings explaining the whole thing." But supporters of the system, while admitting that committee work can be tedious, still believe in it. Says one: "The complexity of our business is such that committees are essential. Jersey couldn't be run by individual executives. Imagine the complications of tax laws in a dozen foreign countries, and the possibility that company action in one country could affect our tax position in another. We have a battery of experts who are paid to know about these things. It would be foolhardy for an executive to act without consulting them."

Growing up in the committee system, Rathbone learned his enormous patience. He surely must be numbered among the best listeners in American corporate life. He also acquired the self-discipline that enables him to go through his days without a trace of emotion or strain. But his greatest attribute he could never have learned in an eternity of committee meetings—his independence of mind. Everybody who walks into Rathbone's office wants to convince him of something. A certain amount of auctioneering accompanies every proposal. But Rathbone, who likes to get to the point without any small talk—with office callers he usually omits the pleasantries of greeting and parting—discounts the sales pitch. With phlegmatic determination he makes up his own mind on the facts, stripped of ribbon and lace.

Rathbone can be doggedly negative sometimes. Bill Stott, whose marketing abilities are partly responsible for Jersey's good showing, recently remarked: "I went to the board with a contract and found everyone pleased except Jack. He kept saying that the period was too long and he didn't like the price fixed so far in advance, even though it was a damned good price. Finally, he threw up his hands and said, 'O.K., go ahead if I'm outvoted.' Instead, I renegotiated. It took six months but I finally came back with the same terms over a twenty-year period instead of thirty years. I couldn't leave it that we had voted him down. It's a good example of the kind of influence he exercises."

Crude for the Customer

Around the oval table, or across the desk in his simply furnished office, Rathbone is forever passing out views and judgments to the groups who come to solicit them. In a recent discussion of outlets for crude, someone mentions that some companies are selling crude directly to customers without processing it.

Rathbone: "Where does the demand for that crude come from? Are the marketers pushing its sale or do the customers want it?" Told the customers were asking for it, Rathbone continued: "We don't want to encourage that kind of consumption. We are in the business of selling fuel oil and not selling crude for fuel oil. But let's make sure that our salesmen will sell crude, if that is what the customer wants. They can tell him the problems involved. But if the customer insists, let's make the sale rather than lose the business. We have to meet the competition, and not say 'If what you want is crude, we aren't interested.' The demand is not something we can control or change. All we can do is be prepared for it."

During long and formal sessions, the meetings sometimes drag. But Rathbone's attention never flags, and to keep others attentive, he has a helpful habit of rephrasing complicated points in simpler language: "What you're really saying is this," he will begin. In smaller groups, Rathbone may allow himself the luxury of a little doodling—tight black-and-white checkered designs, which he tosses away when his visitors leave—while he patiently hears a proposal through to the end before framing questions and making decisions. He displays no easy enthusiasm to suggested change—indeed, as what he describes as "a standard technique to keep these fellows on their mettle," he often plays the devil's advocate, pointing out all the unfavorable aspects of the proposition in front of him before giving his verdict. But in groups big or small, he is clearly in the lead, traveling over many topics, sprinkling judgments like spangles.

"A Good, Solid Figure"

Across his desk, Rathbone was explaining some aspects of Jersey's financial philosophy. "Where there is a capital market of respectable size—meaning big enough so our project won't sop up all the capital in the country—we encourage our affiliates to borrow locally. It's good business to give business to the local markets. And sometimes we can protect ourselves against inflation by borrowing locally: if you have to pay back funny money ten years from now, you're protected. But if these advantages don't enter in, and cash reserves are adequate here, our affiliates need not borrow outside. They get their money from Jersey, and they pay interest, and the amortization schedules are more flexible.

"Jersey believes in a strong cash position. In our business, it's a must. We never worry about going out of business because we think energy is here forever. But we may have serious interruptions sometimes. Our balance of cash and marketable securities is drawn up with a view to keep us from worrying when those interruptions occur. We set that balance at around $1 billion. Even considering everything that could reasonably happen, that's a good, solid figure. If we go substantially below that amount, we do something about it—perhaps reduce capital expenditures. This policy has been sharpened and clarified in recent years."

Responding to a proposal that Jersey might want to build its own office building in New York, partly because "that would be a form of diversification," Rathbone did some financial clarifying: "I don't agree. The only purpose of diversification is to get at new sources of customer money, not simply to use up our own." Aide: "But we could have our own building financed." Rathbone (shrugging): "That wouldn't make any difference to me. It doesn't change the basic point."

On how long Jersey should stay in a foreign country when politics start to go sour: "I don't doubt for a minute the wisdom of our policy of staying in business just as long as we possibly can. If we hadn't done that in the past, we wouldn't be in many places in the world today. We rode out Perón in Argentina. Things were better under Frondizi. Now there seems to be some doubt again. But we'll stay if we can."

Rathbone on Jersey's international rectitude: "Every once in a while we miss out on a concession because we won't pay a bribe for it. But we turn that kind of thing down—and not because I consider myself an especially moral man. It would make our position impossible all over the world. The oil business is full of joint ventures between companies, but in such ventures we avoid companies that we suspect may be leaning toward improper practices. We think they make bad company in the international oil world, and that after all is the world we live in. Money is heady wine for some of these poor countries, and some of these poor people. But we can't get into bribery. We've faced some hard temptations. But I'm convinced we've been absolutely right."

Muses a colleague of twenty-five years' standing: "Sometimes Jack seems hard to me. I have come away from some meetings with him sorely hurt and disappointed. He is always measuring people, testing to see if their edges jibe. Yet that tendency to measure objectively—he is an engineer with a T square—has great merit. In a company like ours, there is great involvement with wives and families. But Jack has never responded officially to what anyone's wife, not even his own, thinks of anybody else. He is a very moral, even a straitlaced man. It is impossible to think of him making a dishonest decision. For him to depart from company disciplines would be unthinkable." Adds another old friend of Rathbone: "There will never be any hidden-ball tricks while Jack is around."

The Harvest of Wisdom

To evaluate what Rathbone has done for Jersey is no easy task. The company pays him $275,000 a year for his services, but his performance cannot be weighed on so simple a scale. No man could dissipate the difficulties that confronts Jersey by means of management, however good. Jersey still faces grave competitive pressures as a result of the oil glut. The erosion of prices for crude and its products is still menacing. In foreign countries, the local people are restless. In petrochemicals, investment opportunities promising good returns are harder and harder to find. But Rathbone's emphasis on developing new markets and enforcing new economies has kept Jersey a tower of strength, in spite of all the problems. In 1959, the year before Rathbone became chief executive, Jersey earned $630 million, or $2.93 a share, on gross operating revenues of $8.7 billion. When the 1962 figures are in, *Fortune* estimates that Jersey will show earnings of around $840 million, or $3.87 a share, on gross revenues in excess of $10 billion. It looks as though, in those quarters where good management can help, Rathbone had run Jersey with telling success.

If Rathbone has a defect as an executive, it comes as an

exaggeration of a virtue. Rarely having a moment alone in his office during a working day, he habitually pores over company documents at home in the evening—too infrequently, according to associates, allowing himself the cherished pleasure of an Ian Fleming mystery. "Jack sometimes takes on too much for his own health and his own good," says a colleague. "He could, and he should, take life a little easier." Another associate agrees, but adds: "Jack basically has an engineer's mind. He's unhappy unless he's looking for new facts. He'll always do a little too much."

Rathbone himself looks back over the years with pleasure. Now sixty-two, he has less than three years to go before he retires. Even for a man like Rathbone, who had the hallmark of success on him early in his career, it took a long time to get to be Jersey's chief executive. But he believes in the thesis that you need a long time to learn the oil business. "All our directors have been with the company a great many years. These days, people seem to mature faster and learn quicker than they used to. But no whiz kid will ever run this company. Some of them are busy now wondering about how to get to the moon. If they were Jersey men, they'd be thinking ahead—wondering what to do when they got there. Working for Jersey has been a great thing for me. I've never in all these years been disappointed in this company. It's been an exhilarating experience."

How Du Pont Keeps Out in Front*_____

BY LAWRENCE LESSING

In the summer of 1962, E. I. du Pont de Nemours & Co. elected a new president, the eleventh in its hundred-and-sixty-year history. The event was solemnized around the huge, oval board table in Wilmington, under the portraits of past presidents, beginning with the Eleuthère Irénée du Pont who fled the French Revolution for the U.S. and established a gunpowder works in 1802 on the banks of Brandywine Creek near Wilmington—and also established a tradition of skilled family management almost

* December 1962

unbroken to this day. Only two presidents in the past century have not been "of the name." One was Walter S. Carpenter Jr., who served through the crowded years of World War II (1940-48) and retired last summer as board chairman; the other was his successor, Crawford H. Greenewalt (1948-62), who this year, at sixty, became chairman. Elected to the presidency was Lammot du Pont Copeland, great-great-grandson of the founder, who has inherited (through his mother, sister of the late Pierre, Irénée, and Lammot du Pont) and returned to the office the square, vigorous, big-boned features of this prolific family.

Thus, with a historic demonstration of continuity almost unique in U.S. industry, the largest chemical company in the world faces the challenges of the second half of its second century. The challenges are considerable. For Du Pont and the industry are entering in many ways a new and difficult era of chemical development. It is an era in which Du Pont's strategies must allow for sharpening competition, the spread of technological sophistication, and new balances of world trade. More than ever before, the company will need solutions to all the problems of bigness. When *Fortune* last looked at Du Pont in October, 1950, in a five-part series of articles, it had just passed the $1-billion mark in annual sales; this year it is pressing toward $2.5 billion.

To stay on top in the new era, Du Pont has a strategy—or rather, it has two strategies. For much of its expansion it will depend on a massive assault on lush foreign markets. At home, where the market looks a lot less lush than it used to, Du Pont will work on the pinpoint development of individual markets.

The Figures That Matter at Du Pont

There is a plausible case to be made that the chemical industry is leveling off to a plateau of sales, earnings, and growth more nearly in line with that of older, more mature industries (see "Chemicals: The Ball Is Over," *Fortune*, October, 1961). Through the Forties and early Fifties, chemicals grew at a rate faster than that of all other industry. Earnings ran to about 20 percent of sales before taxes and were used to finance the unremitting plant expansion and heavy research on which all the growth depended. It was a fairly small, compact industry to begin with, and had such high technical standards for entry and so much undeveloped territory that the pioneers rarely encroached on one another. Competition within the industry was nominal and gentlemanly. But following the technical explosion of World War II, and attracted by high profits, nearly everyone and his brother seemed to be getting into chemicals, led by the big oil companies and including representatives from the distillery, aircraft, utility, and machinery industries, and even W. R. Grace, the shipping line. In the classic pattern, overcapacities began to appear, and sharp price cutting and internal competition assailed the industry. *Chemical & Engineering News* estimates, in a recent study of ten of the industry's leading companies, that price cutting since 1952 cost the industry at least $3 billion in sales; roughly half of this may be considered lost profits. Since 1955, when many indexes peaked, industry margins have dropped to 13.6 percent before taxes. Dollar sales in 1955-62 grew at an average of 5.5 percent a year, only a little over a point above the rate for all manufacturing. Though sales this year are rising sharply to about $33 billion, some are ready to write chemicals off as a growth industry.

The more optimistic view of the industry holds that, after unparalleled growth in a relatively short period, it has just paused, for the first time, to digest a lot of new elements. This is more likely to be an interruption than a leveling off. Some of the more narrowly based, ill-conceived, hasty excursions into chemicals may be dissolved in a painful shake-out. Even some of the giants may feel a certain temporary and localized constriction. And profit margins may never be quite so fat as they once were. But, the industry's optimists believe, the dynamic nature of the chemical sciences is such that major discoveries are always in prospect, and one or two of them could get the industry to exceed even the growth rates of its immediate past. Chemicals, like other new technological industries, are not bound by the old nineteenth-century patterns of industrial growth.

Applying growth percentages to a billion-dollar corporation like Du Pont can be an interesting but not entirely meaningful exercise. When Walter Carpenter passed the presidency to Greenewalt in 1948, he sportively pointed out that it was a tradition for each Du Pont president to double the business of his predecessor. Annual sales than stood at $783 million, and at the end of Greenewalt's long tenure sales were almost exactly tripled. However, Greenewalt refrained last summer from passing on the same challenge to Copeland. At $2.2 billion, doubling sales obviously begins to get difficult.

Copeland's first year has been a good one for Du Pont. Sales this year will be about 10 percent above 1961, much of it from the intensive development of new markets. And Du Pont pretax earnings from operations, which have declined since 1955 from 30 to about 23 percent of sales, still far above the industry average, will be up sharply this year, probably to a healthy all-time record of around $600 million.

The figure that really matters at Du Pont is another index, the return on investment—which Du Pont defines as net earnings from operations on total current assets and plant, i.e., not counting the G.M. investment. And by this standard DuPont has performed brilliantly over the last decade, and the one before that too. It has averaged a remarkable 10 percent return. "I don't think any apology has to be made for how Du Pont has done in this period," says Greenewalt, in modest understatement. "To show the growth we've shown and to maintain a rate of return around 10 percent takes some doing."

Furthermore, despite all talk of overcapacity, there is no letup in new investment, on which Du Pont fully expects to earn its usual return. One of Lammot du Pont Copeland's first acts as president was to confirm record capital expenditures for 1963 of something over $300 million—not just to set a record, he carefully explained, but simply to take care of Du Pont's regular round of plant improvements and requirements for new products and processes, which happened to reach a peak this year. Since 1955 capital expenditures have averaged $200 million a year, and for the rest of this decade they may average $225 million to $250 million. Obviously Du Pont is not operating on the premise that this is a leveling-off industry.

Chapter Four: It's Getting Harder

Du Pont is now setting out on what may be thought of as the fourth phase in its long history. The first phase lasted roughly throughout its first century. Du Pont then was based wholly on gunpowder and explosives, becoming the biggest explosives combine of its day in the settling of the new republic. In this primitive phase of the enterprise, industries were conceived as operating on a single, stable, almost immutable line of products. It ended for Du Pont in 1912 with the historic antitrust decree that broke up the company into three separate entities (Du Pont, Hercules Powder, and Atlas Powder) and strengthened its determination, undertaken some time before, to get into other lines in the then budding chemical industry.

The second phase, therefore—roughly from 1910 to 1930—

was marked by diversification through acquisition and merger. Striking out logically from its nitrocellulose base, Du Pont acquired a host of smaller companies to give it a position in paints and finishes, dyes and pigments, acids and heavy chemicals, cellulose plastics and coated textiles, and, through rights purchased from France's Comptoir des Textiles Artificiels, in rayon and cellophane. Also, between 1917 and 1919, Du Pont put some $50 million into the early General Motors Corp., an investment that, with later additions, came to represent 23 percent of G.M. stock, today worth something over $3 billion.

The third phase began toward the end of the Twenties when Du Pont initiated a broad, farsighted program in basic research, signaling the end of its growth through acquisition and the beginning of growth through internal development. In this period, extending down to the present, the mainspring of the modern business became innovation. While the acquisitions gave Du Pont a broad base and a background in established markets, on which applied research soon built many improvements and a structure bigger than the whole of Du Pont before the breakup, basic research into the internal molecular structure of matter gave Du Pont its most spectacular growth. Out of this came neoprene, the first U.S. commercial synthetic rubber, nylon, the first all-synthetic fiber, and an endless stream of new products with which Du Pont moved out well ahead of the competition and became a noted developer of new markets.

The new phase of development is likely to be a period of intensive consolidation and intense competition. This period began with another big antitrust jolt. Belatedly, last year, the courts decided that Du Pont's holding of G.M. stock, some of which it had owned for over forty years, was wrong. Du Pont had fought the suit hard for thirteen years. First it had fought for the right to retain this investment; then, as the decisions went against it, it argued for a plan of divestiture that would not involve excessive taxes (and massive dumping of Du Pont stock to pay them). Last July, Du Pont began the divestiture by distributing about a third of its 63 million G.M. shares to stockholders (the rest must be disposed of by 1965), under remedial legislation that reduced the tax penalty by designating the stock a return of capital. A large penalty will fall on Christiana Securities Co., holder of du Pont family investments, for which a different tax base was worked out. Christiana's total tax bill may run around $65 million.

As it happens, this mammoth divestiture will have almost no effect on Du Pont's own operations or financial position. For years the G.M. investment has been carefully segregated in Du Pont's balance sheet and all income from it has been passed directly to stockholders. The only major effect of the divestiture might be to reduce Du Pont's dividend. So far in this booming year, however, quarterly dividends have been running along at usual $1.50 per share, and the total at year's end, when G.M. earnings are paid over, is not likely to be much under last year's record $7.50 per share.

A Strategy for Continuing Growth

There is no doubt, however, that Du Pont is operating in a business climate far more competitive than any it has seen in the past. Whereas only a decade ago Du Pont was the only major chemical producer of all-synthetic textile fibers, today there are seven companies making nylon yarn (one of them, Chemstrand Corp., was inducted into the business by Du Pont itself), four others making polyester fibers, and six others in acrylics and modified acrylics—all major new fibers pioneered by Du Pont. A decade ago Du Pont and Union Carbide were the pioneer U.S. producers of polyethylene, the biggest postwar plastic; today there are over twenty companies in the business. Du Pont will continue to come up with new products, of course. But the long lead time on which it could once count to cash in on such products is dwindling, as more competitors gain the research resources to move in fast on anything new and drive prices down. And while opportunities to exploit new products are shrinking, the cost of discovering them is rising. Lammot Copeland laconically sums up this new climate as one in which "it's getting harder to make a dollar"—but one in which Du Pont shows no diminishing talent for making it.

Always ready to recognize the facts of life, Du Pont has been wheeling and changing with the times. But the corporation's basic institutions seem admirably suited to the stresses of the new era. In its tradition of management, under which presidents have resigned at sixty or earlier and executive replacements are ready in depth all down the line, Du Pont ensures great flexibility and resourcefulness. Around the new president is an executive committee that has been almost completely renewed since 1950, with the last of its older members, Henry B. du Pont, due to retire next summer.[1] The operating departments have risen in number from ten to twelve in the same period, and, with only two exceptions, they have a fresh set of general managers. Meanwhile, moving steadily up the line is other executive talent, including younger, eligible du Ponts, a fair representative being Irénée du Pont Jr., engineer and currently assistant production manager in the Film Department.

The elevation of a new president brings no great change, for it is the executive committee that really runs Du Pont. Indeed, Lammot Copeland, who had been a member of the executive committee since 1959, participated in making most of the policies that he now implements as the committee's chairman. The committee operates in a way that is deliberative, democratic, and almost timeless and unique to Du Pont. The president as chairman has only one vote on this committee, and he is surrounded by members who have moved up from the operating departments, engineering, and research. All but one on the present committee hold degrees in chemistry or engineering (Copeland himself holds a degree in industrial chemistry from Harvard), and they bring to the task technical or research-oriented backgrounds in Du Pont. Each sits as adviser to the departments in some broad area, such as research, engineering, finance, or sales, but none can issue orders on the operational level to any department. The operating departments run their own businesses, each as big as or bigger than many individual companies in the industry. And that is Du Pont as it has long continued to run.

Financially, Du Pont works from an equally flexible position in depth. Du Pont, of course, is financially something of a phenomenon. It has had no debt whatever since the early Twenties (when it borrowed $30 million for one of its G.M. stock purchases), and it finances all expansions and capital expenditures out of earnings, while still turning over some 80 percent of net income to dividends. To the argument that it would be cheaper to borrow, it has always turned a deaf ear. Its cash and short-term marketable securities available to meet contingencies run along

---

[1] Present executive committee: Lammot du Pont Copeland, chairman; T. Crawley Davis, up from treasurer; David H. Dawson, up from the Textile Fibers Department and research; Henry B. du Pont, up from the Engineering Department; Robert L. Hershey, up from the Plastics Department; George E. Holbrook, up from the Elastomer Chemicals Department; Samuel Lenher, up from the Organic Chemicals Department; Charles B. McCoy, up from the Explosives, Elastomer Chemicals, and Electrochemicals departments.

at some $350 million year in and year out. And its average oper-
ating investment per employee (total: 90,000) now stands at an
estimated $37,000.

Its financial conservatism is related to a broad, deeply rooted
policy of restraint in pursuing growth. Du Pont never pursues
growth just for its own sake. It does not as a general rule, for
instance, "integrate backward" to raw materials, as others have
been doing, except where it is demonstrably profitable to do so,
preferring in general to keep flexible by buying basic chemicals
outside. And Du Pont does not venture into new products unless
it has thoroughly explored the markets for them. Unlike the rest
of a largely production-oriented industry, built up in the past
mainly on basic chemicals, Du Pont has been market-oriented
from the beginning of its earliest modern phase. "Growth per se
is meaningless," says Crawford Greenewalt. "Rather, it's a question of soundness and worth." And for Du Pont, soundness means
hewing to the line of a 10 percent return on investment.

To maintain this in today's harsher competitive and economic
situations obviously requires an extraordinary efficiency, and Du
Pont never stops trying to rationalize its operations still further.
To keep costs down and ahead of competition, it has kept plants,
processes, and engineering up to new heights of technological
efficiency. It has just completed a total modernization of its
sulfuric acid plants. The largest chunk of the current construction
program, some $70 million, will go to a new nylon raw-material
plant in Louisiana and to improvements in other nylon plants at
Seaford, Delaware, and Martinsville, Virginia, which have been
expanded and practically rebuilt at least six times since their
openings in 1939 and 1942. At the same time, Du Pont has hard-
headedly closed out businesses that no longer pay. It has shut
down all but one of its black-powder plants, the product that
started the business, while explosives generally are down from
less than 10 percent of sales in 1950 to less than 3 percent today.
And by next June, Du Pont will have closed down all operations
in rayon, the product that provided its start and mastery in synthetic textile fibers, and that became the biggest operating department in the company. Lopping it off was a great sentimental
wrench, but it was lopped off all the same.

The company has also worked hard on several organizational
efficiencies. Within the past year Du Pont has set up a Consumer
Products Division to consolidate and strengthen the development
and marketing of consumer products. It has set up a New Ventures Division to cull promising new businesses from the interplay

of products and processes in its regular operating departments. (The first new venture to come out of the division was a line of analytical and control instruments developed for the company's own processes, and now ready to be sold outside.) Du Pont also has bought a minority interest in a small Massachusetts electronics firm, Block Engineering, Inc., which is especially strong in infrared technology. And Du Pont has been tightening and deploying the organization of its industrial departments—stripping Plastics down to the single interest of plastics production, separating out Elastomer Chemicals—for a more concentrated attack on broad market areas.

But in a company that is already as well organized as Du Pont, the payoff on new efficiencies is necessarily limited. Any larger payoffs must await the results of Du Pont's big new move abroad and its new strategic approach to the U.S. market.

The Big Common Market Adventure

Until the mid-Fifties, Du Pont's foreign business never amounted to much more than 6 percent of total sales. This was made up mainly from licensing fees, some exports, one Mexican explosives plant, and three joint ventures with Britain's Imperial Chemical Industries, Ltd., in Argentina, Brazil, and Canada. (These joint ventures were struck down in 1954 by another antitrust action.) Du Pont's hands, capital, and skills were too preoccupied with exploiting the vast U.S. markets. But as those markets began to reach a high state of development, and with mammoth growth in the U.S. increasingly likely to get antitrust attention, Du Pont suddenly picked up interest in the foreign field. Decisive to its new interest was the remarkable growth of the European Common Market, which finally created markets, previously repressed by national boundaries, large enough to fit Du Pont's mass-production skills. In 1958, Du Pont set up a full-scale International Department. Today it has thirty-five foreign plants in thirteen countries, employing close to 16,000 people, with a total investment of $320 million. Total foreign sales this year are estimated at some $400 million—i.e., over 15 percent of Du Pont's total, and greater than the total sales of the entire company in 1940. The total foreign operating investment is climbing at the rate of 12 to 15 percent a year.

Du Pont has moved especially fast in Europe; from nothing in 1958, the European investment has shot up to $100 million. The company started in 1956 with a decision to build a neoprene plant in Northern Ireland, completed in 1960, and since then has been moving into Holland (Orlon, Delrin plastics, and Lycra spandex fiber), Belgium (paints and finishes), France (herbicides, isocyanates), Germany (pigments), Sweden (paints), and Spain (fungicides). A central sales and export company also has been set up in Switzerland. Some of these plants are owned wholly, others in partnership. This fall Du Pont wholly acquired Germany's Adox Fotowerke, employing some 2,000 persons, to give it a strong European base in photographic products. In addition, it took over its half of the joint I.C.I. companies in Latin America and Canada, has added companies in Mexico and Venezuela, and has entered into two new joint companies in Japan, one in polyethylene, the other in neoprene. And expansion is in progress in all these foreign areas, from Europe to the Far East, to the tune of $10 million to $20 million each.

One reason for Du Pont's speed is that it was behind other U.S. chemical companies in moving into foreign markets. Another reason is that the European market has been growing so lustily; it became clear that if Du Pont did not get into plant construction on certain of its products, then others, particularly the Germans, would. Since Du Pont has no patent preemption on most of these products, it has had to move even faster than it would in the U.S. Competition in the Common Market is no less fierce than it is at home.

So far, Du Pont's foreign manufacture, which is wholly for foreign sales, has not tended to cut down its exports; rather surprisingly, the reverse is true. Du Pont has found that when a new plant is first announced for a country, there is a surge of export business, with customers' interest in a product whetted by the knowledge that it will later be available locally. In the case of its neoprene plant in Northern Ireland, for example, Du Pont found that, in the period between announcement and completion of the plant, the volume of its neoprene exports to the United Kingdom exceeded the cost of the plant two or three times over. Furthermore, exports hold up well even after the new plant is built. Du Pont's explanation is that the new organization abroad has a base for an effective sales effort that can move products besides those manufactured there. The payoff has been dramatic: while most of Du Pont's rise in foreign sales this year is from its new plants, export volume also is up over 1961.

As exports approach a volume at which further foreign manufacture becomes justified, total exports may yet be cut. But the bigger base thus secured will still leave a net gain for Du Pont.

"It's like having another whole new U.S. market open up," one executive-committee member says. It is a market for products whose big costs—i.e., development, processes, and plant designs—have already been incurred in the U.S., so that the returns on investment abroad are healthy.

Du Pont is understandably excited and bullish about its foreign adventures. It has engineers carefully investigating new products, locations, and markets over the world. One area it is seriously looking at is India, another is Australia, and it even has some ideas cooking in Africa. "It's fantastic," says the new International Department's general manager, W. Sam Carpenter III, son of the former president, "the range of places and things we can go to and do."

The Battle on the Brandywine

Meanwhile, back on the banks of the Brandywine, Du Pont is pressing the much more complex battle of U.S. markets no less vigorously. The frontal attack is on synthetic fibers, plastics, films, and rubbers, which together account for some 50 to 60 percent of its business. This, indeed, is the heart of the business, not only economically but chemically, for all four of these product divisions are essentially plastics or resins in different physical forms. (Nylon, for instance, is both a filament for gossamer hosiery and a solid for tough, abrasion-resistant gears.) All four are based on the great discovery of the Thirties, in which Du Pont played a leading role, of the means of putting together big, long-chain molecules or superpolymers, a discovery that accounts for most of modern chemistry's spectacular growth.

The situation today is not simply that there are more competitive companies in polymer chemistry, but that there are many more competitive molecules or products within the industry itself, created by the amazing versatility of chemical synthesis. Historically, the role of chemistry has been the replacement of natural products, and this is still the major competitive battleground. But now, with half a dozen major families of synthetic fibers in production, and over a dozen families of plastics and films, there is a great overlapping of properties, a great many applications in common, so that the scramble has sharpened considerably within the synthetics themselves. For instance, competing with cellophane today are a host of polyvinyl, polyethylene, polyester, and polypropylene films, unrelated chemically, all of which Du Pont itself makes to maintain a broad base in films. This is called "supplantive competition," on a functional rather than a chemical basis, and it is increasingly rough.

Du Pont's strategy is to press on to new refinements of specialization, tailoring the basic-product molecule to specific end uses, to ensure a place above the competitive ruck. Take nylon, for instance. Twenty-three years after its introduction, it remains the star of Du Pont's market creations, with over thirty types of nylon filament and yarn developed for specific uses. Among them is a range of "BFC" nylons, specifically developed for loop-pile carpeting, overcoming "pilling" and other drawbacks, which since 1958 has opened wide the rug market to nylon. And a new development in tirecord yarn puts nylon in position to bid for the original-equipment market (it already has a big part of the replacement market) by eliminating its tendency to "flat spotting" when tires stand too long. (Much the same sort of pinpoint market development is going on in Du Pont's other major fibers, Orlon acrylic and Dacron polyester.) Hence, contrary to the impression of some that it is a product long past its youth, nylon is still among the biggest of Du Pont's products in volume and earnings, and is still growing.

The Boiling Pot of Polyolefins

The same intensive development is going on in Du Pont's biggest plastic, polyethylene, which will reach a volume of close to 400 million pounds next year. The polyethylene market offers a good example of the present uneven state of industry capacity, as well as of the sharp infighting of supplantive competition. Polyethylene shows the most precipitous growth of all plastics since World War II, up to around two billion pounds this year. A waxy, supple, versatile material, it is the leading member of a growing class of plastics called polyolefins, derived from relatively cheap and plentiful petroleum gases, which is what has attracted over twenty producers into the business. It is rolling in overcapacities, with prices ranging from around 14 cents a pound for off-grades to about 36 cents a pound for high-quality material. Conventional or high-pressure polyethylene, the first type in the business, is relatively in balance, but some overcapacity is disturbing linear or low-pressure polyethylene.

Complicating the situation since 1957 is the entry into the market of polypropylene, a close polyolefin relative of polyethylene, with many similar properties and uses, which currently is staggering under a large overcapacity. Seeing the spectacular growth of polyethylene (1961 sales: $1.6 billion), some producers and financial writers jumped on polypropylene as the next big, glamorous "growth" plastic, with special advantages for films, rug and rope filaments, and a new textile fiber. Today some 450 million pounds of annual capacity has been built in polypropylene, spread among more than half a dozen producers, led by Hercules Powder Co. and including a foreign invader, Novamont Corp., wholly owned subsidiary of Italy's Montecatini, early developer and promoter of polypropylene. But for 1962 polypropylene sales will be only about 140 million pounds—a mere 30 percent of capacity—and no one yet has made a profit.

Du Pont thinks this is a fantastic situation. It makes no polypropylene of its own at present, though it has been doing basic work on it since 1954. Instead, it is buying small quantities of the plastic from Hercules for resale, in a cautious attempt to find its right niche in the fast-moving polyolefin market, which is bursting with still other developments. Polypropylene, though superior to polyethylene in some applications, such as special packaging films, has certain disadvantages, the chief one being its cold-brittleness, which has kept it out of containers, a major polyethylene field. And as a fiber, polypropylene not only has some technical difficulties still to be solved, but it is yet to enter the most costly phase of textile development. It is a situation to be watched, however, and Du Pont has a wary eye on it. This fall it plunked down, as a challenge and a test, a basic catalytic patent in polypropylene, which it believes covers all present production. In the uproar that followed, Montecatini calmly announced a $26-million expansion and development of its U.S. subsidiary.

Du Pont elected to stay with polyethylene, and to keep its head above the situation by intensive market development. It now has over fifty types of polyethylene. In coating resins alone, for bonding protective films to paper, boxboard, metal foils, and the like, it has fourteen different types, each fitted to a particular application. Among them is a new plastic coating for milk cartons, which is replacing wax and rapidly taking over the business, estimated for Du Pont and others at some 130 million pounds a year by 1965. This is the kind of mass marketing—supplying an improved wisp of material to a universal commodity—that Du Pont likes to get into. At Parkersburg, West Virginia, where the rest of Du Pont's plastics are made—the Lucites (acrylics), Zytels (nylons), Butacites (polyvinyl butyral for safety glass), Teflons (fluorocarbons), and newest Delrins (polyformaldehydes)—a big computer is required to juggle production schedules for over 100 basic types and 2,700 formulations. All plastics are still growing in volume at a rate of 12 to 15 percent a year, and Du Pont is getting its share.

The Duel Over Delrin

No matter how fast and smartly Du Pont moves, however, it can no longer count on enjoying a new market alone for very long. The industry, which has been heavily based on production of basic chemicals in the past, is rapidly shifting to follow Du Pont's lead in market orientation and development. If nylon were invented today, for instance, it would not have clear sailing for about fifteen years—as it did—but for something less than ten. Du Pont introduced its new plastic Delrin in commercial quantities in 1960, and only two years later Celanese Corp. jumped in with Celcon, a plastic arrived at by a slightly different route but much the same as Delrin. And in even shorter time than that, only about a year after Du Pont introduced Lycra—a yarn with unusual elastic-like properties built into its molecule, now moving in on the girdle, bra, and swimsuit trade—the company found itself facing a half-dozen competitors.

Delrin is the classic story of the industry in these changed times. It took over ten years and $10 million in research and technical development, including three years spent in careful market evaluation—exploring over 500 end uses in cooperation with some 250 companies—to get Delrin into production; the total development cost was some $50 million. The comparable cost for nylon was $27 million. Yet Delrin, a tough, high-strength plastic for replacing metals in many applications, is not another nylon so far as volume is concerned. It is an engineering plastic for specialized uses. The estimated market is some 200 million pounds a year by 1970, all of which Du Pont might have expected to supply in a happier day. When Celanese announced its entry, Du Pont almost immediately slapped down a patent-infringement suit. The polymerization of formaldehyde had been attempted unsuccessfully for many years in many laboratories, and in doing it first Du Pont believes that it has a clear priority in composition, covering all methods. Celanese says it too had been working on its material independently for a long time. Du Pont's strong feelings about the case have been reflected in the tough new patent policy adopted to protect its innovations. The company may, if successful, exact royalties, collect damages, or shut down Celanese's operation entirely, as a warning to others. For, if three or four producers were to get into polyformaldehyde, Du Pont maintains, it would not be a profitable business.

Meanwhile, Du Pont, with at least two years' headstart and some 30 million pounds in plant capacity, has been busy cultivating Delrin's market. As sales developed, it rapidly cut prices from 95 to 65 cents a pound to widen markets still further. So far, with the biggest share of polyformaldehyde sales, running this year to well over 15 million pounds, Delrin is developing about as projected. It is gaining new commercial uses at a rate of about two a day, mainly in replacement of die-cast zinc, aluminum, and brass.

In addition, Du Pont has taken an entirely new tack in development. After arduous extension of Delrin's tough, corrosion-resistant properties, it has just built a new plant in Tulsa, Oklahoma, where Delrin pipe will be extruded for the oil and gas utilities fields. And Du Pont is building a plant in Holland that, until it is backed up with chemical production, will take Delrin polymer from the U.S. and extrude it into rods, sheets, tubes, and other finished shapes. Ten years ago Du Pont would never have carried a product like this into the finished state, for it was a fixed policy to stop short and allow others to develop end markets. This is still the general policy—Du Pont could hardly afford to get embroiled in such big, well-established industries as textile weaving or automotive parts—but the exception is significant of the competitive times.

The Troops of Research

To keep up this pace over an immense range of products, Du Pont pours in supporting research and development on a scale that few competitors can match. Indeed, the weight of this kind of research and development grew so great, tending to distort Du Pont's reporting of what is regards strictly as basic research, that three years ago it decided to separate all of its research into two categories in order to simplify accounting. The first and still primary area, now designated pioneering research, is devoted to the discovery of new knowledge, new products and processes, pursued entirely separately from the going business; this is running along at some $60 million a year. The second category, called supporting research, is the improvement and market development of established products and processes, closely tied to industrial operations; it is not reported separately, but it easily exceeds the primary-research budget.

The new concentration on supporting research is visible in a $20-million technical-service laboratory complex that has risen on a campus site at Chestnut Run, near Wilmington, since 1954. Here eight operating departments now have laboratory buildings loaded, not with test tubes, but with all the types of production machinery used in the industries their products serve. On this equipment new products are tried out and their deficiencies defined, new uses are developed for existing products, new manufacturing processes are explored, new markets are evaluated, and customers are aided without charge in solving the problems of using and developing Du Pont products in new businesses.

Chestnut Run is Du Pont's insurance in navigating the increasingly costly, competitive, volatile, and hazardous currents of market development. That the risks can be high was illustrated just before the first technical-service laboratory arose—the Textile Research Laboratory—when Du Pont made one of its few big market miscalculations. In 1951 the first Orlon plant, designed to produce continuous filament, was barely completed at Camden, South Carolina, at a cost of $15 million when the company realized that the fiber was too silky to succeed as a rugged outdoor and industrial fabric, the markets for which it was projected. The filament piled up in warehouses, and the plant was finally shut down completely in 1956. Fortunately, however, Du Pont had a second Orlon plant in process, completed in 1952, designed to make staple or short fibers. And staple proved to be a whirlwind in sweaters and knitwear, the acrylics, all told, capturing same 50 to 60 percent of the market. While it is still trying hard to develop other markets for Orlon, Du Pont has nimbly run its staple capacity up from 30 million to some 120 million pounds a year.

All this has engendered a slight shift in Du Pont's research viewpoint. There is naturally more research of all kinds—the population of the central Experimental Station, fountainhead of pioneering research, has gone up in ten years from 2,600 to 3,300, of whom 1,143 are scientists or technicians—but, to keep on innovating, Du Pont has had to turn more attention to smaller research gains. "You can't count only on the great big developments to keep you profitable and healthy," says Greenewalt. "They're damned important, but the unsung smaller and more numerous research accomplishments are what make your business grow and prosper."

Probing for New Markets

Nevertheless, Du Pont keeps moving on ever newer markets. Nothing as big as nylon is yet on the horizon. Nylon was a great basic discovery, the first conscious design of long-chain polymers, and such coups do not come frequently. Moreover, when a market becomes as well developed as the synthetic fibers are, with a broad choice of available types and properties, it becomes harder and harder to develop a new material. Du Pont has examined—and continues to examine—thousands of possible fibers without yet seeing one unusual enough to warrant the tremendous investment needed to get it into textiles. Still, synthetic fibers have captured only about a third of the total textile market, and plenty of opportunities remain, particularly in the huge domain of cotton used for sheeting and the like. Plastics have only begun to cut into the building and construction fields with materials of any stature or volume. And the whole exciting field of biochemistry is still largely frontier.

In a dozen directions, Du Pont is always probing with new products to find new markets. It has just announced a multi-million-dollar plant, scheduled for completion in 1964 at Old Hickory, Tennessee, to make a new plastic material, already widely market-tested, to compete with leather in shoe uppers of all kinds. A "poromeric" or breathing material, closely resembling natural leather in feel and appearance, it probes the kind of mass market Du Pont seeks. The company plans to enter the amateur photographic-film market for the first time next year with a new color film, to be distributed by Bell & Howell.

Du Pont is in production in Baltimore on a new high-temperature alloy known as TD nickel for jet engines, rockets, spacecraft, and process equipment. This is based on the discovery that dispersal of thoria or other oxides uniformly through the crystal structure of such metals as nickel, copper, aluminum, cobalt, iron, tungsten, and molybdenum markedly increases their operating strength at high temperatures—in the case of nickel, tripling or quadrupling the strength of 2,400° F. It also is producing new columbium alloys for space use with useful strengths above 2,500° F. And it has new high-temperature nylon, polyolefin, and Teflon plastics of remarkable strength coming out of development, mainly for space, but available later for entirely new developments in buildings, appliances, pipe, and structures of all kinds.

On the Unending Frontier

Not to be neglected is the pioneering research from which new products flow. Out of it recently, for example, has come a new discovery in magnetism: it was shown that a brittle, gray manganese antimonide compound becomes magnetic as temperature rises above a precisely determined point, contrary to the pattern of all other known magnetic materials. And out of Du Pont's increasing interest in the biological sciences have come two even more recent discoveries. One is the separating out of nitrogen-fixing chemicals from bacteria and a demonstration of the processes by which living cells create nitrogen compounds, the building blocks of all life and growth. The other discovery is of compounds that uniquely short-circuit the energy-transfer systems of living cells, as in photosynthesis, the process by which green plants synthesize starches and grow. Out of this may eventually come new, highly specific weed killers, insecticides, or drugs, nontoxic to other forms of life.

What the industry's gloomy analysts do not yet understand is that there is literally no end to these scientific discoveries, from which new developments and products will come, and hence there is no end to growth. Discoveries cannot be ordered or scheduled, much less imagined beforehand by the practical and literal-minded; but to the receptive they come. Du Pont might easily double its present size by the early Seventies, given a climate in which bigness per se is not considered evil. "It would be footless to try to say what our sales will be in the future," says the eminently pragmatic Crawford Greenewalt, "but I would predict that our health will be excellent."

Textron: How To Manage a Conglomerate*

BY STANLEY H. BROWN

A Textron executive named Jerome Ottmar left his house in Attleboro, Massachusetts, one day recently and set out on what

* April 1964

was, for him, a routine business trip. He began by flying to a Textron plant in Gastonia, North Carolina, where he looked over some production equipment installed to manufacture a new chain saw. The next morning he drove with the Gastonia production manager across the state border to Greer, South Carolina, where the company has another plant. He talked with the manager there, and inspected facilities in which the company makes outboard motors and portable pumps and generators. Later that day he flew on to Augusta, Georgia, where Textron makes electric golf cars, for another fast conference. Toward the end of the day Ottmar flew down to Boca Raton, Florida, to visit a vacationing division president. Over the weekend they talked business, played golf, and then went to Boynton Beach, for a look at the company's marine-engine test station. On Monday morning Ottmar flew into New York for a meeting with the head of the company division that produces cold-flow metal parts and fasteners. They considered the possibility of a European venture and explored some licensing problems that would involve. Ottmar spent part of the next day at his desk in Providence, Rhode Island, where the company has its headquarters. Providence is only a forty-minute drive from Attleboro, but Ottmar never did get home that night. Instead, he dined in Boston with some investment bankers who wanted a line on Textron's stock. The next day he flew to Montreal to help the management of one of Textron's Canadian companies with some plants to buy land and build a chain saw, pump, and generator plant that will replace three others. That took the better part of two days, and Ottmar didn't get back home until Thursday night. The next day he was off again, this time to Springfield, Vermont, where Textron had just bought a major machine-tool maker. He met the president of the new unit and also the head of an older Textron division that makes machine tools. Together they began to discuss the delicate subject of eliminating duplicate products.

As all these problems and industries forcibly suggest, Ottmar works for a most unusual corporation. Actually, he is one of only three executive vice presidents; together they oversee twenty-seven separate divisions and 113 plants. Although Textron is still often thought of as the textile company founded by the famous entrepreneur, Royal Little, it is now completely out of textiles and in so many other lines that it cannot be identified by any one of them. Its most important single product is helicopters; the Bell Helicopter division, in Fort Worth, sold more than $100 million of them last year, principally the UH-1 for Army use in Vietnam. But helicopters represented less than 20 percent of sales, the rest being distributed over such wildly dissimilar products as chicken feed, chain saws, and something called the Identi-Kit, a device by which witnesses to a crime help police create a picture of the criminal by putting together separate eyes, noses, hairlines, etc. A sampling of Textron's other products would reveal its wide diversification. It may doubtless be viewed as the biggest conglomerate in U.S. industry.

Managing Textron is a unique business problem, but the job is done by only a handful of executives at headquarters in Providence. Headed by Rupert C. Thompson Jr., chairman and chief executive officer, Textron's supervisory and staff executives work in a small, simple suite of offices that look more like, say, the local branch office of a medium-sized insurance company than the executive offices of one of the largest U.S. industrials. There are, for example, no data-processing machines at headquarters (although several divisions have them); instead, Textron relies on plain old black loose-leaf binders, filled with budgets, reports, and forecasts of the operating divisions.

The Assorted Diversifiers

Thompson himself bristles at the word "conglomerate," with which, he says, his first and only association is "mess." (He suggests "non-related diversification.") His sensitivity seems to reflect a widespread feeling that Textron actually was something of a mess in years past. The present company was put together out of more than fifty different large and small corporate entities, and its direction has changed more than once. To understand its present character, it may be useful to contrast Textron with some other diversified corporations.

Some degree of diversification is, of course, the rule among big corporations these days, and has been for some time. General Motors was making locomotives, refrigerators, and oil heaters decades ago; it also controlled Eastern Air Lines for a time in the 1930's. Bendix and Borg-Warner, to name two other long-established companies with broad product lines, were originally conceived in mergers and went on to diversify further. But in these and most other such corporations, there has been a limit: the diverse units either have made minor contributions to total sales or else have been closely related to the company's original products, technology, or markets.

In the postwar years there have been some special pressures and temptations to diversify. High corporate income-tax rates gave profitable companies a strong incentive to buy ventures with tax losses (and vice versa). The trend of antitrust enforcement has made it difficult for many corporations to expand in their own industries; Ford, for example, presumably felt much freer to buy Philco in 1961 than it would have to buy, say, Studebaker. The moves of W. R. Grace and National Distillers into chemicals were typical of those inspired by concern that the original business had only routine prospects. Some immensely profitable corporations have diversified simply because their original business could not absorb their mounting reserves of investible cash—e.g., Kern County Land (which went into auto parts), Gillette (into home permanents and ball-point pens). Neither of these companies has abandoned its major product lines, however.

More like Textron in this respect is Philadelphia & Reading, which got out of its original business altogether in 1961, when it sold its remaining anthracite operations. After nearly a decade of buying, selling, and backing new ventures, the company is now largely in apparel, boots, and toys. (P. & R., of course, doesn't hold a candle to Textron in number of products.) Glen Alden is another old anthracite producer that set off in new directions. Now run by Albert List, a onetime textile-mill liquidator turned conglomerator, Glen Alden still has some coal mines, but the company is also heavily in textiles, movie theatres (the RKO chain), warehousing, and tanning.

Philadelphia & Reading and Glen Alden have been profitable, but many conglomerates have not; they have been put together by men like Meshulam Riklis (See "Who's to Blame for Riklis— Riklis?" *Fortune*, October, 1963) and Leopold Silberstein, whose talent lay in thin-equity deals rather than in management. At its peak, Riklis' conglomerate included a chain of more than 1,300 stores, an electrotype maker, orange groves, children's wear makers, and a plastic-bag producer. Silberstein's Penn-Texas, later renamed Fairbanks Whitney (the present management is proposing still another change, to Colt Industries), has been unprofitable almost from the beginning, and has, like Riklis' Rapid-American, been buried under the heavy debt charges incurred in the original acquisitions. Thompson's resistance to "conglomerate" rests on a strong aversion to the frantic finance associated with such companies.

The Conservative Conglomerators

Textron's own operations and finances have a distinctly un-frantic look about them. Although it sold its textile division a year ago (the unit had produced $71 million in sales in 1962), its total volume increased by 7 percent last year, from $549,493,000 in 1962 to $587,048,000; the current rate is about $650 million. Net income was up 22 percent to $18,047,000. The income figure was a company record, and especially significant because it was set in a year when Textron paid federal income taxes at the rate of about 44 percent, using up the last of its tax-loss credits. Thompson has suggested that 1964 earnings will set another record, probably reaching close to $20 million. Meanwhile, Textron's long-term debt is down to $33 million, obviously no great burden for a company with more than $150 million of stockholders' equity.

This conservative financial policy represents a considerable change at Textron. So, indeed, do Thompson's operating policies. All in all, his approach affords a stark contrast to the freewheeling ways of the promoter and builder who was his predecessor.

The company goes back to 1923, when Little founded an enterprise called Special Yarns Corp. It was strictly a textile company and remained one through twenty-nine years and three name changes. In 1944, Little renamed the company Textron, which he thought was modern-sounding and connoted both "textiles" and such synthetics as rayon and nylon. During World War II, Little set out to change the character of the company; in place of a simple textile manufacturer, he proposed to create a huge combine that would be completely integrated from raw fibers to finished apparel. By the end of 1949 he had his combine built—and discovered almost immediately that the concept would not work. The company was too big and slow-moving, and could not change the styles of its finished garments fast enough to compete with the hundreds of small dress manufacturers; unlike Textron, they were not tied to the long-term commitments and lead time of a company that wove and finished its own fabrics.

Undaunted, Little began to pull the company apart. In 1952 he got his stockholders to approve a charter change that would let him look outside the textile industry for future Textron acquisitions. He then took what looked like a step backward into textiles when he moved to take over American Woolen. The deal took more than a year to complete and *Fortune* called it "the stormiest merger yet." But American's huge tax-loss credits and bulging bag of liquid assets gave Little the money he needed to carry out his diversification program.

During the next five years Little bought most of the other units that now constitute Textron, making enough sound investments to cover his few big mistakes. His flamboyant methods continued to offend more conservative businessmen. Little himself recently recalled the time he tried to buy Brown & Bigelow, the calendar and advertising-specialty company, which, as it happened, was run by an ex-convict. "We got it approved by our board," Little later recalled, "but when their board considered it, they didn't want to be associated with me."

Decency in Management

As the conglomerated Textron began to assume its present shape, Little recognized that his real interest had been in putting it together. He didn't care for operations, and so he decided to bring in some people who did. Early in 1956 he persuaded a young Wall Street lawyer named George William Miller to leave Cravath, Swaine, & Moore and come to work for Textron. Miller is now Textron's president and chief operating officer. About the same time Little approached Thompson, who was an old friend, had been a Textron director for a time after the war, and had also been one of its bankers (at the Industrial National Bank in Providence). Thompson came on as vice chairman of the executive committee, taking over the management of Textron's non-textile divisions.

Little's acquisitions, for the most part, brought financially sound companies into Textron, most of them in manufacturing. He sought businesses with competent managements and insisted that these come along as part of any deal he made. One old associate recalls Little's emphasis on good management vividly. At one session he finally turned town a bargain-priced company with the observation, "If you had a decent management to run it, you wouldn't be giving it away."

Textron's new units generally could be supervised effectively by people who had only general experience in manufacturing. But acquisitions that required special backgrounds in other fields usually fared poorly. Textron got into one of these fields in 1956, when it bought the SS. *La Guardia,* a converted transport, from the federal government and chartered her to the Hawaiian Steamship Co., which renamed her the SS. *Leilani.* Little had intended the deal purely as an investment, and certainly had no interest in Textrons running the ship. But Hawaiian could not make her pay, and eventually defaulted on its payments. Textron did wind up running her, through a subsidiary of its own, Hawaiian Textron Inc. The company's 1957 annual report accordingly suggested that stockholders consider "a holiday to the Hawaiian Islands" and the *Leilani* "as an economical, carefree way to Hawaii." Not many stockholders took up the suggestion, however, and the federal government repossessed the ship after Textron had lost $2,300,000 operating her.

Textron's management has also learned that developing new inventions is not one of its strong points. The company tried to get into the photocopying business in 1960 by backing the inventor of a process called Photek. In 1961, Textron staked the operation to a brand-new plant. A year later Thompson decided to sell the division to a supplier after Textron had dropped $2 million on the venture. (However, if Photek does finally make it, Textron will participate in its success through a royalty arrangement.) "Now you would have a hard time getting me to start from scratch with a company," says Thompson. "I'm a great believer in a record."

Textron has also had some large problems with an electronics subsidiary. Little had been shopping around for an electronics company for years, but had never found one whose stock did not seem overpriced (i.e., because of the high price-earnings ratios on electronics stocks). In May of 1959 he decided to solve this problem by *creating* one. Accordingly, Textron Electronics, Inc., was chartered. It immediately acquired from the parent company its MB Manufacturing division, a former maker of mounts for propeller-driven aircraft engines that had switched to producing vibration-analysis and testing equipment. Subsequently, two other small Textron divisions were also sold to T.E.; Textron itself ended up owning 75 percent of the stock, with the rest publicly owned and traded on the American Stock Exchange. In 1959, the year it was formed, T.E.'s own price-earnings ratio went as high as 55 (vs. 9 for its parent), and this helped it to pick up a few other small outfits. However, the severe price cutting that plagued the industry in 1960-61, combined with internal management problems, created big losses and sent the stock tumbling. Lately the company has begun to turn around, and Textron's management has abandoned any thoughts of selling or merging it.

A Bargain in Bell

When Little made his biggest acquisition—Bell Aircraft's defense business—word went around that he had finally been outfoxed. He had become concerned that Textron did not have enough government contracts. Defense was then about 8 percent of sales, most of it done through the Dalmo Victor division, which made airborne radar antennas. Little wanted to raise the figure to at least 20 percent. John E. Bierwirth, chairman of National Distillers and a former Textron director, brought Bell Aircraft to his attention (Bierwirth was also a Bell director). In July, 1960, Textron concluded a deal for Bell's helicopter division, its rocket and guidance system maker (Bell's Agena engine is the nearest thing to a stock item in big-payload rocketry), and a small manufacturer of servo controls.

The mistake was supposed to be the price Little had paid: $32 million for a business that in 1959 had earned only $4 million before taxes. However, Textron had put up only about half the purchase price in cash, the remainder being borrowed by Bell Aerospace (as the business was renamed). In any case, the Bell earnings have risen sharply since Textron took over the properties. Thompson says, "We knew we had our objective—25 percent pretax on our investment—from day one." He admits, however, that he and Little had never expected anything like the huge increase in helicopter orders that added $50 million to Textron sales in 1963. All together, the Bell companies alone accounted for more than $160 million of corporate sales last year, more than a quarter of the total. Contract backlogs make it probable that these units will increase their sales and profits, despite the current military cutback programs.

With Bell under Textron's belt, Little retired and Thompson took over as chief executive. At first he got Little to agree to hang around as chairman of the executive committee. But, Thompson says, Little never was much for committees and meetings. "The minute he wasn't going to run it alone, he left."

Thompson had started building his own operating system in 1958. "At first," he recalled recently, "I did it as Little did. Roy operated out of his hat." But that quickly proved unsatisfying for an ex-banker who liked things orderly and didn't like to be called at midnight by a division president with a problem. When Little left, Thompson quickly and quietly began making it clear that he was the boss and put the finishing touches on his own program of centralized control and divisional operation.

Its essentials were frankly copied from General Motors, whose management Thompson had studied carefully. Thompson also adapted the G.M. concept of relating the profits from any venture to the invested capital it required. Return on investment is the standard applied to each of Textron's diverse operations. It is a standard applied consistently and unsentimentally.

One unsentimental move was made about a year ago, when Thompson took the Textron company completely out of its original business. This happened when it sold its Amerotron textile division to Deering-Milliken for $45 million. Amerotron, an efficient textile operation, was returning only about 11 percent on investment (before taxes). "We felt we could make more by investing that textile money in other types of businesses," Thompson recalled recently. He used the proceeds of the sale to cut the company's long-term debt, to increase the working capital of some fast-growing divisions, and to pick up a few more companies, including Jones & Lamson, the Vermont machine-tool maker, and Parkersburg-Aetna, which makes oil-field equipment in Kansas, ball bearings in Illinois, and metal buildings in West Virginia.

No Surprises for Thompson

Thompson expects Textron's money to earn a lot more than 11 percent before taxes. Indeed, he insists that a 25 percent return (i.e., operating profit before taxes or corporate charges) be immediately attainable, or at least clearly foreseeable, in any company Textron buys. All Textron divisions taken together are averaging about that right now. On an after-tax basis the company has been doing better than big U.S. industrials in general, whose median return on invested capital has run under 9 percent in recent years. Little once set a long-term corporate objective of 20 percent after taxes for Textron, on the rather ambitious premise that Textron should do as well as General Motors in this respect. Thompson now regards that objective as "somewhat lofty."

To ensure that the division attain their investment objectives, Textron watches over their operations closely. "We foster the thought of autonomy," Thompson says, "but our association with the divisions is intimate." Thompson also says, frequently, "I don't like surprises." He wants the divisional forecasts to be realistic—and to be met. This is the responsibility of operating head Bill Miller. He has two principal means of minimizing surprises: one is the monthly, quarterly, and annual budgets, forecasts, and reports that each division must submit to Providence; the other is the fieldwork of the three executive vice presidents and the other group executives.

The divisional reports are detailed ones. Division presidents are responsible for submitting and sticking to annual budgets, complete to such details as contributions to a local community fund. They can hire personnel and fix salaries themselves only under the $15,000 level. Capital expenditures of more than $5,000 must be approved by Providence. If they involve assets of $25,000 or more, they get a careful second look six months after the facility has been installed; a postcompletion report must then be made, detailing the operating economics of the item and the actual return on investment. Depending on their size, appropriations for personnel or capital must be approved by the division's group executive, by its executive vice president, by Thompson and Miller personally, or by the executive committee of Textron's board. (Since the executive committee meets twice a month, no division ever has to wait very long before getting what it needs.) Providence must also be notified of any *sale* of a fixed asset, and must approve those involving more than $5,000. Not very surprisingly, much of the humor at Textron's top executive level turns on the vigilance exercised by the boss in watching over the dollars. Thompson's executives kid him about his alleged slowness in reaching for dinner checks, and he repeatedly reminds them, half seriously, of the old New England motto, "Use it up; wear it out; make it do; or do without."

Divisional operating figures and forecasts are formally reviewed by headquarters management once a month. The scene of the review is a room on the second floor of Providence's Hope Club, on the corner of Benefit and Benevolent streets. Despite the number and variety of divisions, these meetings are generally finished in half a day, with most of Thompson's and Miller's attention given to the exceptional cases in which forecasts have not been met. "We manage by exception," Miller explained recently. He and Thompson do not rely only on the monthly meetings to keep abreast of divisional operations. They are in more frequent contact with any division that has something especially big in the works, like, say, the Sendzimir mill for rolling stainless steel now being built at the company's Waterbury Farrel division in Connecticut for delivery to Sharon Steel (price tag: $1,500,000, excluding the electric-power system).

Checking Over the Homework

The other part of Miller's supervisory apparatus is the work of the three executive vice presidents, who report to him. Harvey Gaylord, who had been president of Bell Aircraft, oversees the defense group; the industrial and consumer products divisions are divided between Ottmar and Joseph Collinson. Ottmar and Collinson supervise some of their divisions personally, others through group executives, but both men spend about half their time on the road offering advice, putting out miscellaneous fires, keeping up with competitive developments, looking for new products, men, and ideas, and simply maintaining contact with division executives. "We expect the supervisors to know everyone in a division who is important, or will be," says Miller.

Ottmar was the first supervisor Thompson brought in. Trained as a chemical engineer, he had spent years as an executive of a New England concern called Metals & Controls and had been president of one of its divisions. On his own, Ottmar has interests in the profitable Attleboro *Sun* and in radio station WARA in Attleboro.

He sees his job with the divisions as "what a board of directors would do, except that we're closer. I know the second level of management as well as the first, and I often know the third too. I go to the plants less often now because I know them well. If a new plant is to be constructed, I want to see the site and talk about the layout with the people planning it. That way I see how well they've done their homework."

A Problem of Painless Merger

Collinson's responsibilities are, if anything, more diverse than Ottmar's. He is a former banker and accountant, and served for more than three years as Textron's treasurer, a background he regards as ideal for his present assignment. "A finance man knows a little of everything," he remarked recently.

His big problems the past few years have been several new acquisitions; it has been his job to integrate them into the total Textron operation. A year ago, for example, Textron bought Continental Optical, primarily a lens maker and a logical partner for its Shuron division, a lens and frame manufacturer. Shuron itself had moved its lens manufacturing the previous year from upstate New York to a new plant in Barnwell, South Carolina. To bring Continental's operation into line with Shuron's, Collinson began, among other things, to arrange for closing one of the Continental plants, moving its equipment to another plant in Rochester, New York, and fusing the management groups from the two plants as painlessly as possible. Thus far, however, the profits of the Shuron Continental division are running below corporate management's expectations; Collinson's job is not finished.

His diverse responsibilities also include Textron's agro-chemical and feed-producing companies. He has sought to boost

Textron's profits in this area by using the feed to produce Textron's own chickens and eggs, instead of just selling feed to producers. One of Collinson's group executives supervises Caroline Farms, which now has four plants that together can kill, clean, pack, and ship 20,000 chickens a hour. The division's egg ranch processes 2,500,000 dozen eggs a month.

Despite the tough reporting requirements, Textron's acquisitions have been delighted with the new association. In almost every case Textron had been able to buy them because their owners had some problem—often it involved a shortage of capital —that they couldn't solve themselves. When Textron bought Waterbury Farrel, for example, all but a small part of the production facilities were housed in a rambling collection of ancient buildings in downtown Waterbury, Connecticut. Textron quickly moved the operation to a new plant in nearby Cheshire (it was important to stay in the area so as to keep the skilled work force intact). More than a hundred old machine tools were replaced with fifty new ones. The company had needed the move and the new equipment years before, but had never been able to afford them.

Divisions that have no sizable problems see very little of headquarters. James L. McDonald, president of the Hall-Mack bathroom-accessories division in Los Angeles, says he sees Miller maybe three times a year and Collinson once or twice. "It's been a good association so far," McDonald points out. "We were profitable before and continue to be. Frankly, I imagine that if the earnings picture changed we'd have more contact."

The Case of the Thrifty Foreman

A corporation as big and diverse as Textron, with so many unrelated divisions, probably could not be run successfully without a good incentive-compensation program, so that all the executives suddenly moved from a small to a big corporation can retain a belief in the importance of their own efforts. The divisional presidents select, although Providence must approve, the executives to be included in the program. They benefit to the extent that their divisions (or in some cases operations within a division) become "profit centers" and raise or hold Textron's return on its investment above a base level. Increases in compensation up to 100 percent of salary are possible under the program. One division man said recently, "Before Textron, we never thought about net worth, only about dollar income and return on sales." But the effect of the program—which may extend down to project engineers, shop managers, and purchasing agents—has been to permeate the entire corporation with an awareness of the return-on-investment concept. "It means our people request only the capital equipment which really pays for itself," says Carroll Martenson, head of the Hydraulic Research and Manufacturing Division. At Hall-Mack, McDonald says, "It's made the general foreman try to operate on as low an inventory as he can. Somewhere there has to be a retention of the prime interest of the owner, and this is the only way of doing it in a big company."

One potential danger of emphasizing return on investment is that managers may be tempted to raise one year's return at the expense of development programs that would pay off later. Corporate management is very much aware of the problem, but is satisfied that it hasn't been manifested yet. Thompson cites several new products and developments to prove that development programs have not been starved; they include Homelite's new XL-12 chain saw, for example, and the four-cycle outboard engine Homelite perfected after it had bounced around from one company to another for years. Thompson says the company will spend close to $9 million on product development this year, but he concedes that he doesn't intend to have Textron finance much basic research. Its most important forays into far-out research— e.g., Bell Aerosystems' developments in the field of hovercraft and vertical-takeoff-and-landing planes (VTOL)—have been financed by government development contracts, which is the way Thompson likes it.

An Understanding on Wall Street

Textron is very much aware of Wall Street these days. Its management obviously feels it has a new and happy story to tell investors, and it is eager for investors to listen. Textron has been giving its brokerage business (it buys some of its own stock for acquisitions, warrant and option conversions, and for an employees' stock-purchase plan) to a number of select Wall Street houses—those that, as Thompson puts it, "take the trouble to understand our company." His eagerness to publicize the company and its stock rests in part on an awareness that more acquisitions are in the works—Lon Casler, Textron's vice president for acquisitions, has a foot-high pile of prospect folders right now— and that any one of them would come cheaper if it could be paid for in a stock whose price-earnings ratio was higher. Thompson frankly aspires to blue-chip status for Textron, and the higher p/e's that would presumably come with it; and he has repeatedly suggested to the Street that it is underestimating Textron's potential at present price levels. (At about 42 recently, even after a long rise the stock was still only eleven times projected 1964 earnings of $3.75.) He says that earnings of $5 a share are in the cards before he retires.

Whether Textron ever does achieve blue-chip status will doubtless depend very largely on its ability to maintain earnings at a high level even in an economic downturn—a challenge the corporation in its present form has not yet faced. Since Textron is itself close to being a cross section of the industrial economy, any sharp downturn in industrial production would plainly pose a serious challenge to it. However, it has some special resources of its own to meet such challenges. One of them, of course, is the conservatism of its present finances. Its main resource, though, is that remarkably cool, efficient, and professional management in Providence.

"To Live and Die for Armstrong" *

BY HUBERT KAY

"The force behind a great company," said the hero of *Executive Suite*, is "the pride of thousands of men. A company is like an army—it fights on its pride. You can't win wars with paychecks. In all the history of the world there's never been a great army of mercenaries. You can't pay a man enough to make him lay down his life. He wants more than money."

There was more than passing suspicion, when *Executive Suite* came out more than a decade ago, that author Cameron Hawley had drawn his inspiration from his years as advertising director of the Armstrong Cork Co. of Lancaster, Pennsylvania. The Armstrong people themselves convincingly deny any connection with Hawley's story of power-grabbing, back-stabbing corporate politics, but they have all but committed to memory his

* *March 1964*

"pride of thousands" speech, for Armstrong is a company that proudly runs on its morale.

Rare is the visitor to the aging headquarters building and main plant, set among the rolling farmlands of the Pennsylvania Dutch country, who does not sense the difference. And the influence is felt as widely as Armstrong's twenty-seven other plants, scattered in six countries around the world. "If you ever listen to one Armstrong salesman," says Albert H. Hoffman, a New York flooring contractor, "you can pick out another Armstrong man anywhere you happen to find him."

The company morale is no accident. At Armstrong, management prospects are hired just out of college, trained in a kind of fraternity-house atmosphere, and all but guaranteed a job for life if they produce. Members of the 500-man management team average forty-five years of age, and have a average of twenty years with Armstrong; 300 of them are members of a stock-option plan. Armstrong boasts of running by a moral code that almost rivals the Boy Scout law; in every office hangs a handsomely printed and framed set of four corporate "operating principles" and employees are admonished to reread them at least once a month. (Principle No. 2: "To maintain high moral and ethical standards and to reflect honesty, integrity, reliability, and forthrightness in all relationships.")

President Maurice J. ("Moose") Warnock, sixty-one, acknowledges that the company "tends to submerge the individual personality and develop the corporate personality" (though asserting in the next breath, "It takes individualists rather than conformists to be good performers"). The corporate personality shines forth in Armstrong's top echelon—mostly earnest, outgoing products of the Midwest and Far West. Warnock, who started as an Armstrong sales trainee from the University of Oregon in 1926 and became president in 1962, fondly remembers his first lessons in "Armstrong Manor" at the feet of his predecessor, the late Henning Webb Prentis Jr.: "Prentis was a great teacher, and he instilled in us the will to live and die for Armstrong."

A Cheering Section in Wall Street

Such manifestations of corporate togetherness have taken their lumps from cynics and sophisticates, and even from competitors, over the years. But when the story is written in figures it finds Armstrong—in today's less socially oriented parlance—

crying all the way to the bank. Armstrong has a glowing record as the outstanding earner in the feast-or-famine building-materials business. Last year saw earnings of other companies in the industry up by a range of 5 to 10 percent over 1962. But Armstrong, which kept right on earning in the 1960 industry slump, was expected to show 25 to 30 percent earnings increase over its 1962 record. With an estimated $340 million in 1963 domestic sales, plus perhaps $40 million in foreign sales, it earnings should run about $27 million (for a return of 8 percent on sales). This kind of news prompted Wall Street anticipation of a stock split; from its 1962 low of 48, "Arm Ck" closed out 1963 at 110½.

Scorning big sales volume for volume's sake, the company keeps its eye so steadily fixed on profit that it even calls its four operating vice presidents "profit centers." With assets of more than $230 million, no debt, virtually unlimited credit for expansion, a solid reputation for quality and service, a habit of successful innovation, a record of having doubled in size on an average of every eight years in the first six decades of this century, and a vigorous new president surrounded by seasoned but mostly youthful lieutenants who give it unusual depth of management. Armstrong seems a good bet to march forward on its "pride of thousands" for a long time.

No one is more fascinated by the company's character, success, and longevity than Armstrong executives themselves; they analyze it endlessly and like to make speeches with such titles as "What Makes Armstrong Different." Partly they credit their location in pleasant old Lancaster (population 94,000), sixty-five miles west of Philadelphia. A homey, historic cross section of the U.S., Lancaster is no company town; though Armstrong is its biggest industry, it has several others, including R.C.A., Hamilton Watch Co., and a stockyard, plus Franklin and Marshall College. It is also the county seat of a fabulously fertile farming area. Says Clifford J. Backstrand (California's Pomona College '20), chairman and former president, "We couldn't possibly be the kind of company we are if we had moved our headquarters to New York."

But beyond location, the "Armstrong family" explains itself— in a manner so fervent as to put contrived image making to shame —as the product of company principle. As laid down, the operating principles add up to a corporate success formula: let all management decisions and behavior be governed by the determination to be good to your customers, stockholders, employees, suppliers, community neighbors, government, and the general public.

Rewards of Virtue

Armstrong traces its principles all the way back to the founder, Thomas Morton Armstrong. In 1860, when he was a twenty-four-year-old shipping clerk, he used his $300 savings to buy out a one-room Pittsburgh shop for cutting corks by hand. At the time most U.S. manufacturing was small and local—not only for lack of transportation and mass-production machinery, but also for lack of trust. The prevailing rule of the marketplace was *Caveat emptor*—Let the buyer beware!—and the smart commercial buyer preferred to buy locally where he could inspect the merchandise in advance, and often check on his supplier's raw materials and processes. In his little cork shop Thomas Armstrong, son of Presbyterian Scotch-Irish immigrants, set out to change the rule to "Let the buyer have faith."

He made his first mark during the Civil War, when the Pittsburgh branch of the Sanitary Commission—a forerunner of the Red Cross—was collecting private donations to buy medical supplies for Union troops. The shoddy quality of most of the supplies created a scandal and investigation. In it, the firm of Armstrong, Brother & Co. was singled out as one that, despite inflating costs, had made good its contract to supply top-grade corks at the agreed price. Virtue was rewarded when a grateful Sanitary Commission physician became an officer of a big New York drug firm and Armstrong got its cork business. Thus began its move toward national distribution with the establishment of a New York branch in 1874.

Thomas scored another point with customers about 1876. According to cherished company legend, an Armstrong salesman boasted that he had finally unloaded a large lot of odd-sized corks, which were priced at 30 cents per gross, for 40 cents per gross. His boss ordered him to go back to the customer and correct his "mistake."

A "brand name" pioneer in the commercial-supply field, Thomas Armstrong began putting his firm's name on its bags of corks about 1864, and soon was putting a written guarantee of quality in the bags. As confidence in Armstrong dependability grew, so did nationwide sales. By the 1880's, Armstrong was the world's largest cork company, with 750 employees. Kindly Thomas Armstrong knew nearly every one by name, visited them when they were sick and helped them out in times of trouble.

Founder Armstrong remained president until his death in

1908. But at the turn of the century, as first vice president and general manager, his son and successor Charles Dickey Armstrong was already beginning to take over active management. Charles soon came to grips with the fact that cork was being driven out of its old markets as a bottle-stopper and set out to find new uses for it.

Ground up, bound with its own resins or other mixers, and flattened or molded, cork formed insulating corkboard and pipe coverings, high-temperature insulating brick, gaskets for sealing automotive and other machine parts, roll covers to replace sheepskin and leather in textile-spinning machinery. More important for the company's future, cork was also used for linoleum, flooring tile, and acoustical ceilings.

When more advantageous materials began popping cork out of most of these markets too, Armstrong used the new materials or came up with better ones of its own. When fiberboard made from such cheap materials as sugar cane and cottonwood began to cut heavily into corkboard sales, Armstrong developed a process for using waste pine chips. When felt replaced burlap as backing for linoleum, the company bought a felt mill and was soon selling the surplus for automobile soundproofing.

One product or use generally seemed to lead logically to another, so that Armstrong's current 400-odd products and its markets are effectively related. Cork tile and linoleum led on to the world's most complete line of resilient floor coverings: of asphalt, rubber, vinyl-asbestos, vinyl, and Du Pont's new, super-resilient Hypalon. Adhesives for laying floor coverings were the forerunners of adhesives for many industrial purposes. Acoustical ceilings led to fire-retardant ceilings, to heating and air-conditioning ceilings, to illuminating ceilings, and finally, in the new Luminaire, to a ceiling that does all four jobs. When bottle makers began producing their own cork-substitute closures, Armstrong— by now with a full line of metal and plastic crowns and caps— bought a couple of glass plants and launched a line of complete packaging materials.

"Luckily," says President Warnock, "cork didn't go out all at once but in one market at a time. It toughened us early to learn to innovate and diversify. We learned to be market-minded and customer-oriented. We learned to live and grow by providing the best solution based on the customer's problem—not on something we owned in a mine, or on some basic patents of a fundamental manufacturing process."

"Prentis' Rah-Rah Boys"

The man who probably did most to set Armstrong on its market-minded, customer-oriented path was one of its first college recruits. A University of Cincinnati M.A., H. W. Prentis Jr. was persuaded in 1907 that some business experience would make him a better teacher of economics. As a young clerk assigned to the sideline chore of writing perfunctory trade-journal advertisements, Prentis soon began producing a spate of the booklets (*Cork—Its Origin and Uses*), engineering manuals, "selling helps," and other instructional and promotional literature that Armstrong has been turning out in prodigious quantities ever since. Appointed advertising manager, he asked the board for a $15,000 annual budget, whereupon, according to legend, the company treasurer pushed up his spectacles and intoned, "This young fellow wants to bankrupt us." ("You can hardly get Danny Kaye to cough for that much nowadays," Senior Vice President James H. Binns says of Armstrong's current TV extravaganza.) But Prentis got his way, and the first of the company's national consumer advertisements proclaimed the new beauty and convenience of Armstrong linoleum in a 1917 issue of the *Saturday Evening Post*.

Until 1920 the company followed the prevailing trade practice of entrusting all flooring sales to a commission agent. Then the agent retired, and Prentis, the new sales manager, got permission to set up his own sales force and distribution system. He stepped up college recruiting and built a sales corps dubbed by dealers "Prentis' rah-rah boys." One of his early recruits, present Executive Vice President C. N. Painter (University of Missouri '24), remembers going through a six months' training program in which "we made the rounds of the plants and offices, sometimes working a little but mostly just watching and listening. Then we went out on the road in teams of two with big display cases, preaching to linoleum dealers about how the product was made by the felt-layer method. Actually the dealers didn't really give a damn how the stuff was made, but I guess they were kind of taken in by our enthusiasm."

Setting out to create a network of independent wholesale distributors who would be loyal allies of the company, Prentis startled the trade—in which price haggling was and still is common—by publishing Armstrong prices and sticking to them. He also established the Armstrong rule that the smallest wholesaler gets a better price than the biggest retailer. When in the 1920's a major mail-order house offered a million-dollar order in return for the wholesale discount, Armstrong—which was still comparatively small and needed the money—turned it down. In 1934, after the company had lost nearly $9 million in three years of history's worst depression, Armstrong's directors summoned Prentis to the rescue as president.

Meanwhile the company's labor policy had been evolving in ways that were to arm Prentis for the major public battle of his life. At first, President Charles D. Armstrong's employee benefactions, like those of his father, were matters of private rather than corporate obligation. In 1909, for example, he joined his three sisters in endowing what may have been U.S. industry's first free dental service for employees.

But soon corporate responsibilities were being acknowledged and implemented in pioneering succession: extra pay for overtime (1913), shop committees to consult with management (1919), paid vacations for all employees (1924), group life insurance (1931). Other fringe benefits, including pensions and group hospital-surgical insurance, were to follow these pre-New Deal employee-welfare provisions.

As a president and favorite speaker of the N.A.M., Armstrong's President Prentis became one of the New Deal's most persistent critics. He did not denounce the benefits New Dealers were seeking for workers. He argued that they were just, but should come from voluntary sharing by employers rather than government compulsion. This, naturally, did not make him a favorite in Washington.

To Armstrong, Prentis brought the greatest period of growth it had yet experienced. In sixteen years as president he raised the number of domestic plants from nine to seventeen, and the number of domestic employees from 5,100 to 12,700. With time out during World War II to manufacture $110 million worth of artillery shells, aircraft parts, incendiary bombs, and other munitions, sales soared from $40 million in 1936, to $50 million in 1939, to $100 million in 1943. They were only a year away from the $200-million mark when Prentis reached retirement age in 1950, and moved into the chairmanship until his death in 1959.

The "Profit Machine"

Prentis' successor as president was Clifford J. Backstrand, an early Prentis recruit who had organized Armstrong's war effort and, later, the diversification and mass marketing of its floorings. Said Backstrand, in effect: "All right, we've had all this growth; now let's make some money out of it."

The new profit drive involved no slackening of innovation. The Backstrand administration began with completion of one of the building industry's biggest research and development centers, and in 1962 (when Backstrand shifted to the chairmanship) nearly half of all sales were of products developed in the previous ten years. What he added was a sharper consciousness of costs and profits throughout Armstrong management. His tool was the Du Pont-pioneered concept of Return on Capital Employed, or ROCE, which can be used to measure the true profitability of every division and product. It naturally followed that ROCE, diligently pursued, helped Armstrong to spot and weed out its less profitable lines, to concentrate on the more profitable ones. And it had the effect of making the profit process an intensely personal one.

"In the old days, before we adopted this tool," says Executive Vice President Painter, "the average sales manager always wanted to carry a big inventory. He always wanted to have excess manufacturing capacity, and he was not much interested in the size of his accounts receivable. All these, obviously, are part of his capital employed, and now our sales managers are extremely conscious of all of them. We've bought the management philosophy of the president's office down to the sales managers' level, and that's a real accomplishment.

"We've got our production and plant managers into this frame of mind, too. Every plant has to make an operating cost budget for the year ahead, and every week it gets a report on its performance against these plans. Naturally, they're interested in meeting or beating their budgets; it's got to be quite a game and they enjoy playing it. Judging his performance by ROCE standards, the plant manager with excessive capacity starts saying, 'Lord, I don't want all that plant.' They've turned in really remarkable performances, saving us several million dollars a year. We used to be known mainly for merchandising and advertising, but now our manufacturing has caught up."

One of the most unorthodox phenomena of Armstrong's Lancastrian togetherness is the "product manager." He is responsible for coordinating the work of research, engineering, production, styling, sales, and all other people concerned with his product—but has no authority over any of them. To make things even harder, he gets an ROCE statement on his product every month, which makes him feel responsible for its profitability even though others determine its cost and price. Vice President Harry A. Jensen (Iowa's Grinnell College '40), who was once on such a spot, explains that the only reason the system works "can't be found on any organization chart. It's really the unseen lines of understanding. We feel we are all part of the same profit machine."

Though the president's office sets the sales and profit goals, the prime responsibility for achieving them rests on the four men whom Armstrong calls "profit centers." Until 1952 the company was organized functionally, with research, production, sales, etc., merging only in the president's office. Now administration has been divided among four line organizations: (1) flooring, consumer products, and defense production[1]; (2) building materials and industrial specialties; (3) packaging materials; (4) international operations. These are each headed by an operating vice president and general manager with authority and responsibility for all operations and earnings in his field.

How does it all add up? In the six years 1958-63, while Armstrong sales were rising by 36 percent and prices were stable, after-tax profits shot up 98 percent.

Second-Century Speedup

President Warnock, who presided over the last and biggest eighteen months of this spectacular profit rise, is primed to keep pace with the fast-moving world of Armstrong's second century. He is a legitimate corporate heir of the first century—steeped in company tradition through thirty-eight years as trainee, salesman, district manager, assistant flooring-sales manager, director of advertising and promotion, treasurer, vice president for finance and for employee and public relations, senior vice president, and president. So firmly does he hold to the Armstrong principles that he declares with some emotion: "I believe that if these principles are fully ingrained in our employees' corporate life they will come to live them in their personal lives as well." But Warnock does not confuse the permanent and the transitory. "Our organization has long known," he says, "that its goal is to obsolete our products, our services, and our distribution systems first—not to wait until someone else does it for us."

---

[1] Armstrong is currently using old-fashioned cork, which constitutes only 1.5 percent of its raw materials, to form heat-dispersing shields for Minuteman and Polaris missiles.

Seeking to "perfect and sharpen" the total organization and speed up decision making, Warnock now has the operating "profit centers" who used to report directly to him report to Executive Vice President Painter. Similarly, all twenty-two staff departments—including ever growing R. and D. and an agency-sized (110 people) advertising department—report to Senior Vice President Binns. Binns and Painter meet regularly with their lieutenants in sessions devoted mainly to new ideas and where they hope and expect to be five years from now. With only control functions such as finance reporting directly to him, Warnock is able to concentrate on long-range planning and over-all policy direction. To improve communication and cross-fertilization in styling and product design, he has pulled these functions out of the divisions and made them company staff departments.

In the important flooring division Warnock had little difficulty in selling his policy of change, for important change had begun to pick up momentum in 1958. It was then that Armstrong introduced a high-styled vinyl product named Futuresq at twice the price ever asked for a linoleum covering. "That was what really broke the price and styling barriers for us," says Harry Jensen, the flooring vice president and general manager. "Wholesalers who expected to get orders from 200 or 300 dealers found themselves getting orders from 5,000. No one who saw it ever again thought that a room with resilient covering on the floor had to look like a kitchen."

So swift are flooring manufacturers to imitate one another's innovations that lead time on a new product has been drastically cut. Once Armstrong enjoyed three years or more before the competition caught up with a new line; now it feels lucky to get eighteen months. "Styling changes come so fast these days," says one flooring man, "that sometimes I feel as though I were in the dress business." After solving production problems for a new flooring, Armstrong used to allow itself a full year to develop a promotional campaign and get the line into distribution channels. For a recent major product, the process was allowed just sixty days.

The Last May Be First

Sometimes Armstrong itself is caught short by a competitor's innovation; it needed six years to match the Sandura Co.'s Sandran rotogravure-printing process that made high style possible for inexpensive resilient floorings. But Armstrong may also lag behind the competition deliberately. When vinyl floorings were developed in the late 1940's, one New York dealer remembers, "A lot of the major manufacturers rushed their products onto the market with full-page ads claiming that they needed hardly any care and no waxing at all. This, it turned out, just wasn't so." Meanwhile Armstrong had laid some experimental vinyl flooring in an executive's home. It shrank, and went back to the laboratories. Refusing to market an unsatisfactory product or to make untested claims, Armstrong was one of the last on the market with vinyl floorings—but is now probably first in sales.

Some of its sharpest flooring competition, Armstrong finds, comes from small firms that specialize in one type at a narrow price range. For example, says Jensen, "Amtico really knows luxury tile, and Sandura is expert in rotovinyl sheet goods."

President Warnock has few worries about low-cost foreign competition; in general, the rest of the world lags behind the U.S. in resilient-flooring techniques and styling, and Armstrong is well established in foreign markets. The company manufactures textile-mill supplies in India, and these are the leading product line of its sales branches in continental Europe and Brazil. It also processes cork in Spain. But flooring is the chief product of Armstrong plants in Canada, Britain, and West Germany. In 1962 the foreign subsidiaries set a new record of $1,200,000 in earnings on $36,300,000 in sales. Last year both sales and earnings were up again.

Warnock can also take comfort from his company's high place in the markets for ceilings, siding, insulation, and other non-flooring building materials. Like almost everyone else, he takes it for granted that housing construction will boom in the late Sixties as members of the postwar "baby boom" begin to have babies of their own. Armstrong is a major supplier of ceilings and insulation, as well as flooring, to the already booming mobile-home market. The Armstrong development of a moisture-proof backing lets resilient flooring be laid in sublevel basements and playrooms and on the concrete slabs that serve as foundations for an estimated one-third of all single-family residences now being built in the U.S. The building-materials vice president and general manager, J. V. Jones (University of Chicago '36), claims that Armstrong ceilings are now dominant in both the commercial and residential markets, and the company probably sells more square feet of ceilings than of floors. And the company is fortified against construction downturns by the fact that half of its building-materials sales go for never ending home repair and modernization.

One product high on Armstrong's list of priorities is a washable synthetic wall covering that would never need painting. Once the company tried linoleum for the purpose, but soap damaged the stuff, and around showers and sinks it yellowed with age. Though these defects were overcome, a marketable product still eludes Armstrong research.

Race on a Fast Track

In the crowded field of packaging materials Armstrong is hard-pressed. "Packaging," says Operating Vice President Roger Hetzel (Pennsylvania State '35), "is a race between materials on a fast track." In the past four years Armstrong and other manufacturers have joined breweries in spending $6 million to $8 million a year to promote the single-trip beer bottle. Though the manufacturers tripled their annual beer-bottle sales to some $24 million, the campaign has succeeded in "slowing down the can" only a disappointing notch or two. So price-conscious are buyers in the hotly competitive packaging market, Hetzel declares wryly, that "if you do come out with some great new development, you can count on your customers' loyalty and gratitude for about six months—when somebody else will be out with it, maybe even at a better price."

Moving cautiously into plastic bottles, Armstrong has also developed surface coatings to strengthen lightweight glass bottles which are used for filling equipment that handles up to 600 bottles per minute. The old Armstrong zest for distribution is a major asset in packaging sales. For breweries, typically "packed tight in cities" with no space for bottle storage, the company has developed huge palletized cartons that can be moved straight from the truck into the high-speed filling machinery. One major distiller allows no more than fifteen minutes' leeway for arrival of the next Armstrong bottle truck.

Warnock's riskiest move has been to lead his company into the battle of the supermarkets. Trying always to come up with something new, Armstrong entered the consumer-products field in 1962 with its now widely imitated One-Step Floor Care, a liquid wax-plus-detergent that cleans and polishes floors simultaneously. The company's own explanation of the move: (1) Armstrong advertising and reputation for quality assured it of strong consumer acceptance; (2) it wanted to become less dependent on fluctuations in the building industry and the national economy by making consumer-level products that would sell in good times and bad. One-Step, distributed by food brokers who could get it on supermarket shelves, captured 10 percent of the floor-wax market in its first fifteen months. Other products are waiting in the wings.

Short Risk, Long Faith

For the short-term future it seems doubtful that Armstrong can maintain the pace of last year's rocketing profit rise. Cost cutting has its limits, and the company may be reaching them. The long-dropping prices of vinyl and some of its other synthetic raw materials show signs of firming up, while its own labor and distribution costs are rising. The company faces major investment in new flooring capacity. It also seems determined to spend what is necessary to push its supermarket consumer products, a costly and often losing process. A new product usually takes three years to begin to break even—and even the best may never make it. Campbell Soup, the Top Tomato of them all, got squashed when it tried to break into the catsup market.

For the long term, Armstrong's future looks bright but strenuous. In flooring its product quality and styling, its unmatched investment in advertising and research, its unrivaled distribution system of eighty-five loyal wholesalers and some 40,000 retail outlets in every corner of the land—all these have given Armstrong acknowledged leadership in the field and the Armstrong team could not imagine it any other way. After all, their corporate principles are more than a code of manners and morals; they are a declaration of faith in an orderly universe. Armstrong Cork has grown and prospered through one hundred and four years of U.S. ups and downs. What could possibly alter such a progression?

The Optimistic World of Edgar Kaiser*

BY WALTER GUZZARDI, JR.

The thick white carpet muffles footfalls. A silvered acoustical ceiling mutes voices, and quiets the ringing of pastel telephones.

* April 1963

But, despite such refined decor, a clamor of activity, brushed with an overlay of genial confusion, is highly audible on the twenty-seventh floor of Kaiser Center—that gorgeous palace in Oakland, California, where the Kaiser companies make their headquarters. For on that floor, in a light-filled office whose entry is concealed by a glittering fretwork of aluminum screening, Edgar Kaiser, amiable but furious-paced son of a fabled father, guides the destinies of the Kaiser organizations. Working from his office—but also from airplanes, hotel rooms, and hasty facilities flung up at the scene of Kaiser operations from Argentina to Zaragoza—Edgar Kaiser is fast fixing a new imprint upon the Kaiser industrial complex. Edgar's father is active and vigorous at eighty—but the Kaiser complex now is being shaped primarily by Edgar's busy hand.

A busy hand is what it takes in the Kaiser dominion these days. The dominion sprang, as all the world knows, from the seeds of Henry Kaiser's construction companies—those dashing outfits that operated on thin capital, finished great projects months ahead of schedule, and then raced on to new bids and new challenges. But now a different stage of growth has begun. The various companies that began as mere suppliers for construction ventures—cement for dams, steel for ships—have outgrown construction and come to a giant size. They are running affairs more intricate than even Henry Kaiser foresaw for them. Change in the Kaiser organization is everywhere, and Edgar Kaiser is the engine of change.

The organization he is leading could hardly be more complicated. Atop the pyramid sits the publicly held Kaiser Industries Corp., which was formed in 1956 out of Kaiser Motors Corp., an ill-starred venture in Detroit ("What Cooks with Kaiser," *Fortune*, July, 1956.) Alongside of Industries ranges a vestige of the past—the wholly owned Henry J. Kaiser Co. These two companies own big bundles of stock in the three other publicly held enterprises: Kaiser Aluminum & Chemical Corp. (42 percent Kaiser owned); Kaiser Steel Corp. (79 percent); and Permanente Cement Co. (39 percent). But Kaiser Industries is also an operating entity through its divisions and subsidiaries, which include Willys Motors, Inc., Kaiser Engineers, an aircraft and electronics division, and a number of other activities ranging from sand and gravel production to Venetian lagoons in Hawaii.

To gauge the performance of such a complex is no easier than to describe it. As a holding company, Kaiser Industries last year collected $7,700,000 on its $297 million worth of stock[1] in the

---

[1] As of March 1, 1963, market value.

aluminum, cement, and steel companies. The biggest contributor was Kaiser Aluminum, which paid its parent $6 million out of near-record earnings. Permanente Cement, a steady earner, paid another $1,700,000. But Kaiser Steel, in deep trouble, paid no dividends at all—it showed a loss of $5 million in 1962. On the operating side, Willys Motors skidded from $7 million earned in 1961 to a loss of nearly $500,000 last year. But other divisions more than compensated for the skid. Kaiser Engineers, made up of both domestic and foreign operations, showed a good profit, and other smaller divisions made solid contributions.

The result of all these varied returns was that, after taxes, Kaiser Industries earned $10 million last year, an increase of around $3 million over 1960 and 1961 levels. Despite that improvement, Kaiser Industries paid no dividends and, indeed, has never paid any. The principal reason is a heavy load of debt inherited at its formation. To put Kaiser Industries on a dividend-paying basis —to make the whole Kaiser complex perform as well as some of its parts—is the cherished but elusive ambition of the present Kaiser management.

The Ubiquity of the Three

The top tier of that management recurs in all parts of the Kaiser empire. It still includes Henry Kaiser, but today Edgar is imparting a sense of unity to the disparate Kaiser organization. Edgar is president of Kaiser Industries. But he is also an active chairman of the board of the aluminum, cement, and steel companies. He has kindled everyone's interest in foreign markets, and he is increasing his own vigorous, even frenetic, activity in that field. It is a rare executive who works harder, or enjoys it more. He is forever on the frontier—not only in his planning, but literally, flying perpetually to Accra, or New Delhi, or London or Paris. "When he wants to travel, and we know the airport of his destination is fogged in," remarks an assistant, "Edgar is likely to say, 'What's the alternative? Where else can we get to?'" Now fifty-four, with thirty years of experience, Edgar is racing, one suspects, partly as a consequence of the formative years he spent alongside a strong-willed parent. "He seems to get new energy," says an aide, "not by rest, but by changing from one kind of work to another. Shifts in the direction of his thoughts—say from a scheme for a new aluminum plant to a plan for a tunnel under the English Channel—seem to revive him." Deepening lines in his face give the only apparent testimony to the long hours he keeps.

Routine traffic of management is not for Edgar Kaiser. Although he will give time to an ordinary problem if it is brought to his attention—and one of his shortcomings, says an associate, is "his willingness to deal with whatever comes before him"—he never seeks out the ordinary kind of trouble. Like his father, he loves to locate a seam somewhere, but he leaves others to mine it. He has found an able assistant for doing so: Eugene Trefethen is another important link in the Kaiser chain of joint command. A lifelong associate of Edgar, Trefethen serves not only as Edgar's right hand in Kaiser Industries, but also as vice chairman on the other company boards. While Edgar is out breaking new ground, Trefethen is supplying the organization with sound and steady day-to-day management, in consultation with the chief executives of all the companies.

Creeds and Deeds

The result of common management is common philosophy. All the different Kaiser companies share the same striking Kaiser creed, as first articulated by Henry Kaiser: faith plus work equals success. Now, as refined and extended by Edgar, the Kaiser creed admits of no such easy summary, but it has three readily identifiable postulates. The first is confidence in people: there is good in every man. The second is decency in dealings: to do the right thing is not only possible, but it is also necessary and important— as important as an increase in earned cents per share. The third is optimism: the world is going to be a better place tomorrow than it is today, and Edgar Kaiser, through the medium of his companies, can speed the process that will make it so. If there is a fourth postulate, it is simply this: nothing in the first three is incompatible with good management, or intensive negotiations, or efficient business procedures.

From this doctrine many things stem. But its most unexpected result comes when it is translated into financial policy. Although the Kaiser creed is a compound of virtues, it does not logically lead to the practice of another, more homely virtue: thrift. Along with the Kaiser faith in the future goes faith in growth. "This country is going to grow, and grow, and grow," says Edgar Kaiser, "and there isn't going to be any end." The best way to prepare for tomorrow's growth, obviously, is to borrow today. High debt thus becomes the most sensible business practice.

So the Kaiser complex has borrowed, in amounts that might frighten less confident men. With George Woods, former president of First Boston Corp. and now president of the World Bank, formulating the concepts and arranging the financing, Kaiser companies have raised around $2 billion since the war. The parent company, Kaiser Industries, carries a long-term debt of $80 million and a $25-million bank loan—mostly an inheritance from the past. But the separate Kaiser companies have also borrowed heavily. Permanente Cement has always been on the outer fringe of traditional debt ratios for cement companies. Kaiser Steel, in an industry whose debt averages 22 percent of total capital, carries a 60 percent debt—"high enough to give Pittsburgh the creeps," says one analyst, but he quickly adds, "Still, why not? We don't live in the 1930's any longer." While this kind of financing adds up to a liberal policy, Kaiser Industries executives balance that policy with a kind of conservatism: they depreciate their capital equipment at the accelerated rate, thus—while taking full advantage of today's tax laws—also reducing today's profits in the name of tomorrow's. "In relation to our holdings, our debt doesn't amount to a tinker's dam," snaps Gene Trefethen. "When you can service your debt, pay the interest out of earnings, and pay a dividend, debt is a plus."

The Blessings of Debt

When that philosophy proves right, it outruns even Kaiser expectations. A conspicuous, even classic example is Kaiser Aluminum, which at one point in its history had a boatful of debt, and one of the highest debt ratios the industry had ever known. That was in 1953, when its first huge expansion program of $200 million was just blooming. This heavy borrowing followed one of the most inauspicious beginnings in the history of American business: when Henry Kaiser was raising money to found the aluminum company, his favorite bankers and friends at the Bank of America said to him soberly, "We'll lend you this money if you insist, and if you're sure you really want it. But honestly, Henry, for your own good, we recommend against it. It will never work out."

Yet look at Kaiser Aluminum today. Started only seventeen years ago, it is now, measured in sales, the third-biggest aluminum company in the U.S., and very nearly as big as the second company, Reynolds Metals. A decade ago, Kaiser Aluminum's sales were $142 million; last year they stood at $444 million. Its earnings moved from $13 million in 1952 to $31 million last year, and its profit on sales was 7 percent. Out of an increase of $20 million in 1962's sales over 1961, Kaiser Aluminum squeezed an extra $7 million in profits. So far as the debt goes, it is now both in line and in hand: in the expansion year of 1953, long-term debt stood at $191 million and equity at $85 million—a then shocking 69 percent debt ratio. But now the debt ratio is down to 49 percent, and while that is eighteen percentage points higher than conservative Alcoa's, it is only four points higher than Reynolds Metals carries. And, since its big expansion is completed and it could increase its 1962 output of 560,000 tons by 10 percent (to its capacity of 610,000) with no added outlay, Kaiser is set for the next few years. With some fabulous growth already behind it, Kaiser Aluminum stands ready for that typical Kaiser tomorrow.

Not that Kaiser Aluminum finds the living easy at the moment. Once the aluminum industry's only problem was production. Now there is overcapacity. Prices have eroded steadily, first behind the scenes and then in published lists, falling from 26 cents a pound for ingot in 1961 to 22.5 cents a pound today. Estimates are that an efficient U.S. aluminum company probably makes at current prices no more than 3 cents a pound after taxes, in an industry that requires a high average capital investment of $35,000 per employee. Foreign competition is fierce, coming both from Canada's Aluminium Ltd. and from Pechiney, the big French company which believes that the way to compete is to undersell—and, thanks to export incentives and tariff protection at home, is apparently prepared to undersell no matter what happens to prices. "If we had known five years ago what today's problems would be," remarks Tom Ready, newly elected chief of Kaiser Aluminum, "I'm not sure how many of us would have bothered to show up for work."

The market is tricky, too. Aluminum is made into thousands of products that the steelmen call "knick-knacks," so that much of its output runs on a kind of job-shop basis, without benefit of the recurring big volume required for high profitability. Kaiser Aluminum had unhappy experiences with both household aluminum foil (still a loss item) and aluminum siding for houses, a market that Kaiser sidled into, lost on, and retreated from some years ago.

To Ready's way of thinking, the way to increase profits is to control as much as possible of the bauxite-to-consumer process. Right now, Kaiser Aluminum is promoting its aluminum siding once more—this time directly to the house owner. The company is also looking for future growth and profits from its new chemical division. Good earnings will continue to come from the profitable and well-run refractory-brick division.

Fairest of Them All

But foreign fields look fairest of all. Here, Edgar Kaiser acts with characteristic passion and energy in the affairs of the aluminum company. Chairman of its board since 1959, he has always turned first to the foreign area, and, indeed—except at board meetings—he pays little attention to other aspects of the aluminum company's business. Edgar seeks abroad for Kaiser Aluminum what he obviously regards as the only real evidence of life: growth. Kaiser Aluminum executives like to support Edgar's conviction by quoting all the usual statistics: annually the U.S. consumes twenty-three pounds of aluminum per person, Western Europe consumes nine pounds, and in Africa the per capita consumption probaby comes to less than the weight of a tribesman's bangle. "As a matter of fact," says Ready, "we give foreign proposals a more thorough study than any others. We have to, because we know that Edgar inclines in their favor."

Edgar's fervor has made Kaiser, among U.S. aluminum companies, first in foreign sales. In just the last couple of years Kaiser Aluminum has spudded in these overseas undertakings: through the medium of the Hindustan Aluminum Corp. Ltd., which is 27 percent owned by Kaiser, it cast its first metal in India; it entered a partnership with Delta Metal Co. to expand James Booth Aluminum Ltd. in England (50 percent Kaiser owned); it began work on a series of aluminum projects in Australia (Comalco Industries Pty. Ltd., 50 percent Kaiser); and it started enterprises in South Africa, Sweden, Argentina, Venezuela, and West Germany. There, with a $15-million fabricating plant in Coblenz, Kaiser Aluminum will soon have a look into the Common Market. Although they have severe tests yet to pass, the far-flung operations of Kaiser Aluminum's foreign division thus far have proved successful. Booth in Britain, for example, gave Kaiser Aluminum a critically important boost a couple of years ago, when the domestic pinch on sales was first felt. Last year, over 20 percent of Kaiser Aluminum's total volume in aluminum was sold abroad.

The most ambitious foreign venture of all is Kaiser Aluminum's entry into Ghana (see "Edgar Kaiser's Gamble in Africa," *Fortune*, November, 1961). There Kaiser has afoot a vast $128-million project, which includes a huge aluminum reduction plant, powered with electricity generated by the Volta River Dam, designed by Kaiser Engineers and now under construction. Edgar Kaiser himself drove the opening wedge into Ghana. His close personal relationship with Nkrumah, as well as his belief that Nkrumah can and will create a tolerable business climate, still forms one of the project's prime instruments. Yet the Ghana undertaking would try the patience of a Ghandi: Nkrumah's intemperate statements and attitudes have caused a deterioration in U.S.-Ghana relationships, and if the result should be the termination of U.S. aid, it would be a hard blow to Edgar's hopes. While the Kaiser companies, whose Ghana agreements are appropriately hedged with guarantees, would not be badly hurt financially if the Ghana plant remained unbuilt, the psychologic blow would send a shock through the whole system. Even optimistic Kaiser ears would have to hear the creak of doubt.

What would happen to Edgar Kaiser's philosophy then remains to be seen. So far, he remains unshaken in his conviction that the only intelligent and practical way for U.S. business to enter foreign markets is with a local partner. Nor does he see any reason why the U.S. company should insist on majority control. "I don't see any special merit in having 51 percent," he says. "If you're in trouble locally, that 1 percent isn't going to save you. They'll find a way of kicking you out anyway." Sums up an aluminum-company executive: "According to Edgar, local partnership is the greatest thing since the wheel."

Earthquake in Argentina

But one seismic jolt to that declaration has already been recorded in Argentina. There, Willys owns 29 percent of, and manages, Industrias Kaiser Argentina (IKA), an independent automobile company making a line of Jeep vehicles and passenger cars in Córdoba. Ever since it began operating in 1956, with old dies from the former Kaiser Motors Corp., IKA has turned a good profit. But, in a typical way, both Edgar Kaiser and Willys' president, Stephen A. Girard, have always been proud not only of IKA's good work, but also of its good works. Edgar has often pointed with pride to the fact that Argentine ownership of a large part of the company has helped local relations, that its higher-than-average wages have lifted the economy of Córdoba, and that IKA's loyal workers, who began by bicycling to the plant, now come in their own cars. The Argentine operation looked like a first-rate illustration of the infallibility of the Kaiser creed.

Then came the jolt. With a deteriorating national economy, the car market dropped, and IKA decided to shut down production for two weeks. Violence flared. A group of angry workers forced about 200 foremen, including North Americans and Argentineans, into the area of IKA's big ovens, where paint is baked on car bodies. Thousands of watching employees made no move to interfere. Then the word traveled to the plant manager: "Start up the plant, or we'll march these men into the ovens—and turn the heat on." IKA's management had to capitulate. Later, after union negotiations, the plant was successfully shut down for two weeks—and, surprisingly, only about 15 percent of the workers accepted IKA's offer for an interest-free loan on wages to tide them over the two-week period. Evidently the threat of starvation was not the motivation for the violence. Now the plant is operating once more. But the atmosphere around Córdoba isn't ever likely to be the same again.

It was enough to give a man the Willys.

Meanwhile, Willys Motors faces an uphill road at home. Edgar Kaiser is under no illusions about Detroit since he went through a test of fire as president of the Kaiser-Frazer Corp. That experience left its mark. "We went through $110 million," Edgar recalled recently, "and then for six weeks I couldn't pay the bills. It was the first time in my life I ever had that experience. Yet it was invaluable. You win all your life, and that's one thing. Then suddenly you lose, and that's quite another." After the loss, Edgar went back to California in 1954, over the next five years gradually to assume control of all the Kaiser industries. But he has always had, according to Steve Girard, "a chunk of his heart in Willys Motors."

Two years ago Willys faced an exacting decision. "Fifty percent of our net," recalls Girard, "was coming from our foreign sales. But we could see that, in the face of so much local foreign production, the export market was going to decline. We knew we had to have something new." But the decision to put out a new line wasn't easy. "This was a big question for us," continues Girard. "We had been badly burned once. There was some real reluctance about whether we should get back into it all. Bankers eyed us very carefully. After long discussions, we finally decided, 'Let's finance it, and let's go.'"

By Detroit standards, the new models are modest enough. They cost $24 million to tool. The key model is the Jeep Wagoneer, a station wagon, available with four-wheel drive and automatic transmission. Together with its companion series of four-wheel-drive trucks, production now stands at 350 a day—volume that Girard says "would just be a nuisance to Ford or G.M., but it means a lot to us." Although orders are backlogged, no dramatic increase in production is contemplated. "With Kaiser Motors, just as we got the production up, demand fell off, and there we were," remembers Edgar ruefully. "I don't want that to happen again." Besides these new models, Willys has recently won a $58-million Defense Department contract for the production of around 1,000 new military Jeeps a month. The Jeep Universal continues to be Willys' "bread and butter business." And Willys is bolstered further not only by the earnings submitted by IKA, and by Willys-Overland do Brasil (which sold around 60,000 vehicles last year), but also by royalties from companies it licenses throughout the world.

Still, the outcome for Willys rides on the new models. Last year's loss at Willys was the first since Kaiser has owned the company. The new models represent Willys' big effort to get back, and stay back, in the domestic black. Once that happens, Willys can push the prosperity of its foreign companies without worrying at the same time about having to export a high number of units from Toledo. Then Willys can get busy paying off the $21 million it owes to its parent company. So Willys, more than any other part of the Kaiser complex, might improve the condition of Kaiser Industries. Edgar Kaiser puts it this way: "Over the years the aluminum, cement, and steel companies will increase their dividends to us. That will improve our situation, but only gradually. With Willys, however—well, the auto business can be cold, but it can also get hot as a fox. If that happens, it could make a dramatic difference to Kaiser Industries." It could also make a dramatic difference if things at Willys went the other way.

The Deal in Steel

Kaiser Steel has never interested Edgar Kaiser in the way that Willys Motors does. Edgar first became active in the steel company around 1959, when he took a hand in its labor relations, and that is still the area which concerns him most. For other matters, he acts as he does toward the domestic aluminum business— as a concerned, but more traditional, chairman of the board. Informed regularly about the steel situation, he leaves all but the biggest decisions in the hands of Gene Trefethen and the executives of the steel company itself. And, at the moment, those hands are very full indeed.

Kaiser Steel was born in debt. It was built during the war by Henry Kaiser with $91 million of borrowed RFC money. Then Kaiser repaid the RFC in 1950, with financing arranged by

George Woods for the purpose. (Kaiser executives, who are very sensitive to the old saw about how Henry Kaiser "backed a truck up to the Mint" during the war, are quick to point out that the $91 million represented "100 cents on the dollar plus interest" for the U.S. Government.) In the 1950's the company went through a $327-million expansion program—slightly bigger than the one the aluminum company went through in the same decade —and it still carries nearly three times as much debt as the average ratio in the industry. In the eyes of some Kaiser financiers, however, that difference simply indicates that the rest of the industry is lagging behind the times. Says one of them: "That debt may bother the college professors, but it doesn't trouble financial people."

But the company's present predicament does. In its early years, Kaiser Steel—serving its seven-state western market from its integrated Fontana, California, plant, and enjoying the same $14-a-ton freight differential that eastern companies charged western customers—boomed along with earnings of 10 percent and more on sales. Then that pleasant panorama swiftly faded. In 1958, Kaiser Steel began to suffer setbacks, just as the whole industry did. In that recession year its earnings fell to 3 percent of sales—but worse was yet to come. Foreign competition, mostly from Japan, began to hit the West Coast and Kaiser Steel, especially in the production of reinforcing bars and continuous-weld pipe. By 1962, 60 percent of the western steel market for small-diameter pipe was in foreign hands. Besides, some West Coast consumers began to move their plants back east, where steel was cheaper. Kaiser Steel's total production had always been relatively small—around 1,300,000 tons a year, which represents about 20 percent of the western market for which Kaiser Steel competes, but only 1.8 percent of the total national output—and these combined difficulties pushed production down to the point of no return.

Or, to be exact, the point of less than no return. Kaiser Steel lost over $7 million in 1959, over $8 million in 1960, and over $5 million in 1962. (Helped by a $16-million tax-loss carry-over, it took a breather in 1961, showing earnings of $17 million.) As Kaiser executives point out, the importance of those losses should be evaluated only after consideration of the high depreciation, which reached $31 million last year; if Kaiser Steel were depreciating at a slower rate, its current earnings record would be better. Still, the situation had changed radically for the worse, and interest payments of around $1 million a month in 1962 seemed a lot more onerous than they had in the halcyon years. By mid-1962, it was apparent that something had to give.

The Misgivings That Gave

What gave was prices. Kaiser Steel figured that foreign imports were costing its customers on the average $25 to $30 a ton less than home-grown steel—a difference so great that no assurance of service or quick delivery could paper it over. Not without misgivings—"it was a little like hitting themselves over the head with a hammer, but they had to do it," comments an observer—Kaiser Steel dropped its prices about $12 a ton in October of last year—almost the amount of the eastern freight differential. That across-the-board price cut has reduced the foreign advantage to around $10 to $15 a ton; at that level, Jack Ashby, president of Kaiser Steel, thinks some old customers can be tempted back into the fold. "With our quick service, they can reduce their inventories, and have quality control assured," he says. "That ought to be enough." Ashby also confidently believes the price cut will be enough to improve Kaiser Steel's position in domestic competition. Whether it will be, however, won't be demonstrable for several months.

Kaiser Steel's other move came in the field of labor relations. According to eastern steelmen, steel labor on the West Coast has never been as proficient as it is around Pittsburgh, where father teaches son how to make steel. And, ever since he broke with the industry to settle the steel strike separately in 1959, Edgar Kaiser had been troubled by the thought that "every couple of years, we have to go through these negotiations, with lots of pressure on both sides. I've never agreed with businessmen who say that since it's management that has to make the money, it's management that has to dictate the labor terms. I wanted our approach to be bilateral." With an eye both to efficiency and continuity, then, Edgar Kaiser joined with the Steelworkers' David McDonald three years ago in setting up a committee to seek a long-range solution to the labor problem. The resultant plant, put into effect last month, showed the original Kaiser touch: in essence, the four-year plan will divide among Kaiser workers one-third of whatever savings the company may achieve by cutting costs or increasing productivity. It will thus pass on to Kaiser workers a part of something that, at present, does not exist, but that they can help to create. The bookkeeping that the plan involves is very intricate, and its results—both to management and labor—are still unknown.

But a big turnaround at Kaiser Steel would involve nothing less than a shift in the California steel market. At present that market consumes principally tinplate and fabricated steel for construction. But Kaiser Steel turns in its most efficient performance in the primary steps of steelmaking, rather than in fabrication; it has an excellent supply of good-grade ore nearby, and it can make good profits through the ingot stage even though, as Executive Vice President Fred Borden says, "with the size of orders we get, we roll 100 tons of steel, and then have to change our rolls, while the eastern companies roll 1,000 tons before they have to change theirs." If Kaiser could raise its volume of manufacturing steel, it might see the light of a happier day before too long. So an important Kaiser objective is to persuade eastern industrialists to open plants near those growing California markets—not so difficult a job, Kaiser thinks, as it might have been before it lowered its prices. If a couple of auto-frame companies moved west, it could make a big difference to Kaiser. But the process seems likely to be slow.

The Solidity of Cement

Another important Kaiser investment is the Permanente Cement Co. Permanente is a 39 percent owned Kaiser enterprise with the usual high debt (and the usual attitude toward it: "It may be high to the bankers, but we think it's conservative"), earnings of $6 million on $75 million in sales in 1962, and a good record of remissions to the parent. Tied to the West—"as the population goes, so goes our business"—Permanente Cement, supported by a gypsum business that accounts for 39 percent of total sales, can look to a solid future. To be sure, some outside Kaiser officers think it's a stolid future, too. "About the only thing you can do when you bring out a new model in the cement business is to change the bag," cracks Willys Motors' Girard. But Permanente's president, Wallace Marsh, is playing a fascinating checker game with plant locations, depleting resources, and shifting markets. The same situation occurs in the Sand and Gravel Division, which remits around $1 million a year to the parent.

Kaiser Engineers also holds an important place in the Kaiser scheme of things. Beginning as an offshoot of the old construction companies, Engineers' growth in its domestic and foreign divisions has been startling. It moved from $123 million worth of work completed in 1959 to $170 million in 1962. Domestically, it had some losses in missile-base construction in 1960-61, but recovered $8,800,000 last year. Engineers does not break out separate figures for the two divisions, but it turned a profit in 1962. It is working on a $130-million domestic backlog, as well as considerable new business for 1963, when the Engineers' performance should be good.

If it turns out that way, it would be a particular source of gratification to Edgar Kaiser. He was twenty-three when he worked with a construction gang on Henry Kaiser's first big project, Hoover Dam. As a result, Edgar, when he can find time, still keeps close to the business of the Engineers. The original lure is there—like Henry, Edgar Kaiser feels a romantic tug in constructing bridges, dams, and tunnels. And the bright bauble of work overseas shows up once more. Led by Edgar, the Kaiser Engineers International Division took on a $115-million project at Snowy Mountain in Australia (it lost money on the first link, a fourteen-mile tunnel); finished in 1959 a $150-million steel mill for the Tata interests near Calcutta (it turned a profit, but had a rough time with its hard-to-satisfy clients); did the design for the big Volta River project now steaming along in Ghana; and is willing to plunge into any other foreign sea where Edgar's travels and the chance to profit may coincide. At home, Kaiser Engineers is busiest with the Atomic Energy Commission, for which it is engaged in a project whose total value is $150 million. Also in the scientific field is the Aircraft and Electronics Division, which acts as a subcontractor on NASA and Defense Department projects, and yielded $1 million in profits last year.

As for Hawaii Kai, that is Henry Kaiser's domain. His earlier Hawaiian project, Hawaiian Village, was sold in 1961 to Hilton Hotels, at a profit of $5 million—although the sale was not entirely Henry Kaiser's choice, since $5 million was needed to fund Kaiser Industries' loans due at the time the sale was made. Then Henry turned to the development of 6,000 acres around Koko Head, a huge project involving, with the usual Kaiser flair, the dredging of a few lagoons and the moving of a couple of mountains. The project disturbs some Kaiser executives, who believe that it will be a long time before it shows a profit, and who think that the present condition of Kaiser Industries makes inadvisable an investment of the size of Hawaii Kai (some $22 million is tied up in it). To increase their anguish, the real-estate market in Hawaii is in the doldrums at present. But Henry Kaiser has been right many times before, and he may be right this time too; in any case,

Hawaii Kai will go on. Henry's enthusiasm for the project is boundless, and—as Edgar Kaiser is aware—it helps keep Henry hearty and vigorous. "I like to be in the stream of action," Henry says.

To Compete—and Assist

In a curious way, all the Kaiser companies both compete with and help one another. In the early years, as Gene Trefethen says, "we purposely drew the curtain down between the companies." Now the aluminum, cement, and steel companies frequently compete with one another: in the recent bidding for California's license-plate business, Kaiser Steel and Kaiser Aluminum executives butted heads in Sacramento. Even more often, one or the other of the metal companies finds itself in competition with the cement company, which is very active everywhere in West Coast construction. And none of the three companies will buy a Willys Jeep unless the Jeep is the right vehicle for the job.

Yet cooperation is growing, too. From abroad, any Kaiser man, from Edgar on down, may generate Kaiser fame and bring back new opportunities for some part of the complex. As an example, Willys Motors recently encouraged a Brazilian supplier to a Willys foreign partner, Renault, to buy some aluminum from the Kaiser company. "None of us just wears a Willys sweatshirt," says Steve Girard. And what Girard calls "the back scratching around here" also goes on through the medium of Kaiser Engineers. When Engineers is doing work for another Kaiser enterprise, some advantages accrue to the total complex. "When we decided that some Kaiser Steel construction had gone far enough, and we wanted to stop it sooner than we had planned at first, it turned out to be easy because Engineers was doing the job," recalls Edgar Kaiser. "We just cut it off at the pockets, and that was that." To be on the safe side, an intercompany committee oversees the propriety of all dealings between Kaiser companies.

An Albatross for Industries

The success or failure of all these variegated undertakings will eventually be reflected at the top of the pyramid in Kaiser Industries. Here the burden of debt weighs far more heavily than in the case of Kaiser Aluminum or even Kaiser Steel. Kaiser Industries was formed when Kaiser Motors had to accept defeat in its postwar bid to become a major factor in automotive production. The Kaisers might have elected to let Motors go into bankruptcy, and concentrated on their other companies and investments. But partly because of the effect that bankruptcy would have had on those other companies, and partly because of a genuine feeling of responsibility to Kaiser Motors stockholders, the Kaisers, Trefethen, and their intimate financial adviser, George Woods, decided in 1955 both to pay off the creditors and to give the public stockholders some interest in the Kaiser future. In the complex stock deal that Woods worked out, Kaiser Motors disappeared, and Kaiser Industries began its life in 1956 with $95-million term debt.

That hard decision was the correct one. But it hung an albatross around Industries' neck. Today, seven years after Kaiser Industries began, it still carries a total of $41 million of inherited debt, and its stockholdings are pledged as collateral. Kaiser Industries has also contracted new obligations: it has lent $21 million to its wholly owned subsidiary, Willys Motors, rechristened Kaiser Jeep Corp., which has a $22-million debt of its own. Besides, Kaiser Industries owns 25 percent of Kaiser Center Inc., which borrowed $37 million in 1957 to put up the Oakland showplace. And the whole situation is made more difficult by the fact that Kaiser Industries is not helped along very much by depreciation. The result is that it has a low cash flow, and debt repayment is slow.

As for the poor Industries stockholder, he has his stock certificates, but he hasn't got much more so far. He's never been paid a dividend, and if he bought 100 shares of Kaiser-Frazer Corp. (later Kaiser Motors) for $1,000 when it was first issued in 1945, he would now be holding twenty-five shares of Kaiser Industries at around $7—worth $175. And, while he can get a sense of comfort from the fact that he owns a share in the big companies which pay those steady dividends to Kaiser Industries—"ringing up that old cash register," as Trefethen says—he may also become unsettled by the ironic thought that his immediate chances once again hang on the automobile business: this time, on the fate of the new models Willys is bringing out.

He might also, with justice, hope that Industries will soon look to its future management. Too much of that organization now turns on the twin hinges of Edgar Kaiser and Gene Trefethen. When the several Kaiser companies were smaller, there was more executive movement between them, but that has slowed recently. As a result, while competent people can be found in the several divisions and companies, few of them have had the opportunity to develop the Industries' outlook. And within Industries itself, management is pretty thin. Both Trefethen and Edgar, who are the same age, must soon start to move executives up to their administrative level to prepare for the day—remote as it may seem—when the duo will be replaced. Indeed, they should have started such preparation before this.

No Pinchbeck Tribe

Yet much in the Kaiser organization merits optimism. Kaiser Industries sits atop no pinchbeck tribe of companies. Most are solid earners that have recently completed expensive modernizing processes, and now stand ready to grow. Even today's big loser, Kaiser Steel, is positioned so that when external improvements come, they will be translated quickly into improvements in earnings. Generally, according to Trefethen, "the period of consolidation is behind us, and a period of profits lies ahead." Trefethen's own careful management should help bring that day of profits closer. But even if Kaiser gets the kind of growth in the world economy that it is looking for, the day when Kaiser Industries will be sufficiently freed of its debt to pay a dividend still seems at least a couple of years off.

Edgar Kaiser is doing what he can to hurry that day along. Whether behind his twenty-foot desk hung with telephones in Kaiser Center, or in his office in New York, or in a dinner jacket in Accra, he is running the complex with the air of a man half-inspired, half-bedeviled, and thoroughly delighted. A man of great good will, Edgar always leaves his office door open, and he sometimes hails passersby, or calls, "You might just as well come in as pace around out there." During a busy day Edgar may stride from behind his desk into a colleague's office, find him in the midst of a business telephone call, and pick up an extension phone to chime in with his views. He drinks coffee all day out of a constantly replenished thermos, and often dials his own telephone calls—to the despair of his long-suffering secretary, who has trouble keeping up with his appointments and his whereabouts. Not without pleasure, Edgar will sometimes call to her as he strides by: "We may have to go to London tonight—I'm not sure yet." The contrast with the composed office atmosphere that surrounds an executive like Jersey Standard's Jack Rathbone —who keeps to a rhythmic schedule of meetings, and every day at two minutes before 11:00 A.M. enters Jersey's boardroom—is startling. Remarks Gene Trefethen, "We don't believe in committee management."

So Edgar Kaiser stands now with his shoulder to the wheel. But he never forgets his father, who was for Edgar the purveyor of the dream. When Henry enters the office, Edgar is likely to call, "Good morning, Mr. Kaiser," and then spring around his desk to kiss the old man's cheek. Remarked Edgar recently, "I'm the lucky one. Dad built a lot of bridges, and he built one for me, too."

Sears Makes It Look Easy*

BY JOHN MCDONALD

Sears, Roebuck is the paragon of retailers. Every one of its 761 stores has plenty of competition, but Sears as an organization is in a very special league. In that league, as Jack Schwadron, merchandise chief of Korvette, puts its, Sears is No. 1 in the U.S., and also No. 2, 3, 4, and 5. On the basis of sales volume, A & P is the only retailer of any kind that is close to Sears' $5.1 billion (for the year ending January 31). A & P may actually be a bit larger than Sears right now (its annual report is due this month), but that situation is not likely to persist very long. A & P's sales, like its profits, have not been growing in recent years, while old Sears keeps on expanding like a small, young growth company. That is just the point about Sears. Most retailers expect to meet increasing difficulties as they grow larger, and more complex; but last year, after ten years in which it had an average rise in sales of 5.6 percent compounded, Sears had a fantastic new rise of 11.1 percent—i.e., of $500 million, which is roughly the size of the Gimbel chain. Right now it shows promise of a lot more growth, with the earnings rising along with the sales.

How did Sears do it? In a way, the most arresting aspect of its story is that there was no gimmick. Sears opened no big bag of tricks, shot off no skyrockets. Instead, it looked as though everybody in its organization simply did the right thing, easily

* *May 1964*

and naturally. As it always has, Sears bucked the entire retail field in just about every line except food, liquor, and autos, in every major U.S. market area. It competed against discounters offering the toughest price competition and it competed against department stores offering high fashion and elegance. And yet Sears kept right on rolling over the competition. At 11 percent, its sales gain last year was more than twice the 5 percent for all U.S. retail sales in Sears' lines.

It is quite possible for a big corporation to make one big mistake and thereby lose its position for years, as Ford did when it stayed too long with the Model T in the 1920's, and as Montgomery Ward did when Sewell Avery insisted on contraction instead of expansion after World War II. Certainly, Sears was favored by Ward's abdication, as General Motors was by Ford's. But Sears' success is obviously based on more than Ward's big mistake. Indeed, its success suggests another moral: that a corporation making the right decisions at the right time can sometimes gain a position of strength that may endure for years. Going back to the beginning of its modern era—i.e., around 1925 —one can make out ten critical decisions at Sears whose effect can still be seen.

• The fateful decision in the mid-1920's to add retail stores to the original catalogue business as the farm population came to town in automobiles.

• The decision to centralize merchandising (all buying, promotional, and advertising operations) in Chicago, and to control store operations from territorial headquarters—a unique management structure that forms the warp and woof of Sears today.

• The decision to control the cost, quality, and quantity of Sears' merchandise by having deliveries made to its own specifications. Sears today is responsible for the design details of 95 percent of the goods it sells.

• The sweeping decision after World War II to expand aggressively, to relocate old stores and put new stores in new locations. Thus Sears very early preempted the prize locations as the population went from East to West and from the city to the suburbs.

• The decision in the mid-1950's to expand its sale of soft goods in retail stores, that is, to go to full-line department stores in place of the old hardware sort of stores featuring tools and fishing tackle.

• The more recent decision to play up style and fashion along with economy, a decision that has modernized Sears' image and,

incidentally, made it one of the largest mink and diamond merchants in the country.
• The decision to set up a service organization, despite its low or zero profitability, to support the sales of Sears' durable goods.
• The decision to diversify into insurance and other financial services in the Allstate operation, which has possibilities of becoming as big as Sears itself one day. (Right now the corporation is about ready to add a mutual-fund selling operation to Allstate.)
• A series of decisions to invest in supplier corporations, which not only increased Sears' prime strength in distribution but has led to some sizable capital gains.
• Finally, a series of decisions to invest heavily in superior personnel, in part through large-scale training programs (200 to 500 college graduates a year go through these), and related decisions to promote from within, to be generous with profit sharing, and also to purchase Sears' own stock for the profit-sharing fund, as a result of which the employees today own about 26 percent of the common. The result of such policies has been that Sears has superior management in considerable depth—indeed, it is the target now of management raids by Ward's.

Not all of these decisions were sharply defined as of a moment. Some took years of evolution. Some decisions seemed to flow naturally out of others. And their cumulative effect was to create an extraordinary powerhouse of a company that nevertheless seemed to be doing nothing more than going about its business in a simple, natural way. Sears has made it appear that you need only start a retail business, give the customer good merchandise at a good price, and give him good service; set up strong buying lines linking factories to stores and merchandise so that the customer gets what he wants; then take your money and set up new stores in growing areas of the country; add new goods from time to time, as in the soft lines; get your employees interested in keeping the show going—and lo and behold, you end up with a growth company doing 2 percent of total U.S. retail sales, and 6 percent of sales in its own merchandise lines. It looks quite easy—or would, except for the fact that Sears was the only company that did it.

Store Buyers in Captivity

Retailing through a chain of hundreds of stores is an extraordinary exercise in management. It is, above all, a business of supervision, and the key to the high performance at Sears is control—control of the merchandise and control of the way it passes through the stores.

The dimensions of the problem may be suggested by a few figures. A single class-A store—i.e., a full-line department store—may have annual sales of as much as $30 million. And all together Sears has 149 class-A stores located in all parts of the country, with thirteen more scheduled to be put into operation in 1964 and nineteen in 1965. That is obviously a lot of different businesses to open up every morning. And yet it is apparent that, somehow, they are all part of the same business. All of them are good-looking, modern, styled in "economic good taste," and obviously well maintained. They vary considerably in some respects. They are splashy with color in the Southwest and California, neat and utilitarian in the old, declined neighborhoods of Chicago, earnestly and sedately economic in New England. At the Sears along the highway in Torrance, south of Los Angeles, the racks of dresses are aglow with a variety of colors, in distinct contrast to the solid, staid, gray-brown checks of the New England stores. But despite these differences, the stores are all unmistakably Sears in character: the company's mark is on the clerks and managers, the merchandise (identical except for some regional expressions, like the colorful California soft goods), the display fixtures, lighting, and store layout.

The heart of the control procedures is the merchandise. In effect, every Sears store manager is a captive customer of a single "seller," namely, Sears' merchandising department in Chicago, and its branches in New York City, Los Angeles, Dallas, and Atlanta. Thus management policy and product policy are decisively interlocked at Sears. All the merchandising decisions, right down to the specifications and price of every hammer on the hardware counters, are made in Chicago.

"The core of Sears is the Chicago merchandise brain trust," says Charles A. Meyer, vice president in charge of the southwest territory, sitting in Dallas. If you had to name the one most critical operating group in Sears, it would be this department, which first creates the product, assigns it a specific place in the catalogue and a specific counter in the stores, and also provides the stores with a "syndicated service" of display materials, advertising designs (including the mats), and selections for special promotions. George Struthers, the merchandise vice president who oversees this operation, is probably the third-highest-ranking executive in the company, after the chairman and president. Struthers is a tall, young-looking executive, now fifty, an ardent fisherman who manages to pursue the sport from Alaska to the Cayman Islands in the Caribbean without ever really losing track of the $5 billion worth of goods that flow through his department. "Everything starts with the merchandise and has to be centralized," says Struthers. "It's obvious—you could hardly decentralize it and realize the economies of purchasing the product and booming it."

The Buyer Who Just Signed

The merchandising department consists of fifty divisions, each representing a category of product—e.g., plumbing and heating, infants' wear, automotive accessories—which has its own supervisor—an executive whose "sales volume" will be anywhere from $25 million (notions) to $300 million (appliances). The supervisors, Struthers says, "are given fantastic freedom to perform." However, their final results are monitored. Each, for example, maintains five-year projections of his category's sales volume, and actual sales are checked back against the projections. Twice a year the merchandise heads meet to establish their general policies and evaluate sales performance by lines of goods.

Struthers' merchandising supervisors are a different breed of cat from the traditional department-store buyer. The latter normally shop around among suppliers and deal with them at arm's length. Sears' buyers, however, are responsible for the product from the original specifications, which they are apt to develop themselves after close work with manufacturers, designers, and Sears engineers, for the factory production, and for the entire merchandising program, including pricing. (To assist the buyers, Sears' centralized staff departments provide a testing and development laboratory, industrial-design, financing, distribution, and marketing expertise.) The buyers watch closely the flow of goods from production to store deliveries to sales. In the fashion-goods lines, where demand is especially volatile, the buyer gets a weekly report on the flow of his goods—or a daily report, if he thinks one is necessary—so that he can correct bad guesses before the company gets overstocked. The more stable lines are reported monthly.

Another kind of report is provided by catalogue sales, which are an excellent harbinger of demand. A buyer may obtain a daily record of catalogue sales for his own line shortly after a new catalogue is delivered. Indeed, in the first week, with only 30 percent of the catalogues delivered, he can often get a fix on the final sales volume of his line. Sears' records of catalogue sales have been analyzed exhaustively, and the effect on sales of the size of a catalogue entry, its color, place on the page, etc., has also been analyzed, so that the buyer can adjust for all these variables in calculating what level of sales to expect. Advance indications from the catalogue sometimes save buyers from over-ordering items. They do not, of course, save the buyer from his first order. One memorable mistake recalled by Struthers recently was made by the buyer who persuaded himself that gardening dresses, at a reasonable stiff price for Sears, would be a hot item. He ordered 50,000 dresses, and then found that there weren't 50,000 women who wanted gardening dresses—as a matter of fact, there were only about 100. The dresses eventually wound up as a donation to a relief program for Hungarian refugees. Asked how a buyer could go for 50,000 gardening dresses, Struthers shrugged and said, "He just signed the order."

The buyers' sales forecasts are a crucial matter at Sears because they set a vast production effort in motion. The buyer takes his original forecast, then decides what proportion of an item to have on the shelf when the buying season begins. This decision commits him: if the stores refuse to handle any of it—as, in theory, they might—or take it but can't sell it, he would have to figure out some way to get rid of it. But the buyer is committed to the factory; he cannot cancel out there. Sears' contracts are devised so that the manufacturer has firm orders for at least six months ahead, and can concentrate on efficient manufacturing. Often he has firm orders looking ahead for years. Even in fashion goods, Sears may have a line of apparel committed to one manufacturer for five to seven years. The commitment would not be for a specific design, of course; it allows for changes in line with style trends. It also allows for some variation in production as the sales forecast changes: in 1963, for example, Sears originally forecasted a 5 percent rise in sales and actually made the 11 percent rise. It got the extra goods produced and onto the shelves by opening wider the spigots of factory production as the signs appeared that the forecast was too low.

This kind of arrangement enables Sears to merchandise its own brands at low cost with effective quality controls. It depends, of course, on close and usually long-term relationships with suppliers. Most of Sears' purchases are made on a "known cost" basis, i.e., Sears is privy to the manufacturer's production data. Where necessary, Sears may also provide engineering and other technical assistance to a supplier. Sears does a lot of buying, but nobody "sells" Sears. The first cost that it cuts out of a supply contract is the selling commission.

The Companies Sears Keeps

A considerable volume—around 30 percent—of Sears' products are not really bought at all, but manufactured by companies in which Sears has an equity of 9 to 100 percent. Sears is, in fact, one of the largest manufacturers in the U.S. It had several motives for getting into manufacturing. Historically, it bought into plants to get an assured supply in emergencies, and to get a line on costs and quality control. Later it encountered "cartels," so to speak, that is, industries in which no brand-producing company would manufacture privately branded goods for Sears. (In new industries, moreover, like television, the manufacturers had their hands full just building up their own brands.)

Sears now owns only one company outright (Newark Ohio), and the supplier firms in which Sears has the largest and the most long-standing investments are in the hard-goods field: Whirlpool (1963 sales: $539 million), of which Sears controls 19 percent, and which sells 65 percent of its goods to Sears (Kenmore and Coldspot appliances); Globe-Union Inc. of Milwaukee (1963 sales: $73,300,000), of which Sears controls 12 percent, and which sells 36 percent of its goods (auto batteries) to Sears; George D. Roper Corp. of Kankakee, Illinois (1963 sales: $41,400,000), of which Sears owns 25 percent and controls another 15 percent, and which sells 55 percent of its goods to Sears (Kenmore gas ranges); and Universal-Rundle of New Castle, Pennsylvania (1963 sales: $19 million), which is 72 percent owned by Sears and makes plumbing fixtures.

Though Sears got into manufacturing only to help its retail operations, a few of its investments have returned handsome capital gains—and Sears' motives in manufacturing are naturally somewhat mixed nowadays. In 1956, Sears sold all its paint and wallpaper factories to DeSoto Chemical Coatings and received in return 92 percent of the DeSoto common and 55 percent of the preferred—with the Sears Foundation picking up some more. DeSoto now supplies Sears with 90 percent of its paint and 85 percent of its wallpaper requirements. It is the nation's largest wallpaper manufacturer, and Sears accounts for close to 60 percent of its business (its total 1963 sales: $70,800,000). Sears has also created a giant TV-set manufacturer, now probably the fifth largest in the U.S. Between 1951 and 1960 it acquired virtually all the common stock of Warwick Manufacturing, supplier of the Silvertone line of TV and radio sets, phonographs, and tape recorders. In 1963, Sears merged Warwick and Pacific Mercury, another set manufacturer. The new Warwick Electronics has a sales level of about $110 million.

Sears has a soft-goods company of about the same size. Kellwood Co. came into existence in 1961, in a merger of fifteen soft-goods companies that supplied up to 90 percent of Sears' requirements in their various lines. Most of these companies manufacture in the South, but Kellwood's management is now in Chicago.

Whether it owns it suppliers or has long-term contracts with them, Sears has been increasingly interested—and successful—in developing its own brands. Last year, for instance, a number of different products for infants were pulled together into one department to be sold, for the first time, with the Sears label. The change was suggested by George Struthers and implemented after a preliminary study by Gordon Heaton, product supervisor for infants' and children's wear, indicated that Sears was offering nothing more than many other retailers of bottles, food warmers, etc., and was not getting a very sizable share of the market. Sears settled on one small manufacturer, Hanks Craft, of Reedsburg, Wisconsin, and gave it a contract to produce a wide range of new baby products. The merchandise, which is just now beginning to show up in the stores, includes a variety of originally designed products, including hourglass-shaped bottles with dials at the top to indicate whether they hold formula or milk. Most of the competing branded items have now disappeared from Sears' shelves.

Sears Gets Organized

Sears' success is rooted in organization. For many years the company had serious difficulties in defining its organization. The solution of these difficulties, in 1948, was a major breakthrough for Sears—and it led, naturally and easily, to a series of other breakthroughs.

A centralized organization was, of course, inherent in the original mail-order business. But the case was not so clear when the stores came along; and a big and critical decision on organization became imperative when Sears opened 324 retail stores between 1925 and 1929. At first, Sears retained its centralized way of doing things; the stores were viewed simply as annexes of the mail-order houses and were managed from the houses; the only real problem seemed to be finding enough people to man the new stores that were opening just about every week. Sears' chairman, General Robert E. Wood, who had been fired from Ward's and hired by Julius Rosenwald (that was in 1924), eventually saw that the problem went a lot deeper than personnel, and ultimately solved it. The decision to open retail stores and the present form of organization are Wood's two great legacies to Sears. But it is a fact that for many years he held out against introducing the kind of organization that made the company's growth possible.

Actually, the basic outlines of the present organization—i.e., centralized merchandising combined with decentralized administration of the stores—were on paper in 1929, almost twenty years before they were adopted. The concept was originally proposed by a Sears committee on organization set up by Wood. After a brief trial the proposed scheme was abandoned. It remained abandoned all during the 1930's, for a number of reasons.[1] One was the difficulty of finding supervisory personnel to administer the territorial divisions. Another was friction between the central merchants in Chicago and the territorial administrations over what functions were to be grouped in the territories. Finally, there was General Wood's fear that the concept would lead to the growth of territorial bureaucracies with their own interests. The depression settled the argument for a while: as the business contracted, Wood ruled out any activity that might lead to duplication of effort, and so the territorial administrations were disbanded. This left Sears with one central merchandising office in Chicago and hundreds of stores reporting directly to the president. It didn't work very well, and was gradually modified by the development of big-city groupings—the pooling of Sears' talent and effort in these cities and in zone offices.

In 1940, Wood made a more serious effort to get the stores under control. He set up a West Coast territorial administration with jurisdiction over Sears' stores in nine western states. Except for merchandising, which was still run from Chicago, this administration was given charge of store and catalogue operations. It seemed to work, and after the war four more territorial organizations were set up, covering the rest of the U.S. The Chicago office ended up with control over buying, factory management, finance, and several staff operations. The five territories became administrative dukedoms of a sort. Each is headed by a powerful

---

[1] A detailed account of the organizational experiments between the 1920's and the 1940's is given in the chapter on Sears in Alfred D. Chandler Jr.'s book, *Strategy and Structure* (the M.I.T. Press, 1962).

vice president, and these five constitute one-half of the corporate officers on the board of directors, the other five being Chicago men: the chairman and president, vice presidents in charge of merchandising and personnel, and the controller.

General Wood's old concern about the growth of special territorial interests has not been borne out by events. In effect, the problem appears to have been solved by engaging the territorial managements so deeply in the administration of Sears policies; a corporate director is not apt to be distracted by regional adhesions. Any one of the territorial vice presidents could be called upon to return to Chicago in a couple of hours and take over the organization, as Chairman Austin Cushman (who had headed the West Coast territory) was a year and a half ago.

The connection between the territories and the parent is secured at several different points. One important point is the controller operation. The corporate controller at Sears, Howard Benthin, has rather extraordinary responsibilities. In a tradition that goes back to General Wood's desire for one central figure man, his office is always available to top officers who want any information—e.g., on marketing or construction costs—that would enable them to work out in detail the consequences of new policies. In addition, the corporate controller closely monitors the reports of the field controllers. Each week Benthin's office gets all the territorial figures on inventory and relates them to the sales budget; any significant discrepancy is followed by sharp and persistent inquiries.

By 1948 the present Sears organization had pretty much taken shape. Inevitably, some organizational details, and perhaps some of the corporate personality as well, change with each chief executive officer; yet Sears is now set up to keep right on rolling under quite different men. The last two chief executives were strikingly different. Charles Kellstadt, chairman in 1960-62, was by all accounts an extremely able chief who was strongly inclined to executive centralization, preferring to make a large number of detailed decisions himself. With Austin Cushman, the present chairman, the pendulum has swung the other way. Cushman is by disposition a delegator and a man shy of the public prominence that ordinarily comes to a Sears chief; he has remained almost invisible while he has guided the organization.

Cows in the Parking Lot

Sears' organization change was completed just in time for the great expansion. If it had not been completed, Wood's decision to expand might not have seemed so brilliantly right. As it was, however, Wood was able to expand furiously and across the board, building new stores in new areas, relocating stores in old areas, recruiting and training a management in depth, and developing lucrative ventures such as Allstate. Wood placed his big bets in the right places—Florida, Texas, and California—the places where the population was going. He insisted on, and got, locations that were in the path of the population growth, even if they didn't always look like good store sites at the time. Cushman recalled recently that he had looked for sites in orange groves and had put one California store on a dairy farm; when it opened there were cows in the parking lot. Once established, such stores had only to perform to the Sears standard in order to grow. The latecomers, e.g., Ward's, had to leapfrog over these stores to locations farther out.

Sears and Ward's had competed neck and neck in the 1920's and early 1930's. Ward's was actually the more aggressive of the two in expanding during the late 1930's. When the postwar competition began in 1946, its sales were almost two-thirds of Sears': $1 billion for Sears that year, vs. $655 million for Ward's. But the spread began to widen rapidly after Sears' expansion, and by 1954 Sears was at the $3-billion level, Ward's at about $1 billion. When Ward's finally turned to expansion, it had trouble finding good locations for new stores and more trouble with its run-down old stores. Its sales were only $1.5 billion last year, while Sears soared to its record $5.1 billion; in the same period J. C. Penney rose from $1.1 billion to $1.8 billion. Ward's percentage sales gain was 39 percent in the past ten years, Penney's was 64 percent, and Sears' was 76 percent. There are some important regional differences. Sears generally dominates Ward's in the big metropolitan areas, but Ward's has managed to stay ahead in many middle-sized cities, and also in a few big ones, including Fort Worth, Kansas City, and Detroit. There is no doubt that, while Sears now competes with thousands of retailers, it still regards Ward's as *the* competition. (Sears goes into shopping centers with Penney's, even though that chain is now full line, but still will not go in with Ward's.)

The decision to expand aggressively after World War II was accompanied by an important decision to push a lot deeper into soft goods. Sears had, of course, been a hard-goods company from the beginning—i.e., from the time, in 1887, when Richard Warren Sears hired Alvah Curtis Roebuck to help him sell watches. The company retained a strong hard-goods emphasis long after its catalogue began to offer economy dresses, overalls, and other clothing staples. But it was a measure of Sears' diffidence about fashion lines that, until after the war, the job of merchandising them was contracted out to an affiliate, Henry Rose Stores, Inc. This arrangement had come into being in 1928, when General Wood had established Rose as the sole agent for buying, distributing, and merchandising fashion lines for Sears' retail stores. Rose got a group of apparel suppliers attuned to Sears' policy of low-cost, economical operations. During the war Sears bought out Rose's interest, made the company a wholly owned subsidiary, and at the same time began to increase its interest in soft goods.

To some extent this decision was imposed by circumstance— the circumstance that hard goods virtually disappeared from the market during the war. In adding the new clothing lines, Sears took some steps to upgrade them. It hired Mary Lewis, a famous stylist and merchandiser who had been at Best's and Saks Fifth Avenue, as a consultant, mainly on sportswear for women. She worked with suppliers to add style to Sears' basic economy and quality, and actually succeeded in making some farm clothes (e.g., denim pants) fashionable.

The emphasis on soft goods inevitably receded somewhat after the war, when the appliance market was big and lush. When the appliance boom began to let up in the early 1950's, Sears turned back to soft goods. In 1954, moreover, Rose himself retired and a new generation of Sears men took over his operation. From then on soft goods visibly got more space in the catalogue and on the counters. In 1963 they represented 40 percent of corporate sales—about $2 billion.

Soft goods have represented some new kinds of problems for Sears. One large problem concerns inventory. In markets where styles change rapidly, how do you go about putting $2 billion worth of widely assorted articles in the places where the customers want them? Says a Sears executive: "It's not a problem with refrigerators, say, where you just turn on a spigot in the factory if you run short. But in soft goods you can't do that; it's difficult to find sources for new materials that suddenly become fashionable, difficult to keep up quality and to get delivery in time at a certain place." Furthermore, the customers keep getting harder to please; with more money in their pockets, greater exposure to fashion magazines, more foreign travel, customers have become sophisticated. Style has become so important to sales, says Vice President Charles Meyer, that "Sears can no longer say, 'Let Federated play with stretch fabrics for two years.' If we're not right on it, it will die before we get around to it. We think it's switched from wool to Banlon sweaters and suddenly it's mohair. The velocity is terrific."

Sears' ads for mink stoles are one sign of the new sophistication. The French and Italian provincial furniture is another. The well-advertised use of Ted Williams as a consultant on sporting goods, and Vincent Price to develop collections of original art, are other symbols of the new Sears. Several weeks ago Sears hired Letitia Baldrige, who had been Jacqueline Kennedy's social secretary in the White House as a consultant on teenage merchandise. The company has discovered that these special programs have a value that goes far beyond the product lines immediately involved. Said one Sears executive, "Fashion makes it easier to sell everything else."

The View from California

Sears' customers have increasingly taken on that middle-class, suburban look. Today only 4.6 percent of the revolving-credit customers, and only 7.8 percent of its easy-payment customers, are laborers, vs. 19 percent ten years ago. When Sears interviewed customers in twenty-five of its stores recently, 28 percent of them reported that they had family incomes of over $10,000, and 20 percent classified themselves as technicians, or professional workers. Sears believes the figures are exaggerated but probably not by much. In any case, it now takes the rich, new middle class for granted, exercising care only not to "trade up" the customers too rapidly. The company recently opened up a posh and flashy new store in Austin, Texas, where it expects to do a lot of business with high-income customers. But another new store in the cotton-and-cattle area of the Texas Panhandle had a subdued decor so that work-clothed shoppers would not feel uncomfortable.

As some of this may suggest, the turn to soft goods has had a lot to do with the transformed look of Sears' stores; at the same time the widening of the merchandise lines has made their operations a considerably larger problem for the territorial administrators. The individual manager of a class-A store is a man with a lot of responsibilities. He is expected to participate actively in civic activities. In the store itself he is responsible for the hiring and training of personnel, for meeting sales targets, and for maintaining profit margins. He will have at least two assistants for merchandise, one for administration and others for credit sales, customer service, warehouse operations, personnel, and security; he will also have his own controller. Beyond these

officials, each of the forty-five departments in a full-line store will
have a "division manager" in charge of the sales force on his line.
Of all Sears officials, he is the closest to the actual selling floor,
and is accordingly held responsible for the display, inventory, and
sales of his line. Perhaps a third of these division managers come
to the job after a year as post-college trainees; the best then make
the "highly promotable" list, which forms the base of Sears'
management in depth.

If the store is in, say, Los Angeles, its manager will be one of
sixteen reporting to that city's group manager. (Los Angeles'
sixteen class-A stores is more than Sears has in any other U.S.
city; the second city is Chicago, with twelve.) The group manager
there is a former class-A store manager; he took over the group
responsibilities when his predecessor was hired away by Ward's.
He now has a staff of thirty, including a controller and managers
for various lines of merchandise, and others for operations, credit,
and advertising.

Advertising is one of the key functions of any Sears group.
Because prices are uniform in the group area, no store does its
own advertising. Instead, the group arranges for all of the stores'
newspaper advertising, most of which is in the big Los Angeles
Times; every store address is given in every ad. Ward's, having
come to this market late, has had to go to outlying communities,
where it advertises separately for each store.

The group reports, of course, to the territorial office, which
oversees all store operations in its nine-state territory. The territorial vice president, through his own staff, governs the administration of all personnel, referring only appointments of class-A
store managers to Chicago for approval. (These are approved, in
fact, by Sears' chairman himself.) Among other things, the territorial chief is also responsible for watching closely over the expansion of credit (and rates of repayment and delinquency) in his
own area; for the state of customer service (Sears' territories will
run down every serious complaint, and sometimes even report on
it to Chicago); for real estate and store locations; and, finally, for
merchandising. The latter responsibility is a crucial one, for it is
the vice president's job to interpret and sell Chicago's views on
merchandising. A Chicago man in each merchandising category
comes to his territory twice a year and shows the new line at meetings of all the store and territorial merchandising men. A vast
volume of printed matter rolls out of the Chicago offices, and every
territorial vice president is an omnivorous reader of it. The most
important literature of all is the "Program for Growth," by terri-

tory and store. This volume, endlessly revised, includes everything down to how much, say, the sporting-goods department in the Fresno store should sell.

Each store has a profit pattern related to its size. The territorial vice presidents know precisely what the operating profit of each department in each store should be. West Coast head Arthur Wood explains: "The averages are known down to each division. And if the division manager is not up to that average, I'll check and ask where he stands."

Back to the Book

Sears' continuous expansion has been primarily "territorial," i.e., it has meant opening new department stores in new places. But other forms of expansion are visible too. The catalogue selling apparatus is being expanded by encouraging telephone orders and opening more "catalogue stores" (there are now 1,055). Something like a quarter of Sears' sales are made through the catalogue nowadays. The big general catalogue offers 170,000 items (vs. about 60,000 in a class-A store) and it is sent out twice a year, but only to customers who placed at least two orders totaling $15 or more in the previous six months. All in all, the catalogue business is not likely to expand as rapidly as the stores, but it is certain to remain a large and profitable segment of Sears' business. The margin on catalogue sales is a bit higher than on retail sales.

Sears is not just a retailer, of course. In addition to its store and catalogue business, it owns and operates an insurance company, a retail-credit subsidiary, a couple of savings and loan associations, an auto-financing company, and those manufacturing subsidiaries, with the mutual fund about ready to start rolling. All of these ventures are profitable. Sears' unconsolidated subsidiaries and affiliates (mainly Allstate Insurance Co. and the Latin-American subsidiaries) paid it dividends of $32,900,000 last year, and also earned for it another $32,564,000 of undistributed net income. For the time being, however, expansion mainly means more standard department stores.

The budget for expansion this year is $175 million; for fiscal 1965 it is $225 million. The money will come, as it almost always has, from retained earnings (about half of earnings are distributed in dividends) and depreciation. All through the 1930's and 1940's, under General Wood, Sears' financial policy was simple: no debt. Properties were sold and leased back, and receivables were sold to banks. But since the mid-1950's Sears has generally been buying its own sites and building its own stores. The turn to owning came after the 1954 tax law raised depreciation allowances, thereby making it attractive to build and own so as to generate higher cash flows. Sears is also developing some of its own shopping centers through a subsidiary, Homart Development. It opened one center in Fort Worth in 1962, and another in Austin last October. In general (though not always), the heavy depreciation charges keep new stores from operating at a profit the first year.

Sears' profits were, in fact, held down considerably last year by heavy depreciation charges on new stores—and by the special start-up expenses on such stores. These were not the only drags on profits, however. Some large new experiments in automation were also costly, and so was a saturation campaign to promote catalogue sales in major market areas. (In evaluating Sears' profit performance last year, it should be noted that these drags on profits were more than offset by a change in the method of handling the investment credit and by a sharp reduction in tax liabilities, which together raised reported profits by $15,525,000. Although the lower new tax rates went into effect only a month before Sears' fiscal year ended, they had the effect of reducing the tax provision for installment sales profits reported in 1963—i.e., because the lower rates will apply when collections are actually made.)

Sears began borrowing in the 1950's to finance its new stores—and its rapidly growing credit business. (Credit sales now represent 56 percent of total volume.) In 1956, Sears found that Wall Street would offer it better terms for $125 million it then needed for credit operations if the debt were not in Sears' name but in that of a separate company: hence the Sears Acceptance Corp., which technically buys all Sears' credit accounts and whose assets are liquidating receivables. In 1958, Sears brought out a $350-million debenture issue. The underwriters this time imposed no restrictive conditions except for one provision that the unencumbered assets of the corporation amount to 150 percent of the liabilities (a ratio that, if it had been allowed in 1956, would have made the acceptance company unnecessary). Sears sees no new long-term financing in the near future, but if it did need money it could get it in several ways: another debenture issue, sales of receivables, issuance of commercial paper against receivables, sale-and-leaseback of store properties, or mortgages.

Thus the company is still financially flexible. Any more bor-

rowing it might do would be managed easily and naturally—the
way Sears does everything.

What Happened at Endicott Johnson
after the Band Stopped Playing*_____

BY STEPHEN MAHONEY

On a night in January, 1961—it was Friday the thirteenth—
three contiguous cities in western New York's Susquehanna Valley
celebrated the rout of an invader. The invader was Glen Alden
Corp., a diversified holding company based in New York City.
It had attempted to gain control of the valley's biggest business
enterprise, the Endicott Johnson Corp., a leading shoe manufacturer. In the space of ten days, the residents of Binghamton,
Johnson City, and Endicott had rallied around the company, buying some 63,000 shares of its stock in order to support local
management in the anticipated proxy fight. Policemen, Boy Scouts,
clergymen, schoolteachers, and shoe workers had bought E.J.
stock at prices up to $35 a share. That day in January Glen Alden
conceded that it could not win a proxy fight. Speaking in Johnson
City, in a community recreation hall built by the company, President Frank Johnson congratulated the valley on the victory, as one
citizen remembers the speech, over "the forces of evil."

The community had good reasons for backing Endicott Johnson, or so they thought. E.J. was the area's biggest employer, with
16,700 on its payroll. The valley feared that Glen Alden might
cut back employment and liquidate some E.J. properties. There
were also sentimental reasons for supporting the Johnson family,
which had run the company from its beginnings some seventy
years earlier and was closely identified with its unique brand
of paternalism, whose benefits were enjoyed by workers and
nonworkers alike. It all made a heartwarming story in the press,
and heartwarming news continued coming out of the company
all through early 1961. In February the Binghamton *Press* re-

September 1962

ported Frank Johnson's "utter confidence in the firm's prospects for spectacular growth." At the March stockholders' meeting, Johnson assured his audience of townspeople that the company, which had taken a loss the year before, would show a profit in the fiscal year ending on December 1, 1961. The stock was then selling for $26 a share.

Johnson admits now, "We were optimistic." The fact is that at the time of the attempted take-over E.J. was careering wildly toward disaster. The 1960 loss, E.J.'s first, had been $1,500,000. When the 1961 figures were all in, E.J. showed a loss of $12,-200,000, on sales of $133 million. (In 1951, the record year, sales had been $157 million.) Production in 1961—29 million pairs of shoes—was the lowest since the 1930's.

The company, with Frank Johnson no longer running it, is now fighting for its life. In June, 1962, it passed its third consecutive preferred dividend. Belatedly, E.J. is taking the cost-cutting measures that the valley had feared Glen Alden would take. The cost of maintaining parks and pools built by the company has been shouldered off on the local taxpayers; the recreation hall in which Johnson spoke has been leased out; the company golf course is up for sale. By the end of 1962 three inefficient plants will have been shut down. Since the defeat of Glen Alden, E.J.'s labor force has been cut back by 2,000. "We got taken," an Endicott waitress said bitterly, expressing what is now the prevailing sentiment in the valley. "The cities took a bath." Recently the Boy Scouts' equity has been down around $16 a share.

Any Number Can Play

Endicott Johnson's troubles had been building up for many years, and the fault has to be laid to its management. In the shoe industry more than in most others, a company's fortunes ride with management. Capital resources are not crucial, for equipment can be rented out of anticipated profits. Technology is slow to change, and materials are available to everyone at the same prices. Anybody can get into the business, and just about anybody does. There are perhaps a thousand shoe manufacturers in the U.S., and the two biggest, Brown Shoe (1961 sales: $298 million) and International Shoe ($294 million), together account for only 12 percent of the industry's production.

E.J.'s board swept in a new management in October, 1961, when it was finally evident that the loss would be immense. It was able to do this because Frank Johnson's position had rested, not on stock control, but on sentiment alone. His grandfather, founder George F. Johnson, owned half the company's original capital. But these holdings were widely dispersed among the Johnson family in later years, and most of them found their way to the market, often to meet inheritance taxes. When his regime foundered, Frank Johnson (who now bears the title of chairman, but has little to say about policy) owned less than 1 percent of E.J. stock.

The new president, the man on whom the company's chances now depend, is Pasquale J. (Pat) Casella, forty-eight, formerly a Montgomery Ward store manager and an R.C.A. executive. Casella was brought up and educated in Binghamton, a fact that doubtless helped to reassure the valley and that was certainly a major factor in his selection to run Endicott Johnson. He was new to the shoe business, however. Frank Johnson had hired Casella to be senior vice president, but he had always insisted that it took years of experience in shoes to gain the understanding necessary to run a company like E.J. Casella, who tends to be thin-skinned, is sensitive on this point. Recently he exclaimed heatedly: "It was people who 'understood' the shoe business who got this company into the shape it was in when I took over."

A short, stocky man with an aggressive manner—"Napoleonic" is the word applied by former business associates—Casella earned a reputation at R.C.A. as a troubleshooter. He was known as an executive who drove himself and his subordinates relentlessly. These qualities undoubtedly recommended him to Endicott Johnson, despite the fact that, at R.C.A., Casella did not have an unblemished record of success. He had joined R.C.A. in 1954, first performing creditably as president of Canadian operations and later as director of an Italian subsidiary. In 1958 he was put in charge of the trouble-ridden consumer-products division and made executive vice president. In this job troubles arose out of a situation something like the one he now faces at Endicott Johnson. R.C.A.'s TV and appliance manufacturing costs were out of hand, and Casella's efforts to cut them resulted in a sharp drop in product quality. His efforts also made him a lot of enemies in the company. He was finally ousted as head of consumer products in June, 1960, after which he took a job with the international division for six months. Then he quit R.C.A., and was unemployed for five months before E.J. took him on, in May, 1961, as senior vice president for sales and marketing.

Casella is struggling now to show a 1962 profit, and the indications are that he will be successful. For the first six months of fiscal 1962 the company showed a profit of $257,034, on sales of $66,200,000. But 1962 profits are being achieved partly through economies that are hampering the promotion of badly needed brands introduced last year, and also hampering the buildup of an adequate sales force. Attempting to get the company on its feet, Casella has a real dilemma: he must economize, but he must also expand operations and increase sales.

Two Men and a Snowball

The disasters of 1960-61 should not have come as a shock to Endicott Johnson, for there had been some strenuous warnings that the company was in trouble. Unfortunately, however, the Johnson regime persisted in viewing the warnings with a large measure of complacency.

Frank Johnson is a mild, gray man who enjoys discussing shoe craftsmanship, the company, and E.J.'s benevolence. Everyone in the community has always felt free to address him simply as "Frank." Like all the Johnson's before him who ran the company, Frank was led by his family to disdain a college education as a waste of time for a man who was to go into business. He had gone to work at an E.J. bench in his teens, cementing soles on tennis shoes. In the 1930's he had become general manager of the rubber and tennis shoe division, and in 1940 he had become a company director. In 1957, after his cousin Charles had a cerebral hemorrhage, Frank became president and chief executive.

His cousin Charles—"Mr. Charley" to the community—appears to have had misgivings about Frank. One director recalls: "Mr. Charley was afraid that Frank wasn't interested in the business or in working." And so the board gave a friend of Frank's, Vice President and Director Ray Mills, a strong mandate to share the management responsibilities with Frank. Tall and slightly stooped, Mills had been born in Endicott and educated at the University of Michigan as a chemical engineer. He had worked for E.J. in the manufacturing division since the late 1920's, becoming a director in 1939. Of the company's troubles, before and after Frank took over, Mills says: "They were like a snowball rolling downhill, growing bigger and going faster till you couldn't stop them." During the years the snowball was going fastest, Frank Johnson and Mills shared top management responsibility.

In their first two years on the job the new chiefs accomplished very little. These years, Mills acknowledges, were "a period of uncertainty." There was no forward planning. Mostly, says one former E.J. executive, only half-seriously, "people sat back and prayed for another war." Meanwhile, sales kept falling: from $151 million in 1956, to $146 million in 1957, to $134 million in 1958. E.J.'s operating profit margin, already the lowest among the industry leaders, fell from 7.5 percent in 1956 to 6.9 in 1957 and to 6.2 percent in 1958.

Four Pounds of Bad News

Some of these figures, and quite a few others, were contained in studies of the company made in 1959 by Booz Allen & Hamilton, the management consultant. Booz Allen had been brought into the picture in January, 1959, when it was apparent to the board that management was floundering. The consultants had received a cold welcome from the old-line executives, and had difficulty obtaining data from the Johnson management on the company's operations. In some parts of the company, giving out data to these outsiders was viewed as disloyal.

Booz Allen took on several assignments. The first was to prepare something new to Endicott Johnson: an organization chart. Organization at E.J. had always been a hit-or-miss proposition. At one time, says Mills, "people *felt* their way into jobs. They sensed what was wrong and took care of it." Then later they waited for Charley Johnson to tell them what to do. But by 1959, according to Robert Horton, one of the outside directors, "no one knew what his job was or what he was supposed to do."

Booz Allen's next assignments were to recruit management talent and to create a five-year marketing plan. The consultants were to map the U.S. shoe market and locate marketing and merchandising areas where competitors were outstripping E.J. They were to explain why E.J. was taking a drubbing and suggest remedies. The final copies of the marketing plan were delivered to the desks of Johnson and Mills on May 10, 1960. The report had more than 300 pages and fifty charts and tables. It weighed four pounds, twelve ounces. Fourteen Booz Allen executives had contributed to the report. It was terribly depressing reading.

To summarize the case, it appeared that E.J. was producing the wrong kinds of shoes, aiming for the wrong kinds of customers, and selling through the wrong kinds of outlets, which were concentrated in the wrong areas. E.J. was still heavily committed to work shoes when work shoes' proportion of total industry sales was declining rapidly. Furthermore, the work shoes the company made were the wrong kind; they were heavy clodhoppers. Work shoes that sold were lighter in construction and also lighter in color than E.J.'s. (Frank Johnson laments today: "Even the men working on the highways here have stopped wearing heavy shoes.") Between 1947 and 1959, E.J.'s share of U.S. work-shoe production dropped from 33 to 20 percent.

Meanwhile, the company was not trying to meet the rising demand for high-style shoes, even though these can be sold for more and provide higher profit margins. A 1959 industry survey estimated that men's shoes retailing for $10 or more represented 41 percent of U.S. production and 60 percent of manufacturers' income. At E.J., however, men's shoes in this price line made up less than 1 percent of total production. In 1959 the average pair of E.J. shoes sold for $5 at retail.

E.J. was also pretty well shut out of the booming market for women's shoes. The shoes it offered women were clumsy, unattractive, and uncomfortable. The company's share of the industry's production of women's shoes had been only 3.6 percent in 1947, but by 1959 it had dropped to 2 percent. Finally, the company was faring poorly in the "youth market," where it had started from a strong position. Like their elders, children and teenagers were wearing shoes with some flair in the postwar years, but E.J. seemed unaware of this. Between 1947 and 1959 its share of the youth market slid from 24 to 11 percent.

How to Lose the Old Family Touch

E.J. merchandising was as far behind as its styling. "After the war," Mills recalled recently, "there were all these new merchandising trends. First there was a trend toward shopping centers. The company did think about getting into them. But along came these roadside stores, and we switched and talked about getting into them, instead. But along came discounting and leased departments." The end result was that E.J. did not get into anything much that was new. In one seven-year period in the mid-1950's, the Melville Shoe Corp.'s Thom McAn stores had a net increase of 247 locations, over 95 percent of them in heavy-traffic shopping centers or roadside stores. During those years E.J. had a net increase of eighteen stores; and most of the new stores, like the old ones, were in relatively low-traffic downtown areas.

With the population increasingly concentrated in urban and suburban areas, E.J. stores remained concentrated in small towns. In the late 1950's two-thirds of E.J. captive outlets were each producing less than $75,000 retail volume annually. (Concentrating on high-traffic locations, the Edison Brothers chain in 1959 had average per-store sales of $251,000, while A. S. Beck stores averaged $348,000.) But it was not only a matter of poor location. The E.J. stores were old and generally shabby, and designed to appeal to a clientele that wasn't doing the buying. One competitor says, derisively, "Lots of their stores are named Father and Son stores, to give them the nice family touch. That's supposed to bring teenagers in?" Some 40 percent of E.J. captive outlets were unprofitable by the late 1950's.

Not all of its shoes were sold through the captives; 40 percent of sales went through small-town, small-volume independents. But the independents had been squeezed since the war by department stores and chains—and for these fast-growing channels of shoe distribution E.J. offered practically no suitable merchandise. Booz Allen described dealers as "virtually unanimous in declaring that Endicott Johnson shoes are wanting in style and workmanship." Typical complaints: "Endicott Johnson's men's shoes are dated. They don't have a good cha-cha boot and they don't have a leather dress boot with a buckle." And "Finish and detail don't compare with other manufacturers' and are never uniform."

The Fast and the Terrible

An optimistic, easygoing man, Frank Johnson probably was staggered by the Booz Allen findings, and he made some efforts to put the consultants' ideas into practice—though sometimes with a few modifications of his own. In a preliminary report, for example, Booz Allen had urged that Johnson appoint a senior vice president for sales and marketing. Johnson appointed his old colleague Ray Mills to the post. The choice was something of a surprise to the consultants, for Mills had spent his career in manufacturing and engineering. Says Mills: "I knew nothing about sales and marketing, but the job appealed to me." To help staff his department, Mills began hiring "fast-shoe" executives whom Booz Allen had spotted working for other shoe manufacturers.

Getting these new executives, and getting the fast shoes themselves, were among the few solid accomplishments of the Johnson-Mills regime. Designed for the popular-price market, fast shoes have pointed toes, paper-thin soles, and buckles and eyelets that may be purely ornamental. One of the new executives, Hugh Warren, now product development manager, exclaimed recently: "Aren't they *terrible*! They sell like hotcakes!"

The fast shoes, and the new men sponsoring them, were a

source of consternation to the "old-shoe" executives who had worked for Mr. Charley. The fast-shoe men were restless, driving, ambitious men in their forties and early fifties. Most of the old-shoe men, on the other hand, were born in the valley, began their business careers assembling shoes at an E.J. bench, and had—indeed, still have—intense loyalty to the Johnson family. They are likely to be close to, or over, normal retirement age; some are seventy. These older men are inclined to mourn for E.J.'s former devotion to heavy, boxy footwear with no nonsense about it.

Perhaps the "fastest" of the new executives was a vice president for marketing sent along by Booz Allen in July, 1959, to work with Mills. He was Edgar B. Mooney, a man with a boyish, scrubbed look and a bouncy, confident manner, who had come from his own marketing firm. A self-proclaimed "idea man," Mooney jotted down thoughts incessantly. He had had a desk of sorts built below the dashboard of his Thunderbird. "I get ideas from my subconscious," he confided. "It doesn't shut off because I'm driving."

Horton Gets His Allies

The first assignment of the new arrivals was to study the marketing plan. In line with its recommendations, a new product-planning department began restyling all 1,500 of E.J.'s stock models in 1960. The five-year plan pointed out that, while E.J. aimed at a generalized mass market, competitors were getting rich by selling to specialized markets. Product planning thereupon created specialized name brands for E.J.: an inexpensive, dressy men's line ("The Man"), a women's fashion line ("Fashion 10"), and a children's line ("Romper Room"). Packaging had been as heavy and clumsy as shoes. In pursuit of the new fashion image Booz Allen called for, a new advertising department restyled the shoe boxes. Mooney advertised the fast, new E.J. look in trade magazines and window displays.

It was a good try by the fast-shoe men, but in 1960 they were not yet running the company. The sales force, scheduled to take spring, 1961, orders in October, did not have samples: the shoes were not in production.

Control over manufacturing, nominally the responsibility of a vice president for manufacturing, was actually in the hands of the plant superintendents. Each superintendent had his own patternmakers, and each persisted for some time in turning out the lines easiest for him to produce with his equipment, layout, and workers—no matter what the product planners said. Finally, when they attempted to produce the new shoes, the plant superintendents found they couldn't. The restyled shoes required new tips, heels, soles, vamps, and linings. Cardboard patterns had to be made; with patterns available, trial shoes had to be hand-lasted; then, with style lines set, metal dies and wooden lasts had to be made. A majority of E.J.'s labor force had to be retrained: stitchers, in particular, lacked the skills the upgraded lines required. The manufacturing vice president, one of the old-shoe men, was not making the necessary changes. Frank Johnson nevertheless stuck by him. "Frank was too loyal, he was too close to all those guys," a fast-shoe man explained recently.

But even if the salesmen had had samples, it is doubtful whether they could have done the job. Says Mooney: "The older salesmen didn't know the names of the department-store buyers. They knew mom and pop in the mom-and-pop stores." Despite the new pep talks at sales meetings, salesmen went right on taking orders from the same old outlets for the same old shoes.

By this time there were four outside directors on the fourteen-man board. More easily swayed than Mr. Charley, Frank had surrendered to Horton's demands for more outsiders. In April, 1959, Joseph Bell, president of New York State Electric & Gas, a Binghamton utility, had been elected a director. In October, 1959, Jacob M. Kaplan, former head of Welch Grape Juice, had come on the board, followed in January, 1960, by Warren J. Reardon, president of Daniel Green Co., a New York state slipper manufacturer. "Always I had been looking around for allies," says Horton. Now he had them.

In October, 1960, the outside directors called in Mooney and Sales Vice President Bill Benjes and invited them to discuss their problems. The two acknowledged that they did not have the shoes they needed. Says Horton: "We landed on management like a ton of bricks." And now Johnson admitted, reluctantly, that changes were overdue.

A Phone Call to Albert List

It was the first of two blows that descended on the Johnson-Mills regime in that period. The second landed in January, when it was announced that Glen Alden had made an offer to buy E.J. stock—and that outside Director Kaplan was in the enemy camp. "Jack Kaplan had lots and lots of ideas about how E.J. ought to be run," says a board member who served with him. "He was a cocklebur." Kaplan had been a board member of Sharon Steel Corp., which suspected him of ambitions to gain control. His reputation on Wall Street was such that, before he came on the E.J. board, Horton sounded him out on his intentions. Kaplan said that he wanted to make money by helping to reinvigorate E.J. from the sidelines—not by taking over. Eager for allies, Horton then sponsored his election to the board. "I had to push Frank and Ray a little," Horton remembers.

Kaplan was a more outspoken critic of management than Horton, and from the beginning he peppered Johnson and Mills with suggestions. For his pains, he was denied access to certain E.J. records; later, he was pointedly refused details on the Booz Allen findings. About some matters, it seems clear, other board members simply lied to him. By the summer of 1960, Kaplan decided he had had enough; he was disgusted, and he told Horton that he wanted a buyer for his stock. He owned 60,000 shares, far more than any other individual; and he wanted to sell them privately, if possible, since dumping them on the market would have depressed the price. Horton suggested that in time the E.J. employee pension fund would buy Kaplan's holdings. Meanwhile, he persuaded Kaplan to remain on the board.

At the December board meeting in Endicott, Kaplan supported a move to omit the common dividend and conserve working capital. Despite some opposition, his arguments prevailed. The board refused, however, to consider his requests for help in disposing of his stock. Kaplan returned to his New York office, feeling that he had been had. He got on the phone with his friend Albert List, Glen Alden chairman.

Another Job for Mooney

Originally a Massachusetts tire distributor, List made his first big money during the depression by acquiring and renovating moribund New England textile mills. Later he bought control of the unprofitable RKO theatre chain and made it pay. In 1959 he merged his holdings with Glen Alden, then the largest U.S. anthracite-mining firm, which was woefully in the red. Eliminating its unprofitable operations, List eased it into the black. Under his management, Glen Alden went on to acquire other unprofitable firms, and managed to squeeze a profit from them. In 1961, Glen Alden had control of firms in aluminum, textiles, and leather tanning. Endicott Johnson looked like a promising addition to

List's mixed bag. It seemed clear that a List take-over would mean a drastic overhaul of E.J.'s weaker operations.

On Saturday, December 31, 1960, List mailed his offer to E.J. stockholders. He offered to buy any number of shares at $30.50—$3 above the market price. Over the weekend Kaplan disclosed to the board that on December 29 he had traded his own holdings to List in exchange for 140,000 shares of Glen Alden (which was then selling at $14.50). This meant that Kaplan, who had bought E.J. at an average price of $34.30, just about broke even. It also meant that Frank Johnson was in for a fight.

What with the chaotic state of E.J. management, Mooney had been taking on unassigned responsibilities all over the lot. He now took on the job of licking Glen Alden. Obviously, if Frank Johnson was to remain in power, the price of E.J.'s stock had to go over $30.50. Mooney spoke to church groups, school-teachers, and civic clubs. He spoke to children—at Boy Scout meetings and high-school assemblies—who might relay the urgency of his message to their parents. The message was an appeal to local sentiment. Mooney recalls: "I said, 'Why have somebody else enjoy the fruits of the community's labors?'"

To cope with the local bull market, Bache & Co. sold E.J. shares at tables in an E.J. cafeteria. A local furniture store offered "free Endicott Johnson stock—this week only—with any $200 purchase." Other stores set up window displays urging people to go "all the way with E.J." The two Binghamton newspapers ran editorials to the same effect. During the two-week life of the tender, the price of E.J. rose as high as $35. "I wanted to sell short," says one E.J. executive. "A broker called from the Street and asked me what I thought the price would go down to. 'Around twenty,' I said. But I couldn't sell short. We were fighting a battle."

Before the price rose, Glen Alden had picked up 20,000 shares on the market, in addition to the 60,000 it got from Kaplan. These 80,000 shares represented some 10 percent of the stock— not enough for control, but not far short. To prevent any big last-minute acquisitions by Glen Alden, Johnson addressed the valley on television on January 8. Speaking from notes supplied by Mooney, he said that Glen Alden's offer was "ridiculously low-priced," and predicted that E.J. would win the fight with the aid of the workers and the community. The following day, petitions were circulated among E.J. workers requesting that $10 million of the $50-million pension fund be made available for the purchase of E.J. stock. Then the day after that, Johnson began touring plants, addressing his employees.

When List capitulated, he sold his holdings to the pension fund at $31.50. The directors were delighted to arrange this deal, for they were still uneasy about having so large a black of E.J. stock available to outsiders. The purchase from List was made possible by changing the trustee agreement so that the directors were able to instruct the fund's manager, Morgan Guaranty, to buy the stock. The fund has taken a licking, of course. List, on the other hand, pulled out of the valley without a loss.

The Road Back to Reality

In the weeks after their glorious victory, the managers of E.J. seem to have been slow in adjusting to the inglorious realities of their business situation. At the March board meeting, there was even some talk about resuming payment of the preferred and common dividends, but the board decided against it. "I put my foot down," Horton recalls.

By summer, it was impossible to ignore the company's problems. E.J. was now six months behind in filling orders, and retailers who had advertised the new models were up in arms. Bill Benjes recalls that he heard complaints from every dealer a salesman had taken an order from. Some shoes that did get shipped fell apart at the seams when they were removed from their new, colorful boxes. Many shoes had shades and qualities of leather different from their mates.

Compounding the production snarl was a great confusion in E.J.'s data-processing system. The computers were housed in a former restaurant built by the company. They had been acquired by the manufacturing division in order to record data on the flow of soles and heels to the plants. When they introduced the restyled footwear, Mooney and Benjes found that they needed information that management had not gathered previously—e.g., what styles were selling, and where. Says Mills: "We tried to program sales and anticipate demand from new territories, but orders got lost in that magnetic tape. I never saw such a mess. We didn't get sales orders on the right tapes. We didn't get the right leather for the shoes we had orders for." There was, in fact, nobody trained to program the computers for the new operations.

With manufacturing snarled, management soon lost control of its costs. In late 1960, sales of $165 million were projected for 1961. In June, 1961, Casella—who had just replaced Mills as head of sales and marketing—asked Johnson what the 1961 breakeven was. Going to his files, Frank said the company would break even on sales of $144 million. "I didn't believe it," says Casella. He took his own look at costs and estimated the breakeven was $185 million (i.e., some 50 million over the sales figure E.J. finally achieved).

As evidence of the Johnson regime's ineptitude piled up that summer, several members of the board grew rebellious. Three more outside directors had been elected at the February meeting, and there were now six all together. One of the three new men was Wayne Cawley, president of Endicott's Cadre Industries Corp., and a strong supporter of E.J. management during the fight against List. The other new directors were Robert Garrison, vice president of a division of Cluett, Peabody & Co., and John Clark, a wealthy local businessman. Says Horton: "If we had all known each other in February as we did in the fall, we might have been able to avoid some of the trouble. Warren Reardon and I knew in February what we wanted to do, but we didn't know whom we had to support us."

The night before the September board meeting, Horton and Reardon were having dinner in the dining room of Endicott's Hotel Frederick. Cawley came into the dining room with some friends, joined his fellow directors for a moment, and to their surprise volunteered to serve in a rebellion against the Johnson management. The next morning two other outside directors, Clark and Bell, were enlisted over breakfast. At the meeting, the inside directors reluctantly agreed that Johnson had to go as chief executive, and they agreed that Pat Casella was the man to replace him.

The Attack on Costs

The Casella regime began with a major assault on operating and overhead costs. Casella set up rigid departmental budgets, and aimed to bring E.J. to the breakeven point by mid-1962. He is succeeding in getting E.J. into the black; the only question his efforts raise is whether the cuts are at the expense of programs E.J. needs for the long pull. Mooney left in January, and the ambitious new marketing program went with him, leaving behind only the restyled shoes as mementoes of E.J.'s first, faltering steps into the modern market.

Another saving, plainly called for, is being achieved by cutbacks in paternalism. Some local facilities built by the company have been leased to the cities; others have been sold. The parks and pools cost the company $197,000 last year; in 1962 they may actually yield a small profit. The medical program for workers and their dependents has been modified. The interest charges on mortgages on company-financed homes have been raised.

More important, nearly $10 million is being pared from operating costs. Eli White, a tough-minded former Genesco executive, who became E.J. manufacturing vice president in October, 1961, began by putting a thousand nonproduction workers—e.g., rack pushers, elevator operators, maintenance men—to work on the bench. Other workers for whom nothing productive could be found were fired. The first plant shutdown came in January.

White has laid out the plants for more efficient work flow and supervised the retraining of workers. In December one factory (named the George F., fittingly) took ten days to turn out a pair of shoes. By May the time was down to six days. Over those five months, the plant's work force was cut from 449 to 397.

White has been relentless in slashing costs. Monthly he examines the long-distance bill run up by each manufacturing supervisor. "It's a clerk's job," he says. "I got to stop doing it. But it tells you who's soft on costs and who's not."

In attempting to get the company back on its feet, Casella has certain advantages. One is the sheer size of the 1961 loss. "The fact that it was a big loss and not a small one," says Director Joseph Bell, "got the three cities willing to accept some of what Pat's doing." Another advantage is the continued presence on the board of Frank Johnson. Says a director, "Except for a Johnson being with the company, labor and the community wouldn't stand for what Pat's doing."

But Casella's ultimate advantage is none of these. It is that, in the role of Savior, he need have no "sentiment" overriding his business judgment—no loyalty to George F. or the valley of the Susqehanna, none to autonomous plant managers or proprietors of rundown stores. His relative freedom may well be to the valley's advantage, too. In time, he may even be able to satisfy those workers, teachers, and Boy Scouts, who hanker for a decent return on their investment.

SUPPLEMENTARY REFERENCES FROM *Fortune*

FORD MOTOR COMPANY

MURPHY, THOMAS P., "How Edsel Lured Those Dealers," September 1957, Volume 56, p. 144.

GENERAL MOTORS CORPORATION

1) BELLO, FRANCIS, "How Strong is G. M. Research?" June 1956, Volume 53, p. 138.

2) SHEEHAN, ROBERT, "How Harlow Curtice Earns His $750,000," February 1956, Volume 53, p. 133.

3) SLOAN, ALFRED P., JR., "A Quarter Century of Glorious Creation—And a Downfall," *My Years with General Motors*, September 1963 to February 1964 (inclusive), Volume 58, No. 3 to Volume 59, No. 2 (six articles).

KAISER ALUMINUM COMPANY

SHEEHAN, ROBERT, "Kaiser Aluminum: Henry J.'s Marvelous Mistake," July 1956, Volume 54, p. 78.

MONTGOMERY WARD AND COMPANY, INC.

MAURER, HERRYMON, "What Did Happen at Ward's?" May 1956, Volume 53, p. 207.

TEXTRON, INC.

LITTLE, ROY, "Why Companies Sell Out," February 1956, Volume 53, p. 117.

WESTINGHOUSE ELECTRIC CORPORATION

STRYKER, PERRIN, AND DANIEL BELL, "What's Wrong at Westinghouse," March 1956, Volume 53, p. 113.